MUHAMMAD AND THE RISE OF ISLAM:

The Creation of Group Identity

5 0664 01028168 3

AUDREY COHEN COLLEGE LIBRARY
75 Varick St. 12th Floor
New York, NY 10013

MUHAMMAD AND THE RISE OF ISLAM:

The Creation of Group Identity

Subhash C. Inamdar

Psychosocial Press
Madison Connecticut

Grateful acknowledgments for permission to use material from the following:

The *History of Al-Tabari*, ed. Ehsan Yarshatar is reprinted by permission of the State University of New York Press, from *The History of Al Tabari*, Vols. VI, VII, IX by Ehsan Yarshatar (Ed.) © 1989, 1987, 1990. State University of New York. All rights reserved.

The Venture of Islam, Vol. I: The Classical Age of Islam, by M. G. S. Hodgson, 1974 is reprinted by permission of The University of Chicago Press.

From *Childhood and Society*, by Erik H. Erikson. Copyright 1950, © 1963 by W. W. Norton & Company Inc., renewed © 1978, 1991 by Erik H. Erikson. Used by permission of W. W. Norton & Company, Inc.

From *Group Psychology and the Analysis of the Ego* by Sigmund Freud, translated by James Strachey. Copyright © 1959, 1922 by the Institute of Psycho-Analysis and Angela Richards. Copyright © 1959 by Sigmund Freud Copyrights Ltd. Copyright © 1959 by James Strachey. Used by permission of W. W. Norton & Company, Inc.

From *Life History and the Historical Moment* by Erik H. Erikson, Copyright © 1975 by Erik H. Erikson. Used by permission of W. W. Norton & Company, Inc.

The Standard Edition of the Complete Psychological Works of Sigmund Freud, translated and edited by James Strachey. Reprinted with the permission of the Sigmund Freud Copyrights, The Institute of Psycho-Analysis and The Hogarth Press.

Copyright © 2001, Psychosocial Press

PSYCHOSOCIAL PRESS ® and PSP (& design) ® are registered trademarks of International Universities Press, Inc.

All rights reserved. No part of this book may be printed or reproduced or utilized in any form or by any electronic, mechanical or other means, now known or hereafter invented, including photocopying and recording, or in any information storage or retrieval system, without permission in writing from the publisher.

Library of Congress Cataloging-in-Publication Data

Inamdar, Subhash C.
    Muhammad and the rise of Islam : the creation of group identity / Subhash C. Inamdar.
      p. cm.
    Includes bibliographical references and index.
    ISBN 1–887841–28–8
    1. Muhammad, Prophet, d. 632—Biography. 2. Umma (Islam) 3. Islamic Empire—History. 4. Islamic civilization—History. I. Title.

BP75.I53 2000
297.6'3—dc21
[B]

00–045723

Manufactured in the United States of America

Contents

Preface vii
Introduction ix

PART I:
THE FORMATION OF A GROUP AND GROUP IDENTITY

1. The Formation of a Group: A Psychosocial Model   3

PART II:
PSYCHOANALYTIC AND SOCIOLOGICAL PERSPECTIVES

2. Psychoanalysis and Sociology: The Links between the Individual and Society   27
3. Theories of Group Formation   43

PART III:
THE WORLD BEFORE ISLAM AND THE BIRTH OF A PROPHET

4. Pre-Islamic Arabia and the Rise of Universal Religions   73
5. The Early History of Mecca and Muhammad's Ancestors   89
6. The Early Years of Muhammad and the Prophetic Call   101

PART IV:
THE RISE OF ISLAM

7.	Migration to Medina—The *Hijra*	133
8.	The Prophet at War	147
9.	The Conquest of Mecca	169
10.	The Last Years of the Prophet	183
11.	The Growth of a Charismatic Leader	189
12.	The Empire of Islam	231

References	241
Name Index	249
Subject Index	253

Preface

Mombasa, the port city of Kenya, and my birth place, has a unique place in history. Indian, Persian, and Arab traders had for over two thousand years carried from here the riches of Africa. Omani Arabs settled here too and ruled from Zanzibar. And it was here that Vasco daGama, a Portuguese explorer, sought an Arab navigator to guide him across the Indian Ocean to India. This seemingly insignificant event marked, however, the beginning of Europe's vast imperial expansion into the East and the beginning of the decline of the Islamic Middle East. Mombasa thus has the distinction of being the site where Africa collided with the seafaring Indian, Arab, and European worlds. Growing up in that crossroads gave history and culture special meaning, and Mombasa engendered in me an early interest in groups and cultures. What made some groups succeed and do better than others? What drew men thousands of miles from home to explore, conquer, convert, and rule?

Later as a medical student it became quickly evident that individual illnesses were very unlike the cases discussed in my medical texts. In the developing world, when medicines are unavailable, a diagnosis is too often a death warrant. Life and its healing are a luxury that depends on what a family, group and its culture could afford and offer. It became evident to me that health was linked to a nation's wealth and its resources.

A group's success and prosperity, but too often its failure, thus circumscribed the sanctity of life. Diagnosis, the process of *knowing through,* has to be extended beyond the individual to the wellness of the world around him. Once again, some cultures provide in greater measure for the well being of their peoples. Why is that so? What lessons do more successful groups offer?

These questions led to a deeper interest in cultures and group psychology; a quest for meaning and answers.

This book reflects this search, over years, to discern patterns in group phenomena. Attempts within the fields of sociology, anthropology, and psychology were often like the proverbial attempts of blind men to describe an elephant. It was finally a biography of Muhammad that provided the necessary and critical clues for the understanding of a group, a religion and a culture—Islam, and its millennium long success. I can only hope this book can provide an understanding of not only Islam, but more broadly of all groups, large and small.

There are thanks that I owe to many individuals. I wish I could thank everyone. It was very meaningful to have had the support of Margaret Emery, Ph.D., editor-in-chief of International Universities Press whose expertise and guidance were essential to the project from the onset. Theodore Shapiro, M.D., teacher and mentor, provided the spark that reignited my interest in psychological theory. He had been kind enough to look at early drafts of this book. My good and brilliant friend, Gregory Siomopoulos, M.D., in Athens, Greece began discussions on theory and its impact in the 1970s. They still continue. This book would not have been possible without these discussions. Finally, my deepest gratitude is extended to Professor Frank Peters. His expertise in Islam, Judaism and Christianity was crucial, of immense help and offered in abundance. His sensitive comments proved of singular importance. He was invariably gracious whether his suggestions were accepted or not, though most were. His book, *Muhammad and the Origins of Islam* provided an important model for this study. None of these colleagues who so generously contributed their time and expertise is, of course, responsible for the conclusions, all of which are mine.

My final thanks are to Robert Cancro, M.D., Professor of Psychiatry and Chairman of the Department of Psychiatry at New York University School of Medicine for his generous support over the years.

Introduction

THIS study of the life of Muhammad will illustrate how a community, or *umma,* as it is called in Arabic, which is defined by a group identity based on Islam, was formed in Arabia in the early seventh century. From a small beginning as a religious association, it developed its own economy and a system of taxation. It maintained internal order, developed a code of law, and a mode of governance appropriate to a "protonation." Under the leadership of Muhammad and the revelations he received as a Messenger of God, a belief system, a ritual and behavioral system, indeed, a culture and the basis of a distinct civilization, were established that are followed today by almost a billion people. The *umma* Muhammad created expanded at an enormous rate. A hundred years after his death a political empire had been established from Gibraltar to the banks of the Indus. It was the first world empire of antiquity that was both religious and political.

An understanding of how Islam grew and developed under the guidance and talents of its leader, Muhammad, provides a model for understanding group formation and *all* group phenomena. What were the necessary and essential requirements for the formation of the *umma?* What are the basic structures and functions of this Islamic community? What were the basic factors that supported the *umma* as a group to form, to develop, and to become immortal?

The need to understand how Islam was formed, developed, and created by Muhammad and his revelations becomes critical, as a brief history of the subsequent impact of Islam on Europe reveals. The political and military power brought together and unleashed under the banner of Islam was an immense and extraordinary historical event. World history for over a millennium has reflected the powerful see-saw battles between the forces of Christendom and Islam. In the seventh century almost the entire Mediterranean world was part of Christendom. Within a few decades after the death of the Prophet Muhammad in 632 c.e., his Arab followers burst out of Arabia and attacked the two great empires of the Middle East: the Christian Roman Empire and the Persia of the Sasanian Shahs. Persia was absorbed in its entirety; and in dazzling succession, Syria, Palestine, Egypt, and North Africa fell. The Romans held Anatolia, but Spain and Sicily were torn from the Western Empire. Muslim armies occupied parts of southern Italy and menaced Rome. One of the Popes was even compelled to pay tribute. Crossing the Pyrenees into France, Islam threatened to engulf Western Europe. In the historical annals of the West, the decisive encounter occurred between Tours and Poitiers in 732 c.e., where the Franks achieved a decisive victory over the armies of Islam.

A famous passage from Gibbon's *Decline and Fall of the Roman Empire* (1776–1788, quoted in Lewis, 1982) illustrates the Western perception of this battle and of the fate which it avoided:

> A victorious line of march had been prolonged above a thousand miles from the Rock of Gibraltar to the banks of the Loire; the repetition of an equal space would have carried the Saracens to the confines of Poland and the Highlands of Scotland; the Rhine is not more impassable than the Nile or the Euphrates, and the Arabian fleet might have sailed without a naval combat into the mouth of the Thames. Perhaps the interpretation of the Koran would now be taught in the schools of Oxford, and her pulpits might demonstrate to a circumcised people the sanctity and truth of the Revelation of Mahomet. (Lewis, 1982, p. 18)

There is, however, no mention of Tours or Poitiers in the Arab chronicles. The rich Arab historiography has lovingly detailed the phases of *Jihad,* the Holy War of the faith against the unbelievers, with an honesty that was meticulous about both successes and defeats. The Frankish victors in what was a major battle for Christendom in Arab eyes, had encountered nothing more than a band of raiders in a minor engagement thousands of miles from home. The expansion of the Holy War in its first great phase was not checked but merely halted in the Frankish land in the west and at the borders of China and India in the east.

It was the Greek defenders of Constantinople, in 668 c.e., and once again 50 years later, who had saved Europe. They had met and halted the fresh, young, and strong forces of Islam at the gateway of Europe. The road to the Rhine through the heart of Eastern Europe was far shorter than via distant Gibraltar, and less arduous than the road to China. Christendom had been saved because Constantinople did not fall.

Muslim scholars of the time saw the world, almost the entire civilized world, with the lands of Islam in the center. In the year 1068 c.e. (2 years after the Battle of Hastings), Said ibn Ahmad, chief justice of the Muslim city of Toledo in Spain, wrote a book in Arabic in which he categorized nations. Eight peoples had contributed to the advances in knowledge: Persians, Indians, Chaldees, Greeks, Romans, Egyptians, Arabs, and Jews. Of the rest of humanity, the Chinese and the Turks were considered the "noblest of the unlearned peoples" and worthy of respect. Said contemptuously dismissed the rest of mankind as the northern and the southern barbarians. Of the European barbarians to the north he remarked:

> The other peoples of this group who have not cultivated the sciences are more like beasts than like men. For those of them who live furthest to the north, between the last of the seven climates and the limits of the inhabited world, the excessive distance of the sun in relation to the zenith line makes the air cold and the sky cloudy. Their temperaments are therefore, frigid, their humors raw, their bellies gross, their color pale, their hair long and lank. Thus they lack keenness of understanding and clarity of intelligence, and are overcome by ignorance and apathy, lack of discernment and stupidity.... (1935, quoted in Lewis, 1982, p. 68)

In the eleventh century, the forces of Christendom began to regain some of their lands in major victories against Islam. Ultimately, by the end of that century they had carried their campaigns, which came to be known as the Crusades, to the Holy Land. The Crusaders ruled parts of Palestine and Syria for over two centuries, but their overall impact on these lands was slight, and they were finally evicted in crushing defeats.

From the fourteenth to the seventeenth century Muslims were engaged, once again, in a Holy War against Christians. This time the leaders of Islam were Turks, newly militant and powerful. Under the Ottomans they captured Constantinople in 1453 and surged into Europe. Ottoman cavalry raided as far as Venice, and the Ottoman navy captured the Italian port of Otranto. If the plan to capture Italy in 1480 had succeeded, just at the beginning of the Renaissance, world history could have been transformed. Under Sultan Suleyman the Magnificent (1492–1566), the Ottoman armies attained mastery of Greece and the Balkans, and invaded Hungary. In 1529 they laid siege to Vienna in the very heart of Europe, halfway between Constantinople and London. The Ottoman navy brought Muslim naval power to the Atlantic, and corsairs from North Africa led raids up to the British Isles.

For the second time, a far more resurgent Islam posed a mortal danger to Europe. In distant Iceland, the Lutheran Book of Common Prayer beseeched God to relieve them from "The cunning of the Pope and the terror of the Turks." As late as 1627, Barbary Corsairs had carried away several hundred captives from Iceland to the slave marts of Algiers.

Not only had Islam attacked Christendom with success and impunity from the seventh to seventeenth century, but it also had economic superiority. Europe had very few commodities to offer that could interest the Islamic world. As late as the eighteenth century, the only products from Central and Western Europe that attracted attention were Frankish weapons, English wool, and European slaves for the marts and harems of Islam.

By the end of the seventeenth century, however, the decline of Islam became evident. In 1683, the Turks failed in their second attempt to capture Vienna. Islam was already on the decline, and with this decisive defeat, it was never again to mount such a threat. The response of Europe to this second great Islamic advance became its own imperialist expansion.

Islam had conquered large parts of Europe and had posed a serious threat to it for a thousand years. Today, a resurgent Islam is posing newer challenges. The task of this study is to understand what is demonstrably one of the most powerful forces in history. But to do so, we have to return to the beginning, to gain an understanding of the life of the Prophet Muhammad, of Islam, the religion he founded, and the group identity he created for those who accepted his message and submitted to his God and became members of his *umma*. Our task, therefore, is to grasp both biography and history and the relations between the two within a given society (Mills, 1959).

The study of history is both a record of and an attempt to understand human behavior. Interest in history, however, has had conceptual cycles which limited and hindered a clearer worldview until breakthroughs occurred. There were the Greek perspectives of Herodotus and Thucydides followed by those of the Christian Augustine, and eventually by the Enlightenment scholar Gibbon and the *philosophes* such as Voltaire and Montesquieu who saw history moving in a linear direction to a rational paradise. Christian evidence for God's role in history was replaced by an equally "religious" search for meaning in the patterns of secular progress.

The next century, however, saw the logical progression of these ideas arrive at a dead end. Whereas the utilitarians at one extreme saw history moving in a straight, rational line, the Hegelian-Marxists saw a spiral, cyclical vision to a "better day." History was straitjacketed within ideology and a sterile, mechanical worldview. A natural reaction to this was a value-free study of history and its minutiae. This, however, led to the blind alley of historical relativism. Since every event and culture was unique and hence could not explain another, it easily led to just facts, a judgment-free history, and ultimately to a form of historical nihilism. Not surprisingly, biographies of Muhammad have not been immune to historical bias based on prevalent worldviews.

The study of history requires that simplistic reductionism or rigid determinism be replaced by a sensitivity to the particular (the individual, the setting, and the period), coupled with an awareness of the universal. This study will focus on particular aspects of the life of Muhammad as he grew up in the historical climate of pre-Islamic Arabia, but with an awareness of larger universals.

Psychological and sociological attempts to understand a historical figure in a social setting have been hampered by limited conceptual frames that have restricted understanding. Moreover, psychological theories have not readily accommodated themselves to sociology and history. Sociological analyses, in turn, have not been empirically and theoretically sound, because their frames of reference failed to include an understanding of nonrational elements or elements of behavior not entirely under conscious control. A satisfactory solution would have to include an understanding of the complex psychic dimensions of personality.

This work belongs to the long tradition of biographical studies based on psychoanalytic theory, a field that attempts an understanding of human nature and has proven more useful and illuminating for biographical research than any other body of psychological theory (Runyan, 1982). Among the founding fathers of psychoanalysis the work of Sigmund Freud, Heinz Hartmann, and Erik H. Erikson on unconscious motives, conflict, and developmental experiences expressed through the functioning of the ego (and its defense mechanisms), as it adapts to the world, is central to psychoanalytic theory, and has had heuristic value in exploring a wide range of hypotheses in biographical studies.

To study the impact of Muhammad on the rise of Islam, requires the application of psychoanalytic insight to systematic sociological viewpoints. While this is justified by the later writings of Freud and supported by the work of Erikson, there is no explicitly formulated sociological position in the psychoanalytic literature, only an implicit and emergent one (Weinstein & Platt, 1973, p. 18). Therefore, the normative sociology of Emile Durkheim, Max Weber, and Talcott Parsons and others must be invoked to cover the serious gaps in any theory that attempts to link the individual to his society.

This study of Muhammad's life will not be a psychobiography in the traditional sense: a study of a great man in history. Rather, it will be a study of Muhammad and how he created a group whose essential elements and identity were defined by him and the revelations he received from Allah. The study will be dialectical as well as diachronic. The impact of the culture of pre-Islamic Arabia on Muhammad as a child, adolescent, and adult will be reviewed, as well as his impact, over time, on the creation of Islam and the world around him.

Part I and Part II deal with theory and theories—the cognitive maps that guide the selection of perception from a profusion of detail. In the first chapter a model will be built utilizing theoretical concepts that link the world of the individual to the world of the group: family, clan or tribe, religious community or nation.

The representational world of the group has a reality sui generis that includes ideal and actual shapes of the group. The representational world of the group has a considerable impact on developments in the individual and his representational world by a process of identification and internalization. A unique individual can affect and transform his world, in a dialectical manner, by meeting not only the basic needs of his group but by fulfilling all their needs.

The second chapter, in this section, examines the efforts made by psychoanalysis and sociology, from opposite ends, to understand the complex and challenging links that tie the individual to society. How and why individuals form groups within societies, the theories of group formation, beginning with the work of Freud, are explored in chapter 3.

This section should be of interest not only to the specialist reader but should appeal to an educated audience receptive to ideas and theory. The assumptions that underlie the proposed model and the links between biography and society within a historical setting are critical to their understanding. Having stated this position, a reader can, however, move directly to chapter 4 and beyond to read about the life of the Prophet, which illustrates the creation of the group identity of Islam based on God-given revelations. It is these very details, in fact, that provide support for a theory of how a powerful and long lasting group is formed.

Chapter 4 will explore the history of events in pre-Islamic Arabia as a setting for the rise of Islam. Pre-Islamic Arabia, isolated by culture and geography from the rest of the world, had been at the center of one of the oldest and longest trade routes in the world. The rise of universalist religions in the Fertile Crescent, which had an impact on Arabia and was a major impetus for the rise of Islam, will be described. These universalist religions finally penetrated the geographical isolation of Arabia. This area had given rise to the great universalist religions of Judaism and Christianity. The set of factors that allowed this is explored. Universalist religions, acting as a unifying force, led to the decline of polytheistic religions, lent relative peace and stability, and supported commerce. Ultimately, the universalist religions became state religions and expanded their proselytizing missions.

Chapter 5 outlines the early history of Mecca, its tribal structures and religion, and describes what is known about Mohammad's ancestors.

The sixth chapter traces the early childhood, adolescence, and young adulthood of Muhammad in Mecca. The first revelations he received as a Messenger of God marked the beginning of Islam. Initially he had a small following. Persecution began after the incident of the "Satanic Verses." As the persecution intensified, he emigrated to Medina with some of his followers.

Muhammad's migration to Medina (the *Hijra*) is described in chapter 7. This is a major turning point in the career of Muhammad, the Messenger of God. A covenant, or the Constitution of Medina, was drawn up between his followers and the Arab (some Muslim and some pagan) and Jewish tribes of Medina. This remarkable document brought peace to the oasis and defined the beginning of a community or *umma* of those who had submitted to the authority of Muhammad.

Chapter 8 outlines the transformation of petty tribal raids into a *Jihad* or Holy War. This transformation marked a major change in the fortunes of the *umma*. The attacks against the caravans and trade of Mecca, which initially began for the economic well-being of the community, led to remarkable successes. Military victories were now associated with economic and political success, as well as the rapid spread of Islam.

The ninth chapter describes the Conquest of Mecca and the statesmanlike reconciliation of Muhammad with those who had bitterly persecuted him. This conquest marked the end of all major resistance to Muhammad and his *umma*.

Chapter 10 describes Muhammad's last years. The "Year of Deputations" describes the consolidation of Islam in Arabia.

A synthesis of events in the representational world of Muhammad as a leader and his impact on the development of a new group identity is presented in chapter 11. Muhammad not only internalized the traditional representational world of his clan in pre-Islamic Arabia, but he also transformed it. Muhammad created one of the most unique groups: a group that was religious, political, and could transcend the barriers of mortality. The revelations received by Muhammad as a Messenger of God, and his role as a leader, defined the initial representational shapes of the *umma*. The role of aggression in the *Jihad*, or Holy War, gave further shape to the representational world of the *umma*, and provided a foundation for building one of the most successful group forces in history.

The final chapter will review the explosive expansion of Islam during Muhammad's life and after his death. The reason for the success of Islam lies in the formation of one of the most powerful groups in history which provided not only for the basic needs of its members but also for *all* of their needs. The community or *umma* continued to be guided after his death by the Quran and the *Hadiths*, the sayings of Muhammad. Some implications for the theory and study of groups and group formation in history are explored. The historical material in chapters 4 to 11 illustrates and supports the theoretical position outlined in chapter 1. There is thus a circular relationship, in the hermeneutic sense, between the parts of the book.

The study of the life of Muhammad and the rise of Islam offers important support for the study and understanding of all group phenomena and group formation. This has critical significance today.

———— * ————

A hundred million lives have been lost in this century in human conflict and war—more than in any other century. Poverty and misery continue to burden parts of the globe, while other areas have witnessed an unprecedented rise in standards of living and wealth. Colonial and ideological empires have collapsed and given rise to new nations: some flounder while others flourish.

Two key traits characterize this century of progress and misery. First, the rapidity of social change has broken down traditional social ties, which have not been effectively replaced with new ones. In addition, the rise of a secular, scientific worldview has marginalized traditional faith and meaning. The resultant fragmentation of human society has led to a painful and dangerous paradox. As science and technology have become more global, our politics have become more parochial. As communication systems have become more universal, people, nonetheless, lack the ability to effectively communicate. As the need to pool global resources has increased, human society had fragmented even further (Isaacs, 1975).

Enlightenment values such as reason, science, equality, and freedom had promised to lead in a linear direction to a secular paradise. Today unambiguous faith in these values lies challenged and crumpled. Intellectuals had been optimistic that race, tribe, and religion would gradually lose power and not impede progress. Primordial ties, however, based on sentiment and passionate loyalty to family, clan, tribe, race, ethnicity, language, religion, and nation have been recalcitrant to such visions. These ties, baffling as they may seem, when combined with advances in modern weaponry, have created havoc and led to lethal regional and global conflicts.

How do we understand these powerful and often destructive ties? Mass human behavior has been difficult to conceptualize and comprehend. Sociological analysis and anthropological observations attempt to describe and define values and belief systems, culture and society. Psychology offers a perspective for an understanding of the individual. Economic models show the role of the utility-maximizing individual. Political science demonstrates the crucial role of elite leaders and governmental apparatus.

Although sociological, anthropological, and psychological theorists among others have sought to conceptualize and understand mass behavior, these attempts have not been completely successful. What is necessary is to add a dimension to this analysis. Common to the major problems on our planet is that these are the problems of groups. It is groups that live together, define commonalities, and create cultures. It is groups that develop economies and build nations. Groups grow, choose leaders, come into conflict, and go to war. A study of the genealogy of group processes and the formation of group identity would then allow a multifaceted approach to the study of family, clan, tribe, ethnicity, class, and nation.

For instance, conventional wisdom prevents a full understanding of recent events, as states collapse and boundaries are redrawn. Theorists who study the origins, rise, and fragility of nationalism, one of the dominant forces of our century, have yet to provide an in-depth analysis of it. The nation has been considered an invention, an artificial construct, or what has even been called an "imagined political community" (Anderson, 1991; Hobsbaum, 1990).

The case has been made even with regard to Great Britain where "the original modern idea of a nation emerged in sixteenth-century England, which was the first nation in the world (and the only one, with the possible exception of Holland, for about two hundred years)" (Greenfeld, 1992, p. 14). And thus, if we accept that "historically speaking, most nations have always been culturally and ethnically diverse, problematic, protean and artificial constructs that take shape very quickly and come apart just as fast, then we can plausibly regard Great Britain as an invented nation . . . " (Colley, 1992, p. 5). If nation states are artificial constructs and invented notions, we can understand why national group identities are difficult to consolidate today as boundaries change and populations shift.

One might go even further. It has been suggested that future wars and global tensions will no longer be based primarily on conflicts between nations, but on clashes between civilizations (Huntington, 1993). As the nation state weakens, civilizations—entities defined by ethnicity, language, history, and above all by religion—would fill the emotional gap in people's identities. With the exhaustion of national ideology, rulers and their rivals have been increasingly appealing to ethnic and religious identities. An appeal to a religious identity would resonate powerfully, since religion is perhaps the most compelling force that motivates and mobilizes people.

Part I

The Formation of a Group and Group Identity

1

The Formation of a Group: A Psychosocial Model

THE pursuit of knowledge, as philosophers of science agree, is defined by the underlying theories held by the observer of the universe being observed. As cognition defines the selection of perceptions among a mass of information and impressions that continuously assail us, we need, in fact cannot function without, a theory.

> It seems to be a characteristic of complex fields—cosmology, evolution, social science, psychology—that large and overarching theories are constructed in an attempt to provide guidance and justification for the investigator in what may otherwise be a disorganized terrain. (Rothstein, 1985, pp. 5–6)

To understand Muhammad and the rise of Islam we need to consider a model of the mind based on the psychology of the individual, an understanding of Arab culture, its anthropological sociology, and the historical circumstances of early seventh century Arabia. The task is to study individual biography and society in its historical context.

This chapter will examine these factors in an attempt to develop a comprehensive theory. This theory combines psychoanalytic and sociological perspectives to review the role of an individual in the formation of a group and a society. The task therefore is twofold: One task is to outline in brief the shortcomings of certain major representative points of view; the other task is to integrate and interpret the virtues of an alternative view.

By long tradition, biographical studies have mainly used psychoanalytic theory, an approach now considered a standard in the field. "Psychoanalytic theory repeatedly proves itself more illuminating or more useful than any other body of psychological theory..." (Runyan, 1982, p. 221). Sociologists and historians have also attempted to use psychoanalytic theory in their work. Psychoanalysis, however, a complex discipline, has not been accommodative to either sociology or history. "The fact that psychoanalysis in its classic form is inherently ahistorical and is characterized by a radical devaluation of the external world are only the most evident reasons for this" (Weinstein & Platt, 1973, p. 1).

Therefore, the model proposed here to understand Muhammad and the rise of Islam, combines a psychoanalytically based understanding of the individual with a study of his historical society at a given moment in time. The model emphasizes the sociohistorical impact of groups on the individual and on society. The model developed provides a way of looking at and thinking about individuals, groups, and history; it is in brief, a theoretical framework. The theoretical frame is a set of ideas that will include subsets of this set of ideas. A unique individual such as Muhammad, in turn, may in a dialectical manner have a profound impact on the transformation of groups, the social world, and ultimately on history.

Any understanding requires theory, which in turn requires abstractions, that simplify, structure, and order reality. The disordered realities of the everyday world, however, do not fit into precise, logically derived categories. Nor does a theory explain every fact. Yet, such abstractly derived categories are necessary to understand the real world and apply some of the lessons learned in this way to a broader universe. One measure of a theory is that it includes in its compass all the relevant facts. More importantly, does the theory encompass and explain those facts better than any other theory? The present volume suggests a relevant and more useful framework, defines some of the more important theoretical issues, and stimulates further thinking about a complex interrelated subject. The study of groups, that link the individual to all societal structures, and should be seen as modules or building blocks of even larger groups, has suffered from too little theorizing.

The purpose of this section on theory and the later review of psychoanalytic and sociological attempts to link the individual to cultures, society, and large groups, is not purely exegetical nor necessarily an attempt at synthesis for its own sake. Integrating several strands of theory may do injustice to the intent of the original formulation. The remarks of Talcott Parsons about his integrative intent has some appreciated parallels.

> The primary aim of the study is not to determine and state in summary form what these writers said... Its interest is not in the separate and discrete propositions to be found in the works of these men, but in a single body of systematic theoretical reasoning. (1949, p. 4)

As such, the model will integrate aspects of different theories to devise one theoretical basis for understanding.

The psychoanalytic understanding of the individual will be based on the work of the founding fathers of psychoanalysis, among them Sigmund Freud, Heinz Hartmann, and Erik Erikson. Unconscious motives, conflict, and developmental experiences expressed through the functions of the ego (and its defense mechanisms) as it adapts to the world around it, are central elements of psychoanalytic theory. Clinical psychoanalysis has led to the development of four familiar, conceptually separable perspectives on the functioning of the human mind. They are the psychologies of drive, ego, object relations, and self. While each perspective emphasizes somewhat different phenomena, they overlap and add to theoretical understanding. These perspectives when developmentally integrated not only allow an understanding of the shaping of the representational world of the individual but are also clinically relevant (Pine, 1988; Sandler & Rosenblatt, 1962).

The representational world of the individual provides an optimal link between his or her inner world and the outer social world. The representational world will also provide a screen where every developmental line will be reflected. The shared representational world of the group has a reality sui generis that exists prior to the individual, influences the representational world of the individual, and survives the individual.

Sociological contributions to an integrated theory will include a Weberian and Durkheimian approach to sociology. Weber's work on the subjective meaning or significance of social reality has to be combined with Durkheim's view of social phenomena as facts. Both views are fitting, but only when wedded together in a Hegelian dialectical synthesis can meaning emerge. Weber's emphasis on subjectivity can lead to idealistic distortion, whereas Durkheim's views alone on the objectivity of phenomena could risk the sociological reification that has been a problem with American sociology.

The model will also integrate Berger (Berger & Luckmann, 1967), Mannheim (1936/1985), and Merton's (1949) work on the sociology of knowledge. Whereas psychology has focused on the unique nature of individual thought, Mannheim considered that society not only determined the appearance but also the content of ideation. Since ideas are not immune to the influence of their social context, the sociology of knowledge is an important method and procedure to use when studying the sociohistorical origins of ideas. To avoid capitulation to the relativity of all sociohistorical issues, Mannheim's term *relationism* allows an awareness that all knowledge is not relative but is knowledge from a certain position (Mannheim, 1936/1985).[1]

Merton's concept of the "manifest" and "latent" function illustrates the important distinction between the conscious, intended function of ideas, and the latent, or unconscious, and unintended meaning. The sociology of knowledge thus analyzes everything that passes for knowledge in society and is particularistic as well as historical.

The social institutions that have the most impact on the individual will be studied as groups, such as the family, clan, tribe, or subculture (or class) and, overarching them, the "national" culture. These institutions should be studied as a "nested series of units, each of which is a population of lower-level units" (Wilson & Sober, 1994, p. 591). Groups and their impact on the individual are best observed as nestled inside one another like Chinese boxes. Links between the groups when studied as a nested series are clearer, and the impact of a change at any level and its impact on other levels, easier to determine than when analyzed separately. The family, or basic group, composed of a

---

[1] The epistemological status of biology, psychology, and sociology, as well as history, is by definition outside the realm of these empirical disciplines and belongs to the realm of philosophy.

number of individuals, is part of a clan or tribe (or subculture and class) made up of a large population of families. Similarly a number of tribes or classes will together form a protonation or nation with shared characteristics. The representational world of each group will have an impact on the groups both above and below it. The largest impact on all groups will be by the ultimate defining group, the "national" culture.

According to Campbell (1983):

> [M]ethodological individualism dominates our neighbouring field of economics, much of sociology, and all of psychology's excursions into organizational theory. This is the dogma that all human social group processes are to be explained by laws of individual behavior—that groups and social organizations have no ontological reality—that where used, references to organizations, etc., are but convenient summaries of individual behavior.... We must reject methodological individualism as an a priori assumption, make the issue an empirical one, and take the position that groups, human social organizations, might be ontologically real, with laws not derivable from individual psychology.... (quoted in Wilson & Sober, 1994, p. 597)

Groups do have the status of a separate ontological reality and the laws of group psychology are distinct, different, and are not derived from individual psychology. This had been assumed as early as the 1940s by Zilboorg (1944) who stated, "Each member of a large mass of people is both an individual and a nonindividual, a particle of a mass subject to many psychological laws different from those under which he primarily functions when alone, at home" (p. 6).

The present approach to the study of groups that allows a comprehensive assessment and understanding, rests on certain central assumptions. The groups studied are long lasting and stable groups. Each group begins with the individual. (The methodological focus on individuals prevents the reification of sociological structures and idealism.) Groups exist in the minds of individuals as well as in the real world. A large aspect of reality, including cultural and social reality, is entirely a construct and a creation of individuals. To see how this is constructed we need to review events in the world of the child, that is, in developmental events.

The first experiences of a child are with a mother. In this first set of experiences, in a dyad, is the beginning of a group.

Over time the mother assumes a directive and organizing role—the role of a leader. It is this role that will be reflected in the role of a leader (and follower) in all subsequent groups that an individual joins.

The mechanisms that tie a child to its mother and siblings were given fleeting recognition in the work of Freud who described reaction formation in childhood. In later life identifications with the leader as well as the members of a group develops. Together with early childhood reaction formation, these identifications allow attachments that are key to group formation. There are also other defense mechanisms that individuals use that are important for group formation.

There are identifications too of a different sort, with all the meaningful symbols offered by a culture, that when internalized form the totality of the symbolic world of the individual. These identifications define important aspects of two merged but separable identities, the individual and group identity. The representational world of the child, a unified concept, includes representations of developmental experiences, individual and group identity, and the entire realm of significant internalized social symbolic structures.

The needs of the group, including its basic needs, stem from and are derived from the needs of its individual members. Society functions to meet these needs, and sets up institutions as structures to serve them. The structural–functional school of sociology receives its importance from the study of both these structures and functions. It is these basic needs of the developing child and the secondary needs of individuals that are important to the study of how groups develop.

Because groups exist only in the minds of people, they need a leader or a subgroup to impress its will and gain a hold on the minds of its members. In order to grow, a group must sufficiently meet the needs of its members or it will lose its grip on their minds and wither. Finally how group functions are integrated to create a cohesive community with mutual trust will define why some groups flourish and others stagnate and decline.

The Representational World of the Child, Family, and Group

A child's subjective world differentiates through the course of gradual development including the process of biological, as well as psychological, adaptation. Freud (1940/1964) had differentiated between the external and internal world of the child. By the age of 5, "[a] portion of the external world has, at least partially, been abandoned as an object and has instead, by identification, been taken into the ego and thus become an integral part of the internal world" (p. 205).

The representational world of the child consists of representations or perceptions of the self and inner world as well as that of the object (or significant other) and the external environment. The construction of this world is one of the functions of the ego, which is both a structure and an organized set of functions. A representation is more than an image in that it includes need and affect (or feeling) representations. It is "a more or less enduring existence of an organization or schema which is constructed out of a multitude of impressions" or images (Sandler & Rosenblatt, 1962). Whereas a self representation is an organization that represents the person as he consciously and unconsciously perceives himself, an object representation is a representation of the significant other or object. Self representations also assume a variety of shapes that depend on the demands and standards of the inner world, as well as the needs and demands for adaptation to the external world.

The "ideal shape of the self" is the wished for shape of the self which would yield the greatest degree of well-being. Thus the "ideal state" for the individual is fundamentally that "feeling-state of well-being which normally accompanied harmonious and integrated psychobiological functioning" (Joffe & Sandler, 1968). Well-being becomes embodied in the "ideal shapes of the self," and discrepancy between the actual shape of the self at any moment and the corresponding or appropriate ideal self will be consciously or unconsciously experienced as conflict or mental pain. In fact, Joffe and Sandler state that "The aim of all ego functioning is to reduce conscious or unconscious representational discrepancy and through this to attain or maintain a basic feeling state of well-being" (p. 451). They further add that "The regulatory basis of the psychological control system . . . (is) based on the maintenance of a dynamic feeling homeostasis" (p. 452). Changes in feeling states are considered to be the "impetus" to the development of all psychological structures. In essence, psychoanalytic psychology is a psychology of adaptation to changes in feeling states. As such the theory is an intrapsychic one that integrates a general theory of adaptation within a fully psychoanalytic point of view.

The representational world of the child, however, is not limited to only the ideal and actual shapes of the self and significant others. Joffe and Sandler include "adaptation to reality as a (biologically predisposed) consequence of a more general principle of regulation and control" (p. 447). Adaptation to reality should therefore include adaptation and reality-mastery over the entire social world of the child. Moreover, if a feeling state of well-being accompanies "harmonious and integrated psychobiological functioning" then by extension well-being related to the social world as well, has to be included.

What follows is that the representational world of the child includes the world of the family, clan, culture, and society, all of which are experienced by the child. The world of the family and other structures around it has unfortunately not been the focus of traditional psychoanalytic thinking; however, there was good reason for it. Given that sociology and anthropology were young disciplines during the early years of psychoanalysis, a conceptual model that could link the inner intrapsychic world to the world outside was premature.

This difficulty has led the traditional psychoanalytic world to continue to stay primarily with the intrapsychic level. Psychoanalysis has tenaciously reflected its origin: a theory based on the retrospective reconstruction of individual intrapsychic events.

How can we link the representational world of the child to that of the family, clan or tribe, and society which have traditionally been the world of anthropological and sociological inquiry (Mills, 1959)?[2] In observing the development of a child in his

---

[2] The task and unfulfilled promise of his sociological imagination was to grasp biography and history and the relations between the two within society.

family and culture, one can identify, describe, and define these links as reflected in the child's representational world.

What sort of world does the child grow up in? All nonhuman species live in a closed world defined and thus limited by their biologically derived relationship to the environment. Man is the only species that can create his own environment. With his capacity for abstract thinking, symbol formation, and language, men together can create a symbolic order that defines culture and society. Models and blueprints of reality can become reality. Man has thus historically created his own cultural and social world. Ultimately the image of a social order provided by a culture becomes the defining element of a society. The large variations in society can be explained by the human capacity to create variable symbolic structures.

According to sociologists, the biological development of a child takes place in an environment that is both natural and human. The developing human being relates to a

> [S]pecific cultural and social order, which is mediated to him by the significant others who have charge of him. Not only is the survival of the human infant dependent upon certain social arrangements, the direction of his organismic development is socially determined. From the moment of birth, man's organismic development, and indeed a large part of his biological being as such, are subjected to continuing socially determined interference. (Berger & Luckmann, 1967, p. 48)

The "socially determined interference" stems from the fact that individual organismic development is preceded by a given social order. This social order is experienced by the child in, for instance, his mother's role as not only a mother but as a woman. This role of woman and mother, an abstract construct, was institutionalized and idealized over time (Berger & Luckmann, 1967, p. 54; the "Reciprocal typification of habitualized actions" is institutionalized as a role.) As such it became part of the history of the social order and a means to direct the role of the individual. A mother who was in any way less than this ideal would experience conflict and be defined as "role deviant." The abstract social construct of the role then is concretely experienced as a reified role, by each and every woman and mother. Man thus creates a social role, which is a historical social product,³ experienced as an objective reality and finally subjectively internalized as a role.⁴

Social order exists only as a product of human activity, and yet a child is unable to distinguish between the reality of social phenomena and the reality of natural phenomena. Language, for instance, appears to a child as real as the nature around him. A thing is what it is called and it is not the same by another name. Roles and institutions appear as immutable givens. Paradoxically, man thus creates the very world and reality that denies him.⁵

Whereas roles institutionalize a set of behaviors and conduct, a set of roles ultimately becomes the entire institutional order. How are these sets of roles that represent the entire institutional order transmitted or carried over to the next generation? Explaining and justifying these roles for the next generation is what makes them legitimate. This is done by a core body of knowledge and values that are passed on in several ways. The most important means of transmission is through vocabulary or language. A child learns that this person is his "mother." A second mode is through maxims, proverbs, and sayings that reinforce the image and role of what a "good mother" is like and should be.

A third level of legitimating would include a body of knowledge and a theory regarding the rights and obligations attributed to roles such as "motherhood." This knowledge and theory would be maintained and elaborated, for instance, by some older woman in the clan who would be the resident expert in the pure theory of "mothers and motherhood." The highest level of legitimation would be the "symbolic universe"⁶ where all the different sectors of the institutional order are integrated in an all-inclusive frame of reference. "The symbolic universe is conceived of as the

---

³ It was Durkheim who insisted on the sui generis character of social order.

⁴ The dialectical process by which this is done is "externalization" of the abstract product, a social role which is then "objectivated" and finally "internalized" as a concrete role. Contemporary American sociology tends to leave out the first step making it undialectical and prone to reification (cf. Berger & Luckmann, 1967, p. 66).

⁵ Dereification, the "seeing through" of roles as roles, is a late development in human history and individual biography (i.e., only after the capacity for abstract thinking in adolescence). The group process of "consciousness raising" can accelerate this dereification process.

⁶ Berger and Luckmann's (1967, p. 96) concept of a symbolic universe is very close to Durkheim's "religion." Religion would be a significant part of the "symbolic universe" of most individuals growing up in traditional cultures.

matrix of all socially objectivated and subjectively real meanings; the entire historic society and the entire biography of the individual are seen as events taking place within this universe" (Berger & Luckmann, 1967, p. 97). Berger and Luckmann clearly define symbolic universes as social products with a history. Unfortunately their reluctance to link intrapsychic events within the individual to social events, because of their concerns that such an alliance would be untenable, reduces the explanatory power of their construct of the symbolic universe (p. 205).[7]

The concept of the representational world of the individual and group serves a better purpose. If we accept that large segments of reality are social but cannot be reduced *only* to the social, we have to look once again at developments in the inner world or the representational world of the child. The inner representational world of the child in constant interaction with the outside world is obviously influenced by the dialectical and historical process of interaction between the child, family, and the changing culture and society around it. Each child, family, and culture changes at its own pace or rate.

The representational world of the child would in the beginning have to be a reflection of the needs and wishes of a child that would be met in interaction with the parent, family, and the world outside the family. The child's most basic needs would be its physiological needs for nurturance and safety, and a parent (or surrogate) to provide for these needs (Maslow, 1954).[8] If the basic needs of a child are not met, the child's future and to that extent the family and culture's future would be at risk. A group that we could call the basic group, defined as the dyad of a mother and a child, is critical, therefore, not only to the well-being, but to the very survival of the child. The addition of another parent, the father, would provide even more for the nurturance, safety, and well-being of the child as well as the mother (Reiss, 1965).[9]

---

[7] Berger and Luckmann's attempt at a genuine dialectical social psychology fundamentally Meadian in orientation falls short as they consider it "unnecessary to seek theoretically untenable alliances with either Freudian or behavioristic psychology." Their self is largely a reflected entity, a "social self" derived from Cooley (1902/1964) and Mead (1934–1962).

[8] The first two of Maslow's five basic needs are also physiological needs, as well as safety and security needs.

[9] The definition of what is family has recently undergone frequent and constant change. The slippery redefinition of family was reflected in Ira Reiss' (1965) view of

This triadic relationship, which contributes so much to the well-being of the child, is central to Freud's developmental oedipal theory (Shapiro & Perry, 1976).[10]

The mother–child dyad, or by extension the triad of mother, father, and child, should be considered as the most fundamental or basic group. However, the family, as we shall note, has surprisingly not been the basis of systematic study of group formation. The representational world of the child would be heavily influenced by the triadic events within this basic group which would be further influenced by not only the needs of the child, but the needs of this group. The needs of the child and this small group should define what *any* group would need. To meet the physiological needs of a child a family would need safe, regular supplies of food and water, warmth, and at a minimum some form of shelter. The social counterpart of the child's physiological needs and the similar needs of the family would define the rudiments or elementary form of an "economy." Second, a child would need some form of safety and well-being within a home that is also safe and secure from external threats. Parents would have to ensure that the home was protected and safe from any threats from the outside. This elemental need could be defined as the need for "security."

Erikson's (1959/1980) important observation that "the human life cycle and man's institutions have evolved together" (p. 250), can be linked to social institutions that evolved to meet the basic physiological and safety needs of a child. The market economy grew to meet physiological needs, and security apparatus or organizations developed to meet the safety needs of a child and family. Erikson's interest in developmental stages resulted in his taking for granted these basic needs and their institutional counterparts. The earliest threats, risks, and dangers that faced a

---

the family as "a small kinship-structured group with the key function of the nurturant socialization of the newborn" (p. 449).

[10] See Shapiro and Perry (1976), for a definition of oedipal theory that is not confined to a sexual (or sensual) libido based theory. In this view triadic concerns of positive and negative, loving and hating attitudes toward the first two significant objects, the parents, take on an overriding significance as the developmental process reaches into latency or middle childhood.

vulnerable child and mother, particularly in unstable social settings,[11] and the social structures that were created to meet them are very relevant, however, to the study of groups.

For Erikson the first developmental stage was when "basic trust" was established and the first social achievement of the infant is a general state of trust. The child has not only "learned to rely on the sameness and continuity of the outer providers, but also that one may trust oneself...."

> [This is] the first task of the ego, and thus first of all a task for maternal care... mothers create a sense of trust in their children by that kind of administration which in its quality combines sensitive care of the baby's individual needs and a firm sense of personal trustworthiness within the trusted framework of their culture's life style. (1950/1985, p. 249)

The faith which parents have in supporting the trust emerging in a newborn has, according to Erikson, its institutional safeguard, throughout history, in organized religion. "All religions have in common the periodical childlike surrender to a Provider or providers who dispense earthly fortune as well as spiritual health..." (p. 250). In a secular culture the state has to assume the institutional counterpart of a religion—become a provider of an environment that can be trusted on faith.

The next developmental stage for Erikson defined the "autonomy" of the child. This stage reaffirms the will of the child given "a sense of rightful dignity and lawful independence on the part of adults around him..." (p. 254).

> [This stage has] an institutional safeguard in the *principle of law and order*. In daily life as well as in the high courts of law—domestic and international—this principle apportions to each his privileges and his limitations, his obligations and his rights... thus the sense of autonomy fostered in the child and modified as life progresses, serves (and is served by) the preservation in economic and political life of a sense of justice. (p. 254)

Freud did not have institutional safeguards linked to his developmental stages but he did make observations about children that included the issues of equality, love, and justice. Freud had

---

[11] Some of these basic needs such as food and water as well as security are often taken for granted. However, throughout history and even today in civil strife, as most social groups collapse, as in Rwanda and Bosnia, children pay a heavy price as families are unable to meet these needs.

noted that when a younger child is born in the family the older child reacts with envy (1921/1955b, p. 86). It is in the reversal of what had once been envy and hostility into its opposite, a positive tie based on identification and a common tie of tenderness with a parent, that is the basis of affective group formation in the family.

Freud had in the process defined two mechanisms in childhood that support group formation—reaction formation (a defense mechanism) and identification. He went on to add: "there grows up in the troop of children a communal or group feeling, which is then further developed at school. The first demand made by this reaction-formation is for justice, for equal treatment for all" (p. 120). Freud also noted that the "demand that equalization shall be consistently carried through" was similar in the other groups he had studied, the church and army, and "that their necessary pre-condition is that all their members should be loved in the same way by one person, the leader" (p. 121).

Freud, in observing childhood events that contributed to "communal or group feeling," not only described two mechanisms that supported group formation, but defined the child's need for a sense of trust, equality, and justice from a parent. Freud also extended the child's manner of relating to the parent into the future. Adults would expect leaders in certain groups to love all their members in the same way. Freud, without being fully aware of the implications, had described what could be considered the childhood developmental origins of a democratic process! The expectation of "justice, for all, equal treatment for all" and the later "demand that equalization should be consistently carried through" is the very basis of individual rights in a liberal democracy and is fully met only when the rights are protected by laws and constitutional guarantees.

It is evident that both Freud and Erikson, using differing approaches, had defined in very similar terms the child's need for trust, equality, love, and the expectation of justice in the beginning from parents and later from group leaders and institutions. A child has to be accepted, liked, and loved in his home, and treated equally and fairly along with his siblings. The basic equality and fairness in the home would then define the earliest forms of "basic trust," and trust in its social counterpart "justice."

The "basic needs" of an individual in a group therefore are: (1) physiological needs; (2) a need for safety and "security"; and (3) a need for "basic trust."

The basic institutions to support these needs would be (1) a free economy; (2) a security structure that would provide safety from internal dangers and external threats (e.g., the police and army); and (3) laws and a legal system that can fairly enforce them.

The meeting of these "basic needs" would be reflected in a sense of well-being in the representational world of the child. When all the basic needs of the family are also met the actual shapes of the family in this regard would be congruent with the ideal shapes of the family for a sense of well-being to ensue in the shared representational world of the family. To maintain this sense of well-being, there would have to be a future dimension, a sense of trust that the well-being and "ideal shapes of the family," as a group, would continue to be experienced into the foreseeable future. This would require that the group maintain a leader who would plan and ensure that these basic needs continue to be met. Because of the vulnerable, helpless state of the child, in the beginning, decisions for the dyad would be made by the mother who would serve as the decision maker or leader. The leader would have to assess the reality of these needs, both present and future, and define and conceptualize an approach to provide these basic needs. The basic group would need a leader, a parent,[12] who would be responsible for conceptualization and planning of, not only the basic needs, but the separate needs of each child and of the needs of the family as a unit.

What is the impact of the parent as a leader on the developing ego of a child? At the individual level, according to Roy Schafer (1967), the interests, standards, and functions of a child:

> [Develop to a significant extent] in relation to parental care and example. The observing parent is not merely someone who opposes instinctual

---

[12] In an extended family which is hierarchical and patriarchal, the task would rest with the patriarch, and in the more egalitarian world of the nuclear family, the leadership could be invested in one or both parents.

expression and fosters renunciation.... (Identification with these aspects of the parent is at the center of superego formation). The observing parent also provides, teaches, and supports effective modes of ego activity, serving in this respect as an auxiliary ego. Simultaneously, the maturing child cannot fail to observe the parent's ego activities in many aspects of life and to be deeply influenced by his observations. Since the parent's activities and child-rearing practices inevitably express his own ego functions, interests, and standards (which, in their specific forms, are also more or less those of his culture), he continuously provides models and encourages the child to develop similar ego characteristics. (p. 137)

If the impact of a parent at the individual level is so significant, it follows that the impact of the parent as leader on the other children in the basic group would be important too. The parent would have to plan not only for the current needs of his family but the future needs as well. The parent would have the responsibility to meet the wishes and needs of the individual members, and guide them in a productive adaptive direction, separately as individuals and together as a family. The parent would define and determine the relations between and among the members of the family. He would have the task of synthesizing and integrating all the varied needs and wishes of the various members so that they would not only meet their own needs and wishes as individuals, but function well together as a family without major conflicts. The leader would thus define the *group relations* of the basic group (the group counterpart of object relations).

Functions, as Freud noted, that the parents carry out for the child and are internalized in the ego include "patterns of reality testing, relating to objects, control and expression of instinctual drives, autonomous ego activity, defenses" (Parens and Saul, 1971, p. 52).

To maintain well-being in any group, the tasks of the leader would be very similar to the tasks of a good parent as described above. They would be essentially adaptive and ideally require a set of adaptive ego skills that would define:

1. *Reality testing for the group.* This task would include assessment and judgment of the complex inner and outer worlds of each member and the group over time. The assessment and meeting of the changing "basic needs" of the group would require constant and accurate reality testing.

2. *Group relations or object relationships in the group.* They would initially be patterned by the leader's affective style of trust, intimacy, and relatedness. This would define a sense of trust, a group sense of trust, which would depend, as Freud had noted, on whether the members feel that they are "loved in the same way by one person, the leader." Good communication encouraged by the leader via the common medium of communication would allow the richness of the representational world of the group to be shared.

3. *The defense mechanisms and styles of the group.* Defenses are unconscious mental processes which the ego uses to cope with and resolve conflicts arising from instinctual drives and internal prohibitions as well as conflicts with significant others and the real world (Vaillant, 1977). Defense mechanisms moreover are stable, measurable, and predictable. Defense styles are conscious derivatives of various defense mechanisms and can be measured (Andrews, Pollock, & Stewart, 1989). Three defense styles have been identified and can be described as mature, neurotic, and immature. Good mental health and adaptive capacity are associated with mature defense style while an immature defense style has been linked to maladaption, personality disorder, and psychosocial immaturity.

Defense mechanisms and styles are a useful approach to the study of groups and group phenomena. Two defense mechanisms, reaction formation and identification, have already been noted to contribute significantly to group formation. The operation of defense mechanisms has proven of enduring utility for psychobiography and political psychology (Post, 1991; Runyan, 1982; Volkan, 1988). Groups also use mechanisms of defense that include denial, displacement, projection, altruism, and acting out (for a description of the use of denial in groups see Milburn and Conrad [1996]; for a use of projection in groups [Hofstadter, 1966; Sagan, 1991]; for altruism see Cohen [quoted in Ettin, 1993]).

Most studies of defense mechanisms are based on inferred intrapsychic processes in the individual. How do we assess defense mechanisms in groups or group defense mechanisms? These phenomena become much more complex as the size of a group increases. Freud, using an inferential process, had defined reaction formation and idealization that was the basis of group formation in a small group of siblings in a family. Intrapsychic events in a larger group can be inferred and assessed by surveys and polls (with all their limitations), and more directly when a group is involved in a fleeting collective action such as a riot or a mob lynching (Schmidt, 1982). It is in the shared representational world of a group of individuals that measurable events occur, however transiently, when a group is involved in shared thought, feeling, and action.

The defense mechanisms used by a group would initially be shaped by the leader. They would be defined by the predominant defense mechanisms which the leader uses to deal with both the world internal and external to the group. Later the needs of adaptation and survival may determine the choice of defense mechanisms of a group as well as the selection (or rise) of a leader.

The above functions of reality testing, group relations, and defense mechanisms are not discrete or separate functions. They are related in complex ways and could even overlap. These functions would ultimately define:

4. *The synthetic or integrative function of the group.* This function would determine how potentially discrepant or incongruent ideas, feelings, or behaviors of the members separately and together are reconciled or integrated to allow smooth biopsychosocial functioning of all its members at any given point. Trust in the leader and between the members would be the central ingredient to forming a cohesive group. Integrative functioning would also allow the group to attain and maintain long-term goals both separately (as individuals) and together.

This set of functions of the leader would serve as a precursor to group functions[13] that would determine for the group what purpose ego functions serve for the individual. While initially they would be heavily determined by the ego functions of the leader, over a period of time they may assume a level of secondary

---

[13] This set of group functions, related to the ego functions of an individual, has some similarity to the Parsons' "action" systems, his well-known AGIL scheme (Adaptation, Goal Attainment, Integration and Latency [pattern maintenance].) For a critique of the limitations of this model see Ritzer (1996, pp. 237–249).

A Psychosocial Model

autonomy. They could become specialized functions and be reflected in the adaptive roles played by subgroups of members.

So far we have traced events in the representational world of the child and the role and functions of the leader of the basic group, the family. How do these functions become autonomous and how are they maintained over time? In brief, how does the representational world of a group evolve?

The concept of the representational world of a group has several advantages over other terms. The concept is soundly based in methodological individualism; that is, the significance of the human agent is central. The representational world of the individual includes his developmental experiences as a child as he grows up in the basic group, the family. The representational world of an individual, a unified concept, thus includes developmental experiences, individual identity, group identity, and significant aspects of the internalized social symbolic world. The family as a group is influenced by and linked (via mechanisms including identification and internalization) to all groups above it as in a "nested series," and their representational worlds, in a dialectical manner. The representational world of a group reflects its history and its entire symbolic order which includes language, mythology, values, and beliefs that are associated with religion and culture. The representational world of a group will reflect the creative impact of innumerable individuals, some in a more significant manner than others.

The medium of communication of myths, rituals, and religion can often define and limit the shape and size of a group. (The development of print media in the 15th century in Europe allowed logical and linear forms of thought and ideas to spread over a vast terrain and reach a broader audience than the more traditional oral forms of communication.)

As a group differentiates over time specializations based on needs and functions to meet these needs emerge. The structures that are formed can become autonomous social institutions that survive the individuals who formed it. Specialized institutions, such as religious bodies and the army, create their own representational worlds. Leaders emerge in each group setting and in some instances an idea, or a set of ideas, such as a constitution or a sacred book lends leadership and flexibility (or fixity) to its representational world. The leader's defense mechanisms will become those of a group when shared and acted upon, and are ultimately reflected in the group's representational world. This may shape and define the future actions of a group.

A group functions with the aid of its specialized and differentiated subgroups and with the logic of its own inner dynamic to adapt to its environment and the world around it. A group therefore functions much as a multicellular higher organism of the highest evolutionary order—the human organism. After all, its needs and functions were basically derived from the individual. A group is greater than the sum of its parts in both its successes and its failures. A group is successful when its basic and other specialized needs are met so that it can function in an integrated, cohesive manner to adapt to the environment. A sense of mutual trust in every level of the group is critical to this integrated and cohesive adaptation. Mutual trust would promote a sense of well-being, a high morale, and pride in the group. This will be most likely when the ideal shapes of the group are close to or match its actual shapes for all or most situations.

As the primacy of childhood developmental experiences maintains a centrality and overriding significance into adulthood, the theoretical model of group formation described above also provides for the basis of a developmental paradigm for understanding an economy, the democratic process and religion. The elemental need of an infant for food, water and warmth provided by a parent and the basic group, in a family, could be the foundation for any developmental theory of economics. Later the need for freedom, equality, and justice for a child and adolescent in the home might give us the basis for understanding the developmental origins of democratic processes and democracy. As noted earlier, Erikson had observed that "all religions have in common the periodical childlike surrender to a Provider . . . who dispense(s) earthly fortune." It is in the powerful need and at times the magical wish for eternal affection and security in the exclusive care of loving, providing parents that we might look for the developmental origins of religion. Finally, this theoretical model of group formation provides substantial support to a general psychology that could link the individual to his entire world.

A Psychosocial Model

The next two chapters briefly outline the history of major attempts within psychology, psychoanalysis, and sociology to link the individual to groups and society. It was the limitations of these approaches that suggested the need and offered a rationale for the present model of group formation.

In later chapters, the life of Muhammad and the rise of Islam will be surveyed in order to reach an understanding of the origins, growth, and success of Islam in the basic principles of group formation. The life of the Prophet Muhammad demonstrates how he as a religious leader, with the revelations he received, singlehandedly created Islam. In empirical fashion how this happened lends support to the present theoretical model for the study of group formation.

The childhood of Muhammad illustrates the influence of the social world of the family, clan, and historic culture of Bedouin life in sixth century Arabia. This influence would be reflected in the shaping of his representational world. As Muhammad experienced conflict between the ideal shapes of his world and its actual shapes, he received revelations from God to form a new religious group that became Islam. When he and his followers faced persecution, they migrated from Mecca to Medina. As a leader, Muhammad's first tasks were to provide for the basic needs of his nascent group. He built basic trust in the group itself. In a new desert setting, with limited resources, he met the other basic needs of his group by initiating raids on rival caravans. The economic as well as the safety and security needs of his group were thus met in this enterprise that ultimately became a *Jihad* or Holy War against unbelievers. As a leader, Muhammad also provided a set of functions for his group; reality testing, adaptive defense styles, and integrative capacities that were critical for its survival. The representational world of the new group was defined by Muhammad and the revelations he received. He modified and merged old tribal traditions and institutions, as well as challenges from the surrounding Judeo-Christian world, to create entirely new structures. It is these structures that defined family, clan, legal systems, beliefs, and religion. This became the basis of a new culture and society, a single Muslim community. The Quran, a record of his revelations, and the *Hadiths,* the Prophet's sayings, were immortalized after his death and became the foundation for almost the whole representational world of Islam. They provide a religious constitution, the guiding principles of Islam. Muhammad had provided for all the needs of his community. The Sharia (or Holy Law) now provided a rule of law and justice for the community. The Quran offered a powerful medium of communication, in Arabic, that tied Arabia, and the expanding world of Islam, across generations, within a new and vast representational world. After the death of Muhammad, Islam functioned for a thousand years, up to the seventeenth century, as one of the most powerful group forces in history. The Holy Wars (*Jihad*) fought to support its Holy Law became the basis of a phenomenal expansion. It was the cohesive, integrated, and adaptive capacities of Islam, first defined by Muhammad, that were the key to this immense success. For large stretches of its history, the ideal shapes of Islam were close to its actual shapes. In fact, until the clashes with the forces of the European imperialist expansion, beginning in the seventeenth century, no culture offered any serious challenge to alter the basic view Islam had of itself.

Muhammad had made a permanent mark on world history. History has often been seen as nothing but the history of individuals, of kings and emperors and the wars they fought. History, however, should be clearly seen as the history of groups and their leaders. History is group history.

Part II

Psychoanalytic and Sociological Perspectives

2

Psychoanalysis and Sociology: The Links between the Individual and Society

Psychoanalysis: The Sociological Implications

FREUD had been convinced that psychoanalysis would allow a mastery of the complex challenges of both history and culture. Over time he developed two somewhat different approaches to address these issues. One theory, complex and elaborate in form, was based on the classical psychoanalytic model and instinct theory. The other view, which was much less developed, was fragmented and rudimentary in shape, and implied a more sociological orientation.

Freud had initially based his theory of the etiology of neurosis in the actual event of a childhood sexual seduction. The subsequent abandonment of the seduction hypothesis and a focus on the sources of fantasy led to the development of psychoanalysis rather than social theory. "This second theory effectively removed social interaction from the center of analytic thought" (Rothstein, 1985, p. 9).

Freud had thus identified infantile sexuality (within the frame of libido theory) as the major determinant of symptom formation and the nuclear Oedipus complex as the basis of neurosis. He went on to add that the variations in the resolution of the oedipal conflict defined not only internal (or intrapsychic) reality but defined activities in the external world as well. The external world was nothing but the inner world writ large. In

Totem and Taboo (1913/1955a), Freud elaborated further on how the oedipal conflict was a phylogenetic inheritance. For Freud, the primal murder of the father by his sons was a real historical event that became an acquired characteristic, by means of a Lamarckian process of inherited psychological characteristics, a theory considered untenable today. Thus changing social and historical reality was redundant, libidinal instinctual life and wishes based upon it were the only unchanging and immutable primary reality.

Society and culture were considered to be a projective screen and nothing but a set of defenses against erotic libidinal wishes and derivatives of the second instinctual aggression based drive. In this view "the essential feature of society—the exogamous family, clan differentiation, hierarchical social structure, political institutions and religion—are all collective responses to the anxiety created by . . . instinctual ambivalence and the tendency to control it through the projection of mythic constructs" (Bergen & Rosenberg, 1971, p. 31).

Freud was evidently not satisfied by such a reductionist position. In a major revision of his theory he formulated structural theory (1923/1961) which refers to the following three structures: id, ego, and superego.

> The id refers to the instinctual aspects, the ego to the reality principle and to the "centralization of functional control" (to borrow a term from brain physiology). The superego has its biological roots in the long dependency on the parents and in the helplessness of the human child; it develops out of identifications with the parents; and it accounts for the fact that moral conflict and guilt feelings become a natural and fundamental aspect of human behavior. The structural formulations, referring to the distinctions of ego, id, superego, have several theoretical and clinical advantages. The most important is probably that the demarcation lines of the three systems ego, id, superego are geared to the typical conflicts of man: conflicts with the instinctual drives, with moral conscience, and with the outside world. (Hartmann, 1965, p. 325)

The emphasis in Freud's thought had now shifted in a major way from the id to the ego, from repression to the forces that repressed, from libidinal drives to relationships (object relationships), and finally from inner to outer reality. The structural theory also "had extraordinary explanatory power . . . (and) . . . led eventually to an emphasis on the centrality of the ego's executive role . . . '' (Rothstein, 1985, p. 10). This shift in thinking was of major import. The relationships to the parents as the first love objects would define the formation and character of ego and superego. The ego and superego shaped by experiences with the parents and the external world clearly allowed Freud to define the possible sociological significance of this new view. "We have repeatedly had to insist on the fact that ego owes its origin as well as the most important of its acquired characteristics to its relation to the real external world'' (1940/1964, p. 201).

While the role played by external objects via identification and internalization clearly affected the character of the ego and superego, the limited and rudimentary nature of Freud's concept of object relationship, and his reluctance to deal with the external world beyond the family, hindered a broader view. The emphasis on inner reality influenced by instinctual drives further hampered understanding and analysis of the external world. Thus both of Freud's models for understanding social and historical events, one a well-developed libido-based theory that allowed an understanding of inner dynamics, and a second model based on structural theory that implicated the external world but not in a systematic manner, failed in allowing an integration of psychoanalysis in other disciplines.

Rothstein (1985) states that

> [W]hile Freud, in a way, saw everything, it is clear that he had biases and predilections which made it difficult for him to give evenhanded attention to matters that today seem of major importance. I refer to such ideas as the developmental significance of the real role of real parents and the culture they represent, . . . the role of dependency, attachment, and safety in development alongside the role of instinctual drives; the central organizing and synthesizing functions of an ego or self; and the importance of nonconflictual aspects of development, to mention but a few. These, and other areas of Freud's opposition or inattention have been the gaps in the standard theory which many of the alternate or revised psychoanalytic theories have attempted to fill. (p. 10)

The classical psychoanalytical viewpoint, with its focus on the genetic view and its emphasis on intrapsychic experience, was relatively uninterested in the real world where these experiences unfolded. Maturational stages were more important to outcome than the vicissitudes of the environment. Gaps in theory had to be filled and theoretical links with the outer or real world established.

Since then, several attempts have been made essentially using psychoanalytic frames of reference to allow an understanding of the mass of unassimilated historical and sociological data. The most significant of these attempts was by Erikson.

Erikson's important and influential work provides another attempt and a model for linking the individual to society. Erikson (1975) had observed that:

> [P]sychoanalysis had broken through to much that had been totally neglected or denied in all previous models of man: it had turned *inward* to open up man's inner world, and especially the unconscious, to systematic study; it searched *backward* to the ontogenetic origins of the mind and of its disturbances; and it pressed *downward* into those instinctual tendencies which man thought he had overcome when he repressed or denied the infancy of individuals, the primitivity of man's beginnings—and evolution. (p. 39).

Erikson developed a theory of the individual at different developmental stages that led to a psychoanalytic theory of psychosocial development. Erikson also challenged basic psychoanalytic assumptions about the biology-based, sex-oriented stages of human development. Through his psychosocial model, he hoped to humanize the biologism of Freudian theory. Considering his work an outgrowth from within psychoanalysis he maintained (1966) that "the psychoanalytic method itself demands that the record proceed from the case history to the life history, from the symptoms of human conflict to the signs of human strength, from man's adaptive and defensive maneuvers to his generative potentials" (p. 646).

In *Childhood and Society* (1950/1985) Erikson suggested that it was the family and society that offered and invited at each stage of a child's development a set of potentialities for his or her growth. The study of identity at each stage would thus provide an understanding of the complex unfolding of the human organism. In fact, he felt that the study of identity would become as strategic in our time as the study of sexuality was in Freud's. Erikson considered identity to be "more than the sum of the childhood identifications. It is the accrued experience of the ego's ability to integrate all identifications with the vicissitudes of the libido, with the aptitudes developed out of endowment, and with the opportunities offered in social roles" (1950/1985, p. 261). The ego for Erikson was "a selective, integrating, coherent, and persistent agency central to personality function" (1964, p. 147).

Erikson's psychosocial model, moreover, allowed for the first time a broader application of psychoanalytic theory to both sociological and historical phenomena. Erikson correctly believed that "the phenomenon and the concept of *social organization* and its bearing on the individual ego was... for the longest time, shunted off by patronizing tributes to the existence of 'social factors'" (1959/1980). Erikson went further than any other post-Freudian analyst in explaining psychological phenomena in social terms.

Erikson's contributions to a sociological approach evolved in several ways. His focus on making adequate or superior functioning plausible instead of a fixation only on psychopathology and dysfunction added a corrective element that allowed a better understanding of how conflicts at several developmental stages are resolved. As psychoanalysis had evolved as a form of a therapy it had to move away from retrospective fixations and a "traumatological psychology" (Evans, 1967, p. 74) to become useful as a normative general psychology that could include data from sociology. To counteract the seeming pessimism, negativism, or fatalism of early psychoanalysis, Erikson shifted his focus on "what, in man's total existence, leads *outward* from self-centeredness to the mutuality of love and communality, *forward* from the enslaving past to the utopian anticipation of new potentialities and *upward* from the unconscious to the enigma of consciousness" (Erikson, 1975, p. 39).

Second, Erikson's elaboration of the psychosocial stages of development, which complemented Freud's psychosexual stages, was clearly the sort of theoretical development that linked the individual to the society he lived in. Erikson's extension of developmental theory beyond Freud's oedipal and latency stages through adolescence to adulthood, further linked the individual to society throughout the life cycle.

The centrality of Erikson's formulations to the fabric of ego psychology was summed up in a sympathetic review by Rapaport as follows:

The crucial characteristic of this psychosocial theory of ego development, and of Hartmann's adaptation theory (in contrast to the "culturalist" theories) is that they offer a conceptual explanation of the individual's social development by tracing the unfolding *of the genetically social character of the human individual* in the course of his encounters with the social environment at each phase of his epigenesis. Thus it is not assumed that societal norms are grafted upon the genetically asocial individual by "disciplines" and "socialization" but that the society into which the individual is born makes him its member by influencing *the manner in which* he solves the tasks posed by each phase of his epigenetic development.... (quoted in Erikson, 1959/1980, p. 11)

Erikson had thus taken the important critical and crucial step in the direction of a psychoanalytic sociological position.[2] However, links to sociological institutions beyond the family which impact and significantly affect behavior beyond the childhood years were not fully developed. In fact social institutions, beyond the family, have a significant impact on the individual at every stage of the life cycle. These institutions have an existence sui generis and in fact, have an existence prior to the individual and survive him or her. They are not, moreover, mere projections or object representations of the original family.

Explicitly aware of social structures and their impact on individual dynamics, Erikson used his psychosocial approach in his well-known psychohistorical studies of Luther (1958) and Gandhi (1969). Despite the significant and important contributions of Erikson, psychohistorical work has its almost exclusive focus on the biography of the individual and often that of the elite individual. "The history of the common man, or of the mass or group is neglected, and the complex effects of social structure on personality are still seriously underevaluated" (Weinstein & Platt, 1973, pp. 12–13). This is because Erikson did not investigate large aspects of sociologically influenced reality. As a result he did not fully develop and extend the compass of his theoretical framework to larger social structures in a systematic way.

In their valid critique of Erikson, Weinstein and Platt state that

this emphasis on the study of individual lives has had one particularly unfortunate consequence ... one finds in such work the acceptance of

---

[2] While many analysts such as Kris and Hartmann had developed an "Environmentalist" position (i.e., influenced by culture and society) this was not *fully* developed.

an implicit assumption that, since great men have helped to shape great events, they must have had special experiences and insights, but that the effectiveness of their leadership must also reflect common experiences, especially of an ontogenetic–familial sort. On the basis of this position one often notes that, when the problem of mass behavior is addressed, the motivation for this behavior is simply and mistakenly inferred from the motivation of the leader. (1973, pp. 12–13)

As such, Erikson's theory of psychosocial development was hindered by his attachment to the ontogenetic–familial model. The obvious and fuller sociological implications of his work were not comprehensively drawn and in his historical studies he limited himself to the analysis of individuals. He created the model of the unique individual with ego strengths that were never defined except in their ultimate accomplishments, nor did he spell out the structure of this model so that it could be applied easily to other individuals.

Several attempts have been made since Freud and Erikson, using defined psychoanalytic frames of reference to make sense of the intractable sociological and historical data. (See Weinstein & Platt [1973] for a discussion of the limitations of two models based on familial–ontogenetic schemas, one developed by studies of the Authoritarian Personality and the other a generational model.) "But each of these [theoretical models] . . . can in turn be shown to be inadequate on theoretical and methodological grounds—and, hence, ultimately on substantive grounds as well (Weinstein & Platt, 1973, p. 2).

Sociological Theory and the Individual

Given the limitations of psychoanalytic attempts to link the world of the individual in a comprehensive way to the vast and varied influences of culture and society, a brief review of the reverse, sociological attempts to study the impact of society on the individual, is necessary.

Sociological thought, and the very formation of the discipline of sociology, began in Europe in the early nineteenth century as the political revolutions ushered in by the French Revolution of 1789 and the Industrial Revolution effected major changes in the patterns of life. With the decline in the authority of monarchy and church, there seemed to be no authority to hold society together. The chaos and disorder in France after the French Revolution had been striking. Industrialization and increased urbanization transformed society by a breakdown of long-established values and ways of living.[3]

The motivation for the sociological thinking of Emile Durkheim not only resulted from a sense of the impending crisis of Europe, but also as an attempt to formulate the central question of sociology—"How is social order possible?" Durkheim had been "haunted by the thought that modern society . . . was a fragile affair, a potentially unstable mix of elements that was always on the verge of dissolving into chaos . . . and . . . he saw himself in a race against time with the gathering forces of anarchy" (Parkin, 1992, p. 59).

In addition to Emile Durkheim, Karl Marx and Max Weber not only formulated similar questions but also provided theories of enduring relevance and concern in an attempt to provide a systematic answer. The social changes in Europe had a profound impact on religious beliefs and practice. For Auguste Comte, the first to use the term *sociology*, sociology itself was transformed into religion. For other sociological theorists, the impact of religion was unmistakable in their work. A large body of the work of Weber (1963) was in fact devoted to the study of the world's religions and a major work of Durkheim (1912/1976) was on religion. Marx (1977), far more critical, was very interested in religious belief and practice.

The growth of the successful physical and biological sciences challenged sociology to be more scientific. Custom, tradition, and religion were seen as full of mystifying superstition when examined in the light of "Reason." The new faith in reason and science was seen as relevant to the organization of human affairs and society. Society and social structures were not preordained and inevitable but were seen as amenable to review and could be changed for the bettering of general welfare. Unquestioned belief

---

[3] Almost two centuries later, with a similar breakdown of long-established values, a sense of urgency is evident in the developing world (and in postcommunist Russia) as it searches for order (Huntingdon, 1996; Kaplan, 1996).

and received wisdom was therefore to be replaced by a scientific awareness based on careful and systematic inquiry.

For Comte sociology was to be the science which would allow an understanding of society and provide a basis for its reconstruction. It would also provide a healthy corrective reaction to the pervasive individualism of the early Enlightenment thinkers such as Descartes, Hobbes, and Locke. In his *Course of Positivist Philosophy* he was insistent that "the scientific spirit forbids us to regard society as composed of individuals" (quoted in Hughes, Martin, & Sharrock, 1995, p. 6). Comte was not denying the existence of individuals, but stressing the relationships among individuals. Individuals were as much products of society, as society was a product of groups of individuals.

Marx also challenged classical economists who claimed that it was the competitive and acquisitive individuals who produced a capitalist society. In Marx's contrary view it was a capitalist society that produced competitive and acquisitive individuals. For Durkheim too, it was the priority of society over the individual. In fact, it was Durkheim who developed the concept of society as a reality sui generis existing over, above, and independently of the individual. He compared society to the human body as being an organic whole with several institutional components just as the body had interrelated organs.

Weber, rankled by the crude materialism and the sweeping claims of economic determinism of Marx and the Marxists of his day, who suggested a single cause theory of social life, challenged a theory that linked all historical and contemporary structures to only economic factors.[4] Weber rejected the view that ideas were a simple reflection of material (mainly economic) interests that determined the ideology of the time. He "turned Marx on his head" by insisting that it was ideas that shaped an economy. Ideas were not simple reflections of economic factors to Weber, but were independent and autonomous forces that could have a profound effect on an entire economy. In *The Protestant Ethic and the Spirit of Capitalism* (1930) he offered considerable evidence

---

[4] Marx's concept of *dialectical materialism* had origins in Hegel's (dialectic) and Feuerbach's (materialism) ideas. Marx's alleged economic determinism has been recently challenged.

that Protestantism as a system of ideas, had a major impact on another system of ideas, the capitalist economic system.

Marxist thinking was challenged by Weber on its prescriptive assumptions as well. Marx was well known for his conviction that social transformation could be brought about only by political means. Pious dreams and utopian visions could not provide the results that only radical and revolutionary action could. Marxist thinking was thus linked to the cataclysmic echoes of the French Revolution. Whereas Durkheim had adopted a more conservative stance and felt that pathological social institutions could be reorganized to improve the conditions of humanity, Weber was dubious and skeptical about interventionist strategies. He did not see any general laws that governed social processes and stressed the possibility of chance and contingency in human affairs. He did not see a role for social reform despite the fact that he was a severe critic of modern capitalist society. Indeed he saw rationality, a liberating principle of the Enlightenment, as a mixed blessing. Progress in science and technology accompanied a soulless bureaucratized world that he called the "iron cage" of rationality.

Weber made a substantive contribution to contemporary sociology by outlining a methodology which attempted to take into account the individual's (the social actor's) subjective interpretation of social reality. Weber's interpretative sociology *(verstehende sociology)* was a powerful critique of the observer's (sociologist's) arbitrary interpretation of social reality that ignored the actor's own definition.

The main problem with and a serious shortcoming of the classical sociological understanding of the individual was sociology's commitment to reason and evolutionary progression based on rational man. This sociological frame of reference could not explain the often nonconscious and nonrational determinants of human behavior. Marx had predicted that the rational and progressive moves of society would inevitably have to face the inherent and irreconcilable contradictions of economically based class interests and end in major conflict. Marx's economic reductionist views failed as workers in the advanced industrial countries did not respond as he had expected. Marxist theories could not explain the stark failure and the lack of a mass radicalization of political action in the direction of revolution. A reason for this failure was Marx's obliviousness to and lack of awareness of most psychic processes including internalization.

A similar problem arises with the work of Weber. Weber made unparalleled contributions to theory and methodology. He gathered substantial historical data, particularly in his massive comparative analysis of religion, in essence, a comparative sociology of civilizations.[5] For instance, Weber's account of the charismatic leader or prophet misses an essential dimension—the charismatic orientation to action is not within full conscious awareness or control. The characteristics, moreover, of charisma are still unclear.

The study of society by classical sociologists such as Marx, Weber, and Durkheim on a systematic basis barely antedates the twentieth century. Within this relatively short life span there have been a number of transformations in academic sociology. Sociology went from a humanistic and reformistic tradition to empirical, value-free investigations. American sociology turned away from historical perspectives to a "scientistic" orientation, from universalistic abstractions to "quantitative" methods. As Ross (1991) puts it, "American social scientists . . . (turned) . . . away from interpretative models available in history and cultural anthropology, and from the generalizing and interpretative model offered by Max Weber" (p. 473). Instead of the study of long-term historical change, sociology turned to the scientific study of short-term process.

Structural-Functionalism in Sociology

Since the work of the classical European sociologists, no theory has been the focus of as much interest as structural-functionalism. It was the dominant sociological theory in the United States from the 1930s to the early 1960s, especially in the work of Talcott Parsons, Robert Merton, and their followers (Ritzer, 1996, p. 233).

One of the most significant attempts at linking psychoanalysis and sociology was the early work by Talcott Parsons. Parsons

---

[5] His studies of Islam were somewhat limited compared to his works on other world religions (Turner, 1974).

(1964) observed that, "In the broadest sense, perhaps, the contribution of psychoanalysis to the social sciences has consisted of an enormous deepening and enrichment of our understanding of human motivation. This enrichment has been such a pervasive influence that it would be almost impossible to trace its many ramifications" (p. 17). He noted that whereas psychoanalysis concentrated on the study of the personality of the individual, sociology "has equally naturally been primarily concerned with the patterning of the behavior of a plurality of individuals as constituting what, increasingly, we tend to call a social system" (p. 18). Sociology and psychology had historical differences based on perspectives and points of departure. As the conceptual schemas of the two disciplines were not congruent, numerous misunderstandings developed.

In an attempt to bring the main theoretical trends of the two disciplines together under a common frame of reference, Parsons attempted what some sociologists have called a "theory of action." He noted that the process of convergence had begun with Freud's concept of the superego. Dramatically convergent with this concept was that of the social origins of moral norms (a formulation developed by Emile Durkheim). This formulation went on to become a cornerstone in the development of sociological theory. Durkheim, whose views on this subject may have slightly antedated Freud's, observed that an individual member of society is "constrained" in making moral decisions not by any coercive external force, but by moral authority. The effectiveness of this moral authority could not be understood without the assumption that these moral values had been "internalized"[6] in the individual personality. It was these internalized moral standards that lent structure and stability to an entire social system.

This internalization process also had important implications for the theory of personality and for the theory of social systems. With a focus on the individual, Freud and his followers had failed to see the interaction of personalities that could form a social system, whereas Durkheim and other sociologists had not recognized that it was the interaction of personalities that constituted

---

[6] Internalization as a concept developed independently in the work of Freud, Emile Durkheim in France, and in the work of sociologists Charles H. Cooley and George Herbert Mead in the United States (Parsons, 1964, p. 80).

this system. Freud, moreover, had too narrow a view in suggesting that the internalization process involving the superego addressed only moral standards. Parsons broadened this perspective by insisting that *all the components of the common culture* are internalized as part of the personality structure.

To Parsons the superego thus provided a bridge, or a bridging concept, because it could not be explained except as acquired from other humans in a social interactional process. Parsons noted that Freud's work had been initially interpreted as having brought "psychology closer to the biological sciences, and to suggest the relative unimportance of society and culture, except as these constitute agencies of the undesirable frustration of man's instinctual needs" (pp. 78–79). Parsons observed that in the complicated evolution of Freud's theories another concept that also provided a bridge was the concept of "object relations"—"the most important area of articulation between the psychoanalytic theory of the personality of the individual, and the sociological theory of the structure and functioning of social systems" (1964, p. 79). His thesis was that there was "in the structure of Freud's own theoretical scheme, a set of propositions which can, with relatively little reinterpretation, be very directly integrated, . . . with the sociological analysis of the family as a small scale social system . . . " (p. 79).

The starting point for the socialization of the child was the action of the mother, the agent responsible for the care of and gratification of the needs of the child. For the infant, "the mother is a *social* object and becomes the most important part of 'reality'—that is, the environment external to him" (p. 92). It is in this process that the mother becomes the "object-choice" in Freud's sense. As the child grows it internalizes the learned aspects of "fundamentals of reciprocal role behaviors in a *dyadic* relationship, the simplest type of social system" (p. 95). It was this "internalization" of "object relations" that provided Parsons with concepts from psychoanalysis that were compatible with and provided linkages to his analysis of social systems.

Parsons thus made the first systematic attempt to integrate concepts from psychoanalytic theory in sociology using the family as a social system. Parsons' contributions, however, have serious limitations and fall short in many ways. Parsons' penchant for grand theory tended to reify the cultural and social system and moved away from the empirical bent of Durkheim and Weber. He dealt with abstract social systems instead of real societies. His work was highly abstract and lacked empirical and historical specificity. He did not develop a comprehensive and detailed framework that specified and defined the various bonds between an individual and society. In describing some of these binding links, he defined issues of stable social structure but he did not work on the problems of conflict, instability, and change. More importantly, Parsons' frame of reference does not allow us to understand how an individual can change internalized mandates to adapt to society or in exceptional situations even mold society to his mandates (see Baldwin [1961] for a critique of the limited view of personality in Parsons' work). Throughout his life Parsons had attempted to integrate a wide range of input into his theory. He was interested in the interrelationships of the cultural, social, and personality systems as the major domains of the social world. In the end, however, Parsons abandoned his synthetic orientation, adopted a narrow structuralist–functionalist orientation, and defined the cultural system as determining the other systems.

Widely accepted by sociologists and anthropologists, structural-functionalism in the work of Parsons, Merton, and others was "without any doubt the single most significant body of theory in the social sciences in the present century" (Turner & Maryanski, 1979, p. xi). Kingsley Davis considered this theory for all intents and purposes synonymous with sociology (Davis, 1959). Although the term *structural-functionalism* is typically conjoined, the terms *structural* and *functional* can be used separately. We can, for example, study the structures of a society without necessarily being concerned with their functions or their consequences for other structures.

Structural-functionalism has suffered from the same substantive criticisms leveled at Parsons. It has been considered inherently ahistorical (a reaction to the highly speculative historical evolutionist views of early anthropologists) and unable to deal effectively with change and conflict. Other criticisms of structural-functionalism have been based on logical and methodological grounds (see Ritzer [1996, pp. 253–259] for a comprehensive view of this critique).

In conclusion, sociological theorists often took the reductionistic position that personality was an epiphenomenon of the structure of society. The personality system was reduced to secondary or dependent status and was not fully developed. Thus the impact of the unconscious and irrational and nonrational behavior of individuals and groups on culture and society still remains outside the purview of sociology. Weinstein and Platt (1973) make the important point that "The classic sociological problems of order and change require for adequate solution an interpretation of personality in all dimensions, and a comprehensive theoretical view must include some notion of psychic processes systematically related to society and culture" (p. 33).

3

Theories of Group Formation

THE first major attempt to understand group psychology was by Sigmund Freud. Until this time there had been little conception of a group except as a mob or collectivity. In *Group Psychology and the Analysis of the Ego* (1921/1955b) he observed "[T]he contrast between individual psychology and social or group psychology, which at a first glance may seem to be full of significance, loses a great deal of its sharpness when examined more closely." He added that "in the individual's mental life someone else is invariably involved, as a model, as an object, as a helper, as an opponent; and so from the very first individual psychology . . . is at the same time social psychology as well . . . " (p. 69). He went on to state that instead of the impact and influence of one person or a small number of persons on a single individual, group psychology was:

> [T]he influencing of an individual by a large number of people simultaneously, people with whom he is connected by something, though otherwise they may in many respects be strangers to him. Group psychology is therefore concerned with the individual man as a member of a race, of a nation, of a caste, of a profession, of an institution, or as a component part of a crowd. . . . " (p. 70)

Freud had thus laid the outline of a special psychology, a group psychology, and raised questions for a theoretical group psychology. What was a group? How did it acquire such a decisive capacity to influence an individual's mental life? And what was the nature of the change it forces on mental life? He went on to debate whether:

> [I]t is easy to regard the phenomena that appear under these special conditions as being expressions of a special instinct that is not further reducible—the social instinct ("herd instinct", "group mind") which does not come to light in any other situations. (p. 70)

He decided, however, that "it seems difficult to attribute to the factor of number a significance so great as to make it capable by itself of arousing in our mental life a new instinct that is otherwise not brought into play" (p. 70). He then explored "two other possibilities: that the social instinct[1] may not be a primitive one and insusceptible of dissection, and that it may be possible to discover the beginnings of its development in a narrower circle, such as that of the family" (p. 70). Freud unfortunately did not explore these two possibilities any further. As a field, group psychology was still in its infancy.

Freud remarked that the classification of different types of group formation would require considerable effort. This important contribution to the study of groups would be based on the morphology of groups. Le Bon (1920), in an early classic, had said that the person who joined a group sacrificed aspects of his precious individuality. He would be more suggestible and therefore susceptible to the contagious impact of others who experienced the invincible power of groups. Le Bon had thus portrayed groups from a negative point of view. He compared the *group mind,* an interesting term, to be similar to the mental life of children and "primitive" people. He described it as changeable, impulsive, and irritable and led exclusively by the unconscious. Le Bon had been careful, however, to indicate that he was writing about large groups or crowds that were like obedient herds thirsting for a strong leader or master.

McDougall, in his book *The Group Mind* (1920), also wrote about crowds that did not have the rudiments of an organization. In a crowd an individual may feel a sense of unlimited power and of insurmountable peril. Such a group was:

---

[1] Instincts in humans comparable to a term used about animals in animal ethology are questionable. The term translated from the German *trieb* is better translated as instinctual drives.

[E]xcessively emotional, impulsive, violent, fickle, inconsistent, irresolute and extreme in action, displaying only the coarser emotions and the less refined sentiments; extremely suggestible, careless in deliberation, hasty in judgment, incapable of any but the simpler and imperfect forms of reasoning; easily swayed and led and lacking in self-consciousness, devoid of self-respect and of sense of responsibility . . . and in the worst cases it is like that of a wild beast rather than like that of human beings. (Quoted in Freud, 1921/1955b, p. 85)

Both Le Bon and McDougall in writing about unorganized groups had been writing about crowds and mobs and had undoubtedly been influenced by the descriptions of the mobs of the French Revolution. The terrors of anarchy that mobs, as groups, created was reflected very well in these early writings.

A well-organized group in contrast to the unorganized had five characteristics according to McDougall. It had to have a degree of continuity of existence as a group; interactions with other groups; traditions, customs, and habits; some degree of specialization and differentiation of functions, and finally the individual members of the group should have some idea of the nature, composition, capacity, and functions of the group.

Freud remarked that McDougall had equipped the group with individual attributes and his observations could be related to "a valuable remark of Trotter's to the effect that the tendency towards the formation of groups is biologically a continuation of the multicellular character of all higher organisms" (1921/1955b, p. 87). Freud suggested that biologically gregariousness was analogous to multicellularity, and that his libido theory allowed an understanding of this inclination, "which is felt by all living beings of the same kind, to combine in more and more comprehensive units" (1921/1955b, p. 118). Freud once again did not explore this important insight except for these two scattered observations.

Freud struggled to understand groups[2] (such as crowds and mobs) and the influence of factors such as "imitation," "contagion," and suggestion. The influence of leaders was related to prestige, and this too was once again linked to suggestibility. He was therefore "prepared for the statement that suggestion (or

---

[2] It is of interest to note that group was translated from the more comprehensive German *masse* which was considered equivalent to Le Bon's *foule* or crowd.

more correctly suggestibility) is actually an irreducible, primitive phenomenon, a fundamental fact in the mental life of man" (p. 89). He later linked suggestibility to hypnosis and repeatedly attempted to understand this powerful force.

Freud then proceeded to study how to distinguish between very different kinds of groups based on the morphology of groups. He noted that there are "very fleeting groups and extremely lasting ones; homogenous ones, made up of the same sorts of individuals, and unhomogenous ones; natural groups, and artificial ones, requiring an external force to keep them together; primitive groups, and highly organized ones with a definite structure . . . leaderless groups and those with leaders"(p. 93). He chose to focus on the highly organized, lasting, and "artificial" groups. The groups he chose, highly unusual for his time but very relevant for us, were churches—communities of believers—and armies.

The church and the army are both long-lasting "artificial" groups that, according to Freud, need a certain external force to prevent major change or disintegration. In both these institutions, however different they were in some respects, there is a head who was seen to love all individuals, equally. In the Catholic church it was Christ, and in the army it was the commander-in-chief, who were the leaders or heads that defined the powerful group binding but ultimately "illusory" relationship. In the Christian church, the family was invoked and believers were "brothers in Christ," whereas in the army the commander-in-chief is a father who loves his soldiers equally.

Trying to understand the nature of the forces that bound an individual to the group, Freud identified two important and intense ties. One tie was to the leader of the group and the other was to the members of the group. These ties bound an individual in two directions by intense emotional bonds. They were powerful enough to result in some lack of freedom in the group and to even cause an alteration in personality that had been noted by earlier observers.

In exploring the nature of these emotional ties further, Freud realized that they were based on "so-called *identifications*, insufficiently-known processes and hard to describe" (p. 104), in their impact on group phenomena. He went on to describe identifications as the "earliest expression of an emotional tie with another person" (p. 105) and that "identification endeavors to mould a person's own ego after the fashion of the one that has been taken as 'a model' " (p. 106). He also noted that in any collection of people the tendency to form a group can become prominent. If identification was the earliest and original form of emotional tie, in a hysterical symptom, where the symptom is the same as that in the person who is loved, "identification has appeared instead of object choice" (pp. 106–107). In attempting to comprehend identification beyond the ties to immediate family members which would lead to the formation of a group, Freud postulated that if members of a group share every new perception of a common quality the partial identification becomes successful as a new tie begins.[3] He went on to add:

> We already begin to divine that the mutual tie between members of a group is in the nature of an identification of this kind, based upon an important emotional common quality; and we may suspect that this common quality lies in the nature of the tie with the leader. (p. 108)

He had earlier noted that "one of these, the tie with the leader, seems . . . to be more of a ruling factor than the other, which holds between the members of the group" (p. 100).

After exploring some of the similarities between the tie of hypnosis (a group of two members) and the tie between an individual and an idealized leader, Freud concluded that groups that have a leader and are not highly organized are primary groups. He noted that "[a] primary group of this kind is a number of individuals who have put one and the same object in the place of their ego ideal and have consequently identified themselves with one another in their ego" (p. 116). In this seemingly tentative manner Freud once again defined two powerful factors that are necessary for group formation—the tie to the leader and a tie to the other members. These vertical identifications (with the leader) and the horizontal identifications (with the members) form the basis of what we should call group identifications. Freud

---

[3] Freud distinguished between three modes of identification, in this study, which was in fact the most thorough exposition by Freud on the subject (LaPlanche & Pontalis, 1973).

was not, however, entirely satisfied with this explanation because it could not explain some of the excesses of behavior that had earlier been described for transient group formations by Le Bon and McDougall.

> Some of its features—the weakness of intellectual ability, the lack of emotional restraint, the incapacity for moderation and delay, the inclination to exceed every limit in the expression of emotion and to work it off completely in the form of action—these and similar features . . . show an unmistakable picture of a regression of mental activity to an earlier stage such as we are not surprised to find among savages or children. (1921/1955b, p. 117)

He went on to point out that:

> [W]e are reminded of how many of these phenomena of dependence are part of the normal constitution of human society, of how little originality and personal courage are to be found in it, of how much every individual is ruled by those attitudes of the group mind which exhibit themselves in such forms as racial characteristics, class prejudices, public opinion, etc. (p. 117) (This insight predates the work of Asch, Milgram, and Janis on how individuals succumb to group pressure and group thinking.)

The troubling and unresolved role of suggestion in these phenomena is brought up again. "The influence of suggestion becomes a greater riddle for us when we admit that it is not exercised only by the leader, but by every individual upon every other individual . . . " (pp. 117–118). Freud in this brief sentence defined the powerful role of mutual suggestion by group members that often maintains even irrational attitudes.

Freud turned next to Trotter's "herd instinct" (gregariousness), which is innate, to see if it lent a further understanding of this complex issue. Trotter claimed that manifestations of this instinct were that an individual feels "incomplete," and small children feel a dread, if alone, and therefore need others. Freud objected to the concept of the "herd instinct" as it left out the central and critical role of the leader. The dread shown by small children could be more readily understood to relate to the missing mother. He then makes the interesting observation that in early childhood for a long time there is no evidence for a "herd instinct." In fact, children are wary of strangers. A group feeling does emerge, but much later, and that too out of the relations of children to their parents, and it "does so as a reaction to the initial envy with which the elder child receives the younger ones" (p. 120).

Freud had described the origins of group formation in childhood developmental events!

> The elder child would certainly like to put its successor jealously aside, to keep it away from the parents, and to rob it of all its privileges; but in the face of the fact that this younger child (like all that come later) is loved by the parents as much as he himself is, and in consequence of the impossibility of his maintaining his hostile attitude without damaging himself, he is forced into identifying himself with the other children. So there grows up in the troop of children a communal or group feeling, which is then further developed at school. The first demand made by this reaction formation[4] is for justice, for equal treatment for all. (Freud, 1921/1955b, p. 120)

Freud goes on to add that:

> [W]hat appears later on in society in the shape of *Gemeingeist, esprit de corps,* "group spirit," etc., does not belie its derivation from what was originally envy . . . and . . . this demand for equality is the root of social conscience and the sense of duty. (pp. 120–121)

Group feeling was thus based on the reversal of what had once been hostility into its opposite: a positive tie based on identification and a common tie of tenderness with a parent.

Freud (1921/1955b) made a final attempt to "understand what is still incomprehensible and mysterious in group formation—all that lies hidden behind the enigmatic words 'hypnosis' and 'suggestion' " (p. 125). It was at this point that he developed his Lamarck-based "primal horde" theory, now discredited along with Lamarck's basic premise, which was discussed earlier (Freud, 1913/1955a). In Lamarckian fashion Freud felt that just as primitive man survived in the individual, the band of fraternal killers (the primal horde) may arise once more out of a random crowd.

Despite Freud's preoccupations with the powerful forces that define transient groups such as rampaging mobs, it was his work

---

[4] Reaction formation, a defense mechanism, in this instance relates to liking instead of hating the sibling. Freud draws attention to the importance of reaction formation alongside sublimation (another defense mechanism) in the construction of human character and virtue (1905/1953, pp. 238–239).

on long-lasting, organized, and "artificial" groups that is significant. Freud's remarkable insights and contributions, however, seem disorganized and scattered throughout the book. His views are tentative observations rather than a discussion of theory, and many of his crucial ideas seem incomplete. One reason for this is that Freud did not describe his new structural theory until 2 years later in 1923. The book has been considered "speculative and ambiguous" to be "both a flawed cornerstone and an enabling event" (Roth, 1993). His work on groups has not been appreciated and several of his significant contributions not fully recognized.

One of his important contributions was an understanding of the morphology of groups, particularly those of stable "artificial" groups, such as the military and religious groups, two of the most powerful group forces in history. His understanding that identification was central to the formation of both these groups has critical meaning. He defined for the first time the ties between the individual and the leader and the mutual ties between the members as based on these powerful identifications. He suggested that it was possible to discover the beginnings of group development in the family and that this tie was "indestructible." In describing these beginnings in the family he linked childhood developmental events and the transformation via reaction formation of sibling rivalry and envy into positive group feelings. The need for equality between siblings becomes the root for a social conscience.

Freud, however, did not develop these critical insights. He did not go further than McDougall in describing the characteristics of stable, highly organized groups. Beyond describing some similarities between the church and the military, he did not even describe the characteristics that McDougall had outlined. He did not define their essential features that would allow an understanding of why some religious groups and military structures are more successful than others. It is puzzling too that in the aftermath of the First World War Freud did not define one of the most intense of identifications, that with the nation state. Strengthened by the post-Enlightenment decline of religion, the nation state had allowed and sometimes demanded an almost religious identification with the nation for which millions died in this devastating war (Hutchinson & Smith, 1994).[5]

Freud discerned the origins of group formation in childhood developmental events, in the family, and linked the mother's role to that of a leader, but did not develop an understanding of these three critical areas any further. He also did not discuss the link between leadership at every level in a hierarchy of groups that all impact the individual—from the family, to the clan, to the tribe, subculture, or class, to religion, and to the nation. Despite his interest in history he did not examine the impact of history on groups nor the impact of groups on history.

Freud had concurred with Trotter's remark that biologically groups are a continuation of the multicellular character of all higher organisms and had observed that living beings combine in more and more comprehensive units. He did not, however, link the need of a vulnerable dependent child for a family and a strong leader in the parent to the needs of a dependent, suggestible individual for a group and a strong leader at every level in the hierarchy of groups. McDougall's observation that groups "have a definite structure, expressed in the specialization and differentiation of the function of its constituents" (quoted in Freud, 1921/1955b, p. 86) was not elaborated on by Freud. The specialization of functions of a larger group represented for instance by the church and army are similar to the specialization of functions that are present in multicellular higher organisms. These specializations at the group level support, supplement, and reinforce the needs of individuals who would be otherwise vulnerable. The army, for example, provides the individual as a member of a group, defense and protection from armed groups of other nations. Because Freud did not define basic and other needs of a group, the necessary functions that meet those needs were not identified. It is group functions that mediate in the service of the needs of the group (and ultimately of individuals), just as ego functions mediate in the service of the needs of an individual.

Freud evidently realized the role of language in fostering identification. He observed that "[s]peech owes its importance

---

[5] The study of nationalism, one of the most powerful of group forces in the modern world, has been relatively neglected. Sustained investigation began really after the 1960s (Hutchinson & Smith, 1994).

to its aptitude for mutual understanding in the herd, and upon it the identifications of the individuals with one another largely rests" (1921/1955b, p. 118). Once again, he did not include identifications with other "sociological" or social symbols that Durkheim (1895/1950) had suggested were just as "real" symbolic objects, such as fetishes and icons in the church and uniforms and emblems in the army. It is these symbolic objects and actions (religious and military rituals) that create stirring, emotional, or affect-laden identifications for which people are ready to offer the most supreme of sacrifices—their own lives.

Freud (1921/1955b) has noted that "it is impossible to grasp the nature of a group if the leader is disregarded" (p. 119). The leader has to be an individual of "superior strength" (p. 122) and while "the members of a group stand in need of the illusion that they are equally and justly loved by their leader . . . the leader himself need love no one else, he may be of a masterful nature, absolutely narcissistic, but self-confident and independent" (p. 123–124). Freud made a few more comments about leaders, but it was his stray remark about the roles of ideas that could substitute for leadership that has broader and more important implications. Freud wondered:

> [W]hether groups with leaders may not be the more primitive and complete, whether in the others an idea, an abstraction, may not take the place of the leader (a state of things to which religious groups, with their invisible head, form a transition stage), and whether a common tendency, a wish in which a number of people can have a share, may not in the same way serve as a substitute. (p. 100)

In this brief, intriguing comment, with once again no further elaboration, Freud had introduced the concept of an idea, or an abstract ideology substituting for the role of a leader. The "common tendency, a wish in which a number of people can have a share" is very similar to the concept of the shared representational world of a group which has a powerful defining impact on the individual as a member of that group. An abstract set of ideas, such as the constitution of a nation, can define what a nation should be. A constitution therefore provides in broad outline the ideal shapes of the representational world of the nation as a group.⁶ A constitution, a set of abstract ideas and values, thus assumes a leading, or "leadership" role, for a nation. It can even structure the role of an elected leader and by surviving the leader provide stability and continuity over time. Religious books like the Bible and the Quran have served a similarly powerful role for their followers.

The vast range—and limitations—of Freud's work on groups and group phenomena only underline the need to develop his rich insights and link them into a comprehensive model. Freud had chosen throughout his career to focus on the individual level, despite several forays over a broader range. As I noted earlier, sociology and anthropology were young fields, using differing conceptual models, and his own work was still in evolution. He had, however, offered brilliant insights for future work that could develop his links between the individual, the family, larger groups, and the cultural surround.

What is the status of the field today? How much progress have we made since Freud? A recent review of the study of group dynamics—the ways in which individual members, their leader, and the group interact, suggests that progress has been limited. Munich observed that:

> [G]roup dynamics is an amalgam of at least three separate disciplines: individual psychology, social psychology and sociology. Each of those disciplines has its theoretical assumptions and distinctive language; moreover, the literature on the interplay between intrapsychic, group dynamic, and contextual factors is sparse and unsophisticated. (Munich, 1993, p. 21)

It is this literature on groups and group dynamics that merits brief review. Scheidlinger noted that:

> [S]ome psychoanalysts do not realize that group psychotherapy bears no direct relation to the psychoanalytic writings on leadership, beginning with Freud's *Group Psychology and the Analysis of the Ego* (1921). In fact, all theorizing on group psychotherapy must entail the integration of two disparate, yet related, conceptual systems, each complex in its own right: (1) The group psychology system involving the question, "what makes groups tick?" which includes the issue of leadership and is applicable

---

⁶ The Constitution of the United States of America defined and continues to define large aspects of the shared representational world not only of the people of the United States but also of the people of other countries who borrowed it, in some instances verbatim (cf. Anderson, 1991).

to all groups, and (2) the group psychotherapy system that is a clinical intervention modality using specific techniques to induce behavioral changes in patients. (Scheidlinger, 1993, p. 6)

Most psychoanalytic writing on groups since Freud is related to group psychotherapy. In the American tradition of pragmatism, group therapy as an American invention, became a planned enterprise to treat personality pathology. Early in this century group therapy was used to treat patients with tuberculosis (Pratt, 1922) and schizophrenia (Lazell, 1921). The impetus for a dramatic increase in the popularity of group psychotherapy was World War II. Faced with an enormous number of war-related psychiatric casualties, both American and British military hospitals were forced to use group treatment as an absolute necessity. Military psychiatrists with this experience later became the leading authorities on group psychotherapy. In the early 1970s there was another powerful growth spurt in the group therapy movement. Surveys suggest that half of all inpatient settings in America use group treatment (Scheidlinger, 1993, p. 9).

Despite this vast increase in size of the group therapy movement, Greenberg and Mitchell in their review of the current state of psychoanalytic theory suggest that "a less reductionistic, more synthetic approach is needed" (Greenberg & Mitchell, 1983) to deal with the complexity, heterogeneity, and lack of communication among the various schools. In a similar vein Klein, Bernard, and Singer (1992) state:

> [T]he history of group psychotherapy is replete with valiant attempts to develop . . . a comprehensive model. Yet it is clear that this process remains incomplete. To a large extent, previous efforts have tended to be partial and fragmented, rather than additive and integrative. (p. 5)

A comprehensive theoretical model that would provide practical guidelines to making clinical decisions seemed remote.

If an integrated theory that supported clinical intervention modalities poses problems, a theory that would be applicable to all groups would seem an even more daunting proposition. In recent years an approach that links the individual to the family and groups, a general systems approach, has attracted the attention of social scientists and scholars of the family. Enthusiasts have made claims that may seem grandiose. General Systems Theory, which has its roots in biology's open systems theory, has been called "a basic reorientation of scientific thinking" (Bertalanffy, 1969). Von Bertalanffy defined a system as a fundamental structure with a particular arrangement of elements that were interconnected. These systems exist within a hierarchy of levels that are not static but complex and dynamic. From the most simple level of a cell to the most complex level of a society, each system is isomorphic—it has a similar structure, function, principles of organization and process. The broadest application of systems theory has been in the area of family therapy. A family as a group and a system clearly interacts with other systems. The therapist's role is merely to correct errors in the system. Critics have found the term *general systems theory* inappropriate and possibly pretentious. They "accuse it of being more 'general' than 'theory' " (Broderick & Smith, 1979, p. 112). It has been suggested that systems theory is without content, mechanistic and reactive. What is missing is an understanding of its self-transformative capacity.

In working with more than one individual, family therapy has attempted to work around the inherent limitations of the individual-based model. Over several decades, family therapy has developed newer models for pragmatic and heuristic reasons. However, these models have also been criticized on several grounds. They had developed concepts "in isolation from one another and loosely strung together to fail as a systematic theory [or lead to] the development of integrated theory" (Bell, 1980, p. 2219). Bell further criticized the field of family therapy for the invention of terms that substituted for conceptual thinking.

The focus of group and family therapy on ameliorative processes in specific cultures did not necessitate a critical need to look at the larger links between the individual, the group therapeutic process, and society. On an everyday basis this was not even necessary as the therapist, and the individual treated in a group, often shared the same cultural milieu.

Parallel to these developments in the fields of group and family therapy, developments emanated from the fields of sociology, anthropology, and social psychology. In several respects these were separate and independent attempts to deal with an emerging and growing climate of concern about how to understand groups. Groups, moreover, were and could be utilized to implement social purposes and change (Lifton, 1968).[7]

Social psychology studied the interactions between individuals within groups to illuminate factors such as motivation and behavior under the impress of social forces. Prior to the 1940s very few scientific attempts had been devoted to the understanding of group process. A scientific attempt to understand group dynamics was ushered in by Kurt Lewin (1947). The lawful nature of group life could be derived by a strict observational approach of the individual under the impact of a group. Group characteristics, cooperation, competition, leadership, and communication were studied. Methods of leadership and the influence on the behavior of members, their cohesiveness, and interdependence in the group were delineated.

Lewin's field theory was the culmination of social psychology's contribution to the study of group dynamics. The perspective of group dynamics, was on the gestalt, the totality or whole as distinguished from the particular. Deutsch (1954), a prominent exponent of this perspective, compared it to:

> [F]ield theory in physics . . . the properties of any event are determined by its relations to the system of events of which it is a component. . . . All psychological events (thinking, acting, dreaming, hoping, etc.) are conceived to be a function of life space which consists of the person and the environment viewed as *one* constellation of interdependent factors. That is, all psychological events are conceived to be determined, not by isolated properties of the person or his environment, but by the mutual relations among the totality of coexisting facts which comprise the life space. . . . (pp. 182–185)

This as an ideal is unassailable, as we should be cognizant of every factor that is influential in a group. In practice, however, determining which factor has greater importance and how to account for all the factors has posed a problem. This field has foundered on this practical issue.

The National Training Laboratory (NTL) founded in 1947 soon had two distinct emphases. One, rooted in the work of Lewin and his associates, continued its allegiance to learning about

---

[7] The thought reform process of group mediated psychological pressure toward ideological conversion was a trademark of Chinese communism. It was one of the most powerful instruments of change.

group development, group dynamics, and leadership roles. The other shifted its focus to human growth, authenticity, and communication among members. The training of leaders to function more effectively and democratically in their own organizations spread group principles and techniques to business and industry. The human potential movement with a focus on human growth and authenticity mushroomed further to include the popular encounter groups that were often commercial enterprises in a nontraditional setting.

Sociological studies of groups had defined them as the building blocks of larger societies. In the "external" or sociological tradition in contrast to the "internal" or psychological tradition, groups were seen to be like cells in a social organism. In this "societies-as-groups" tradition there was an explicit awareness of the types of relationships among group members. In a well-defined dichotomy, groups were seen either as "primary" or "secondary."

In primary groups members have warm, intimate, and personal ties with each other. Such groups are small, have face-to-face relationships that are based not on calculation but on sentiment. Interpersonal behavior is devoted to common or mutual ends. The friendship group, the gang, and the family were the best examples of these primary groups. The primary group received its classic and often-quoted description from Charles H. Cooley (1909) who wrote:

> By primary groups I mean those characterized by intimate face-to-face association and cooperation. They are primary in several senses, but chiefly in that they are fundamental in forming the social nature and ideals of the individual. The result of intimate association, psychologically, is a certain fusion of individualities in a common whole, so that one's self, for many purposes at least, is the common life and purpose of the group....
> Primary groups are primary in the sense that they give the individual his earliest and completest experience of social unity.... These groups, then, are springs of life not only for the individual but for social institutions. They are only in part moulded by special traditions, and in larger degree express a universal nature. (pp. 23–28)

Cooley in these words had described not only the essential features of the primary group but suggested their functions for society.

Secondary groups, in contrast, have characteristics that are the opposite of primary groups. Relations among them are rational, formal, and impersonal. Individuals participate with their specialized skills or training and the group is a means to achieve other ends. These groups are large, with often written rather than verbal contact. Bureaucratic corporations and professional organizations are examples of secondary groups. The primary/secondary group distinction in the sociological literature is somewhat similar to the dichotomies of *Gemeinshaft* (community) and *Gesellshaft* (society or association) of German sociologist Ferdinand Tonnies, "Societies of Status" and "Societies of Contract" of Henry Maine, and the "Folk Society" and "Urban Society" of anthropologist Robert Redfield.

Sociologists since then have done studies on crowds, mass behavior, reference groups, organizations, and leadership in groups to list just some of the many areas in the study of groups. A common shortcoming of sociological attempts to understand both individuals and groups may be reflected in the comments of Olmsted and Hare (1978). In their candid review of research on the effect of groups on the individual they state that:

> One of the two major shortcomings of this research... in the study of the group–individual relationship, the group side of the "equation" has been left largely unspecified; research has, on the whole, neglected matters of internal group organization and process. But the individual side of the "equation" has perhaps fared no better—and this constitutes the second shortcoming. (p. 80)

It is evident that one major reason that the study of groups has been a problem, as described earlier, is the lack of a fully developed conceptual or theoretical model that links the individual to a culture and society. A second possible reason has been the decline of powerful group phenomena in industrialized nations in the post-Enlightenment era. In a secular age with the development of a rational, scientific worldview, the older feudal ties to extended family, clan, religion, and kingdom had given way to nuclear family, class, and nation state. The decline of primary groups, with less concern for the traditional family and the local neighborhoods in small towns has been a long-standing concern, but these social concerns are still with us. The very stability of the nation state, with its standing army, resulted in a major reduction in internal threats and conflict (McNeill, 1982) and a superior level of public peace. Intense conflicts between groups became rare. Rapid industrialization, in a stable setting, led to the development of more impersonal secondary groups of trades, professions, bureaucratic corporations, and the nation state itself. These areas became the traditional domains of sociology. The rest of the nonindustrialized world largely conquered and subdued by imperialist armies became the domain of interest of anthropologists who studied "primitive" tribes and cultures.

The powerful affective ties that bind groups surfaced and continued to surface episodically in the emergence of mobs and riots, odd cults (Galanter, 1989), and financial manias (Mackay, 1980). Interest was aroused but died just as quickly in these relatively brief quirky events within the fairly stable world of strong nation states.

The relationships between nations, however, were far from stable. Two world wars and the horrors of the Holocaust, shook faith in the rational ideas of the Enlightenment. Europe woke to the loss of Empire and a multiplicity of new nation states. For a few decades Cold War ideology was still a powerful presence as Marxist-Socialism extended its sway over the minds and societies of large areas of the globe. The collapse of Marxism in the Soviet Union and the end of the Cold War revealed forces that had been slowly emerging but were now more fully exposed. The rational forces of a secular egalitarian post-Enlightenment world now faced powerful and age-old verities. Like a receding tide revealing long submerged hulks, the world would once again witness ancient loyalties of clan, tribe, ethnicity, race, religion, and civilization engaged in irrational and brutal conflict (Huntington, 1996). Europe itself faces the specter of being wracked from within by religious and ethnic conflict.

The loyalties to clan, tribe, and race had troubled Erikson, who gave the term *pseudospecies* to these powerful but artificial distinctions. He saw a clear need for a comprehensive model of human consciousness to understand this phenomena.

He pondered the following paradox:

> [I]t is one thing... to cultivate the proud rationality of the Enlightenment, of which Freud was probably the last great representative, and to

crown it by insisting that irrationality and the unconscious be included in the study of what can be understood rationally. It is another matter to derive from such study a comprehensive model of human consciousness. (1975, p. 107)

He then defined the formidable task ahead.

Having begun as clinical art-and-science, psychoanalysis cannot shirk the question of what, from the point of view of an undivided human race, is "wrong" with the "normality" reached by groups of men under the conditions of pseudo-speciation. Does it not include pervasive group retrogressions . . . [that] . . . represent a joint fixation on historical formulae mortally dangerous to further adaptation? (p. 109)

The term *pseudospecies,* defined by Erikson:

[D]enotes the fact that while man is obviously one species, he appears and continues on earth split up into groups (from tribes to nations, from castes to classes, from religions to ideologies) which provide their members with a firm sense of God-given identity—and a sense of immortality. This demands, however, that each group must invent for itself a place and a moment in the very center of the universe where and when an especially provident deity caused it to be created superior to all others, the mere mortals. (Erikson, 1975, p. 176)

It is this pseudospeciation, in the shape of groups that "retrogress" and are then "mortally dangerous," that lends a special urgency to our understanding of how groups are formed.

Erikson's vastly influential work on psychosocial development touches on two promising and important group issues: the formation of a "group identity" and how groups saw each other as threatening *pseudospecies.* Beyond expressing grave concern and alarm about the formation of pseudospecies Erikson did not explore how pseudospecies are formed nor why some are more of a mortal danger than others. Erikson (1950/1985) also wrote about group identity, or rather the loss of group identity, in his empathic anthropological observations about childhood among the Sioux and the Yurok. This would have been an ideal setting for extending the framework of his psychosocial model beyond the family to larger group structures such as the tribe and nation. But beyond the expression of his sensitive concerns and observations the promise of his psychosocial approach to groups remained unfulfilled.

He wrote that the peoples who are collectively called American Indians "as stable societies . . . are extinct" and that while "remnants of their timeless cultures can be found . . . these ways are no longer a part of a self-supporting societal existence" (1950/1985, p. 112). One of the most challenging and urgent of tasks today is that whereas we have some understanding of why some societies as groups grow and thrive, we know much less about why others shrink and die.[8]

A nation is the largest community or group that commands men's loyalties. The study of nationalism, one of the most powerful of forces on this planet, however, has been an area of relative neglect. It was only after the 1960s, with the rise of anticolonialism and increased ethnic nationalism, that the subject received academic recognition and attention from several disciplines. Historians had dominated the study of the nation, but now members of several disciplines, including sociologists, social psychologists, anthropologists, political scientists, philosophers, and linguists among others, are studying the possible causal factors that underlie nationalism and the various facets of national identity. Prior to this, "other concepts and phenomena, long held the attention of most scholars—class, capitalism, the market, industrialization, the state, Marxism, parties, kinship, tribes, and communications—and we begin to grasp why the systematic study of nations and nationalism has only recently begun to develop" (Hutchinson & Smith, 1994, p. 3). Sociology and anthropology with their ahistorical bias and analytic (as opposed to synthetic) approaches could only study segments of reality until the disturbing impact of ethnic and national conflicts compelled greater attention.

Nationalism has been described as the basis of this world (Greenfeld, 1992, p. 3). To distinguish nationality from other types of identity, "Nationalism locates the source of individual identity within a 'people,' which is seen as the bearer of sovereignty, the central object of loyalty, and the basis of collective solidarity . . . the only foundation of nationalism as such . . . is an idea" (Greenfeld, 1992, p. 3).

---

[8] Hundreds of tribal groups (and their languages) face extinction, with at first a loss of their group identities, as they fail to adapt to the advances of technologically developed cultures. This is an immeasurable human and cultural loss.

As we noted earlier, well-defined nation states are new in human history, first emerging in sixteenth century England. With the possible exception of Holland, England was the only nation for about two hundred years (Greenfeld, 1992, p. 14). The ambivalent emergence of nations could not have been expressed with greater clarity than by Benedict Anderson:

> The century of the Enlightenment, of rationalist secularism, brought with it its own modern darkness. With the ebbing of religious belief . . . few things were (are) better suited to this end than an idea of nation. If nation-states are widely conceded to be "new" and "historical," the nations to which they give political expression always loom out of an immemorial past, and, still more important, glide into a limitless future. . . . What I am proposing is that nationalism has to be understood by aligning it, not with self-consciously held political ideologies, but with the large cultural systems that preceded it, out of which—as well as against which—it came into being. (Anderson, 1991, pp. 11–12)

Anderson considered nations to be "imagined communities," and cultural artifacts of a particular kind, but was impressed by the deep and passionate attachments of individuals to nations. Gellner (1964) claimed that "Nationalism is not the awakening of nations to self-consciousness: it *invents* nations where they do not exist" (p. 169; emphasis added). Nationalism, however, was seen as a progressive cause, a movement against dynasty and empire and a struggle against privileged descent.

The dawn of nationalism had coincided with the dusk of religion in Europe. The doctrine, for instance, spelled out in *Action Française* defined Catholicism as one of the attributes that defined and separated a true Frenchman from a spurious one (Kedourie, 1993, quoted in Hutchinson & Smith, 1994, p. 51). Thus powerful and tenacious ties of religious beliefs shared in common for centuries were conveniently transformed by nationalists into a nationalist ideology.

These powerful emotional ties of nationalism, however, were to have unfortunate consequences. The links between nationalism and war were clearly underlined and confirmed by the intimate and central role played by nationalism in the two world wars. This was apparent as early as 1792 in the battle of Valmy when a mass citizen army of conscripts, the *levée en masse* went to war in defense of *la patrie en danger*. Nationalism reached its apogee with the injection of racist ideology in the middle of this century. Nazism and fascism brought nationalist ideas and practices to their logical conclusion. The belief in racial imperialism, the *Volk,* the appeal to brute instincts and collective will, heroic struggles, and homage to charismatic leaders, had immense and tragic consequences that culminated in the Second World War (Hutchinson & Smith, 1994, p. 9).

National ideas and ethnic ties seemed obsolete and discredited after the catastrophic horrors of this war. Ethnic revivals, however, came to the fore soon after in anticolonial movements in Asia and Africa. Recent events in Eastern Europe and the former Soviet Union have brought ethnic and religious conflict into the heart of Europe (Pfaff, 1993). Nationalism is now firmly at the center of world affairs. At the end of the twentieth century the greatest threat to the structure of an international order based on equality and justice are the widespread, intractable, and explosive upheavals of ethnic conflict and nationalism (Hutchinson & Smith, 1994, p. 11). These intense conflicts pose continuing dangers for regional and global security. Economic inequality, the easy access to mass communication, and the appeal of nationalist identities for other dissatisfied ethnic groups is not likely to reduce the proliferation of conflict.

It is not a surprise then that nationalism has been pessimistically considered "the pathology of modern developmental history . . . (with a) . . . built-in capacity for descent into dementia . . . and largely incurable" (Nairn, 1977, p. 359). Anderson too observes that nationalism "makes it possible, over the past two centuries, for so many millions of people, not so much to kill, as willingly to die for such limited imaginings" (1991, p. 7). He then goes on to ask the central question posed by nationalism. What force is it that generates such "colossal sacrifices"?

Nationalism clearly is one of the most challenging of *group forces* and its fuller comprehension an ongoing and urgent task. If nationalism is based on an idea, and nationalism is located in an individual identity within a "people," the study of group psychology and the development of group identity should add a dimension to the understanding of nationalism.

Harold Isaacs (1975), in a pace-setting work, was at the forefront in the recognition of ethnicity as a force to reckon with both in the development and destruction of nations. Isaacs found in Erik Erikson's notion of "group identity" an overarching concept and a rich approach to the elusive study of ethnicity. Erikson had been uneasy with the concept of group identity because it was a serious impediment to Enlightenment values and resulted in the formation of "pseudospecies." Isaacs, however, saw group identity as emotionally intense and as complex as Erikson saw individual identity. Moreover it could not be wished away. Erikson thought that people would no longer need the shield of a group identity when they resolved their conflicts about their individual identities. Isaacs was certain that it was often the other way around: people consolidated their individual identities through an emotional commitment to a group identity. Isaacs had also noted profound linkages between individual identity and group identity. Personal identity problems, heightened by anxiety and insecurity, only enhanced the links to group identity. It was this linkage that lent intensity to conflicts around ethnicity. Whereas most studies of ethnicity had accepted group identity as a given and then investigated its role in human relations, and political phenomena, Isaacs studied the very origins of group identity. He studied the elusive but fundamental basis of its formation. He explored the importance of the body (including skin color) and the significance of names, language, history, myths of origin, religion, and nationality to the formation of a group identity. He was dismissive of liberal and Marxist claims that the removal of class and economic obstacles would remedy problems of race and ethnicity. He correctly saw the problem as more primordial and therefore resistant to easy solutions.

Isaacs' work on group identity included several previously neglected aspects. He included a large range of important influences from the developmental (including body image), to the importance of religion, to the most ultimate and inclusive of factors that contribute to basic group identity: the nation. His work, however, was largely descriptive and limited by a focus on the "social" contributions to group identity. The basic psychological reasons as to why people need groups and join groups or how group identity further develops and is maintained is unclear. He left unexplained the role of individual leaders like Muhammad, Luther, and Gandhi in creating almost complete group identities.

The concept of the representational world of a group provides a broader and more overarching concept than group identity to allow some answers to these questions. A brief review, however, of prior attempts to conceptualize this complex issue is necessary.

Freud made several passing references to what he called the "group mind." In a comment on McDougall's *Group Mind,* Freud noted that human beings rarely come together in fleeting or transient groups without possessing "the rudiments of an organization." These individuals must possess:

> [A] common interest in an object, a similar emotional bias in some situation or other, and ("consequently," I should like to interpolate) "some degree of reciprocal influence." The higher the degree of "this mental homogeneity," the more readily do the individuals form a psychological group, and the more striking are the manifestations of a group mind. (Freud, 1921/1955b, p. 84)

McDougall (1920) had described panic as the plainest function of the "group mind." Freud noted the paradox that one of the most striking manifestations of the group mind was when it did away with itself, for panic meant the disintegration of a group (p. 97). Freud used the term *group mind* once again in a more suggestive and important context. He observed that

> [E]ach individual is a component part of numerous groups, he is bound by ties of identification in many directions, and he has built up his ego ideal upon the most various models. Each individual therefore has a share in numerous group minds—those of his race, of his class, of his creed, of his nationality, etc. (p. 129)

He had added earlier that we "may lose courage, in face of the complications that are revealed, to attempt a comprehensive exposition" (p. 129).

Freud had used the term *group mind* in two contexts. The first was to describe the powerful coalesced mental states of individuals in a state of joint panic or acting together in a mob. The second and more complex context was to describe the more stable and defining ties to various groups the individual belongs to. A more useful term to describe these ties, however, would be *group identities* rather that *group minds* (Erikson, 1950/1985).[9] Group mind poses the risk of reifying the term *mind* even further.

Another concept that has been used in sociology and anthropology, is ideology. The term *ideology* was used to understand and conceptualize cultures. Clifford Geertz's (1973) formulation viewed ideology as providing "maps of problematic social reality" by describing aspects of it without which societal arrangement would be meaningless and the individual's place in it unclear. The term *ideology* had been coined in the eighteenth century by a French philosopher, Destutt de Tracy (Bell, 1960). The decline of religion had led this Enlightenment philosopher to seek an objective truth freed from the compulsion of faith, derived from religion, and authority, from the state. De Tracy believed that ideas could be purified by direct linking to sense perceptions. He called this new science of ideas "ideology."

Marx had concluded that it was existence that determined consciousness. Since gods were a creation of men's minds and only appeared to have independence, they were a false consciousness. Religion, therefore, was an ideology that marked the particular interest of specific groups (Marx & Engels, 1847/1970). Nineteenth century ideologists went further to deify science, progress, rationality, and the inevitability of determinism. They infused their followers with passion and competed with religion. Ideology soon became an all-inclusive system of comprehensive reality that included a set of beliefs, infused with passion, and sought to transform a whole way of life.

Ideology had turned full circle from examining belief symptoms and religion to becoming a secular religion itself. Ideas had now become weapons and social levers. Ideology invaded by passion and a commitment to action had thus undermined abstract philosophical inquiry that had abhorred passion. Ideology was the translation of ideas into action. The disillusion of individuals, however, with these nineteenth century ideological visions, rooted in the French revolution, of the total transformation of society, led Daniel Bell in his influential book *The End of Ideology* to the view that the dream of organizing societies from complete

---

[9] Erikson had borrowed from Freud's single use of the term *identity* to build a theory of individual and group identity formation.

blueprints had failed. As newer ideologies of industrialization, modernization, ethnicity, and nationalism were being fashioned, Bell gave in to despair about a term so broad it blurred all distinctions. The term was beyond terminological retrieval. Despite these terminological limitations and the complex history of often pejorative usage, the concept of ideology retains some influence. The major problem with the term, however, is that a relatively fixed construct is used in a procrustean manner to define the protean symbolic order of cultures.

The concept of the representational world of a group has many advantages over similar conceptualizations. It can include aspects of the unique individual identities of outstanding leaders that are shared by the group, the group identity, internalized aspects of shared "ideology," as well as the internalized aspects of the entire symbolic order of that society.

What do we know from these historical studies about groups so far? Groups have been classified into fleeting groups, such as crowds and mobs, and long-lasting or artificial groups such as the church or army. The primary or secondary distinction, and its variants provided by sociology define the quality and intensity of emotional ties in these groups. Freud had hinted at the origins of group formation in childhood and in the family, with the parent as a leader, but he did not delve further and develop these critical insights. Sociology has outlined the importance of the role of the charismatic leader, but the characteristics of charisma and the qualities of leadership are still open to debate. Freud provided a description of the psychological mechanisms that underlie group formation. Reaction formation (the reversal of hostility into its opposite, a positive tie with the sibling) in childhood and identification (with the idealized leader, as well as identification with members of the group), later on in life, are some of these mechanisms. Freud did not describe, however, except for language, the role of identifications with many other symbols and icons that are the bearers of historical culture. Freud, as we noted, did not describe the influence of history on groups nor the impact of groups on history.

Erikson's major contributions to the study of groups were his concept of *group identity* and his valid concerns about groups that threaten each other as pseudospecies. Isaacs, influenced by

Erikson, explored further the formation of group identity, and broadened its study from its developmental origins to its powerful presence in ethnic, religious, and national strife. Freud had described in some detail group formation in the church and army, but did not elaborate on what function these groups served for the individual nor in turn the role they played in the most ultimate and inclusive of groups, the nation. It is this group, the nation, that Freud curiously neglected. As Freud had not defined the needs of a group, the functions that the church and army serve were not fully understood.

What is missing so far in the analysis of groups is the role of several critical factors that are necessary to understand group formation. All individuals from birth are tied to groups, from the basic group or family to the largest of groups the nation state. The origins of groups are based on childhood developmental events that also define the defense mechanisms that underlie group formation.

To summarize, the basic needs of an individual in a group are physiological needs, the need for safety and security and basic trust. Without these essentials a group is under severe threat and can founder. The basic needs of an individual define the needs of a group. These needs are met, as McDougall observed, when a group develops "a definite structure expressed in the specialization and differentiation of the function of its constituents" (Quoted in Freud, 1955b, p. 11). Groups therefore specialize, differentiate, and develop structures to meet the needs of both the individual and the group. An example of a structure developed, as a specialization of function, to protect the individual and group is the army. How does this structure evolve and how are its functions maintained over time? This itself becomes a specialized set of functions, from the selection of soldiers to the creation and evolution of symbolic emblems, uniforms and flags, to the beliefs, values, and training practices. An army will also have its own history describing its early origins and proud descriptions of battles fought and won. All these varied functions in the beginning are abstract designs, plans, and constructs that become social realities and together form and define the representational world of that army. It is this historical representational world that will ultimately influence and shape the performance of the army and the daily life of every single soldier. The individual and group identity of a soldier in turn will reflect facets of this representational world.

The specialization of functions as they evolve to meet the needs of a group further help the task of adaptation to a changing world. A medium of communication is vital in the recording, maintaining, and transmission of the values, beliefs, and ideal shapes of the group to future generations. The representational world of the group is where all the elements that are critical to the functioning of this group will be reflected.

Finally, the leader of a group provides the planning and reality testing for the group and defines the quality of relations within the group and the world outside. The leader also provides initially the defense mechanisms that are used by the group and supports the integrative functions of the group. The life of Muhammad in the next chapters provides ample evidence of how he gave birth as leader of a new group to the rise of Islam.

Part III

The World Before Islam and the Birth of a Prophet

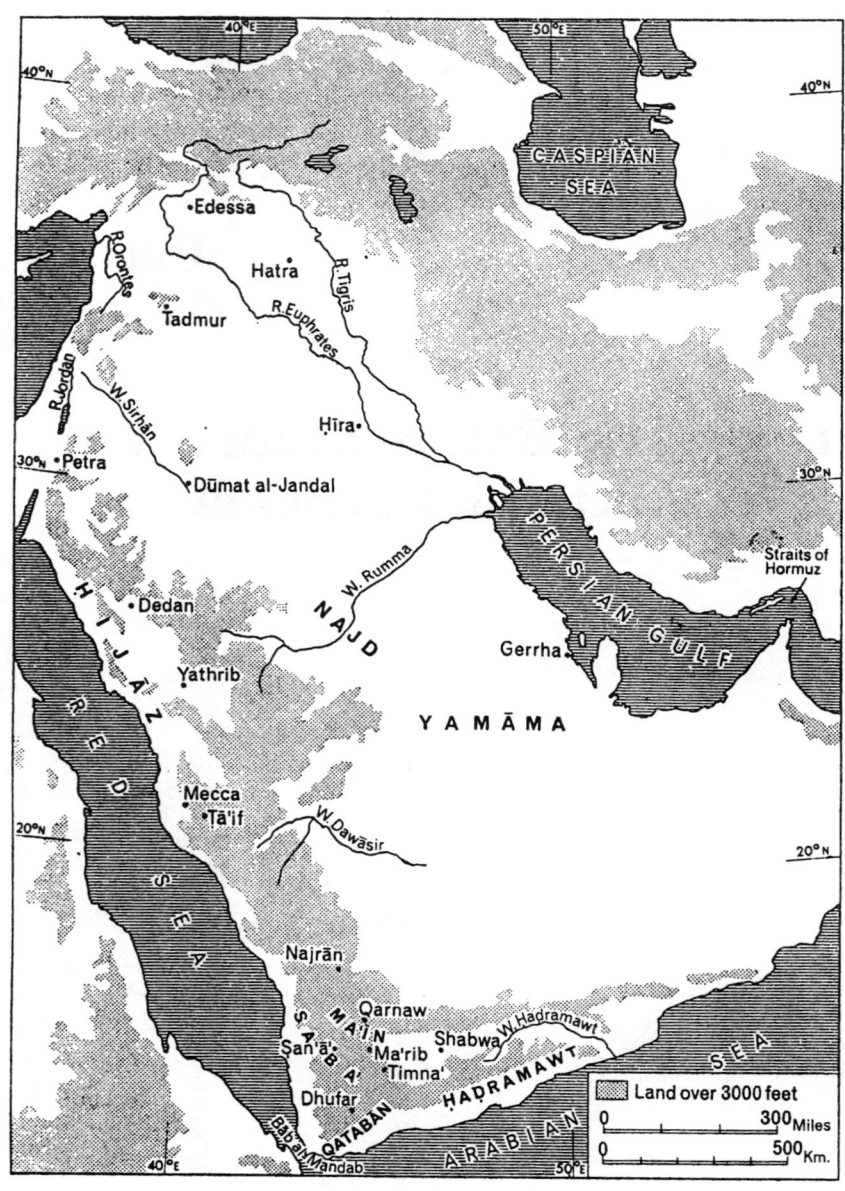

Map I. Pre-Islamic Arabia and the Fertile Crescent

4

Pre-Islamic Arabia and the Rise of Universal Religions

UNDERSTANDING Muhammad and the rise of Islam necessitates looking at the social, cultural, and historical traditions of the clans and tribes that lived in and around Mecca, the birthplace of Islam. Arabia was just south of the Fertile Crescent, the home of the oldest cultures and civilizations, the battleground of the most powerful world empires, and the setting for the birth of the earliest universalist religions. How did these social, political, and religious influences reach Arabia, and what was their impact on the relatively isolated desert tribes of the Arabian peninsula?

Geography, particularly climate, has been a decisive factor in the history of Arabia, a huge quadrilateral mass—1,300 miles long, 750 miles wide, with an area of over 1.25 million square miles—positioned between two continents. It has narrow, forbidding, inhospitable coastal regions and few good harbors. The seas surrounding it are full of coral reefs or shoals; its vast landmass contains rugged mountain terrain in the west and scorching desert or steppes in the east. But for a single exception in the south, it has no major rivers.

Water, or its absence, defines life in Arabia. Most of the peninsula is devoid of lakes or rivers, yet the contrasts are immense. Ample rain in the southwest has created a luxuriantly fertile area, but adjacent to this land is the Empty Quarter, a hell on earth: a savagely arid land with the largest body of continuous sand on this planet.

The two climate extremes have defined the forms of human adaptation to the land. In the arid areas hardiness shapes the capacity for endurance and survival. The Bedouin tribesman, pasturing either his flocks or herds, is constantly on the move. "His life is a competitive struggle for existence . . . waged by tribes to which the individual bedouin must belong if he is to survive at all" (Holt, Lambton, & Lewis, 1970, p. 5). In the ring of oases surrounding the arid areas, perennial springs supported some agriculture and allowed the nomads a form of sedentary life dependent on the hardy date palm. The Bedouin of the desert and their sedentary cousins represented the dwellers of the arid north.

In the southwest the wet climate brought a rich flora, a cornucopia of vegetation that defined life and its history. Sedentary forms of agriculture, intensive irrigation, and dams supported a large population and the growth of towns and cities. South Arabia could provide life's basic necessities as well as luxuries, and this wealth gave rise to its political form and kingdoms and a highly material culture.

The environmental conditions influenced the language and ethnography. The people of the south spoke Sabaic, a Semitic language of their own with dialectal variants; the northern Arabs of the arid areas and oases spoke Arabic *(arabiyya)*, also a Semitic tongue. The Sabaeans and other peoples of the south, though related to the Arabs of the north, were ethnically different. These two peoples were in constant contact, but the enterprising south was dominant for a thousand years or so before the rise of Islam, in Mecca to the north.

The fertile south became the center of an entrepreneurial empire linking the lands of the Indian Ocean, India, and Africa and their rich products which were carried and traded with the Fertile Crescent and the Mediterranean to the north and west. Their products, including the "gold, frankincense, and myrrh" of the region, contributed to the romantic image of Arabia among classical authors as *Arabia Felix*. The South Arabian empire, which supplied many of the luxury articles of the ancient world, relied on keeping the geographical discoveries and trade routes to India and Africa to themselves. The success of this trade also required maintaining a peaceful cohesiveness among the city states of the region as they depended on developing overland trade routes through the arid Arabian peninsula to the northern markets.

South Arabia was successfully able to manage this vast commercial empire because it was a "sea-girt and a sand-girt fortress far removed from the historic routes of world conquerors and protected by inhospitable seas, scorching deserts, and forbidding distances" (Holt et al., 1970, p. 11). Because of its geographical isolation, the states and kingdoms of South Arabia were remarkably long-lived in spite of constant wars and political instability.

The city states that developed in South Arabia were ruled by *mukarribs* or "priest-kings" who were followed by more secular kings or *maliks* who had military power. The king was surrounded by powerful chiefs, the famous *qayls* who headed their own tribes *(ashb)*. The tribes in the south were sedentary and territorial, tied to their members by kinship and labor or trade, and encompassed all classes, including slaves.

Religion played an important role. An astral triad of the sun *(Shams)*, the star-god *('Athtar)*, and the moon characterized the religious pantheon. Saba' was the most dominant of the four kingdoms in the area. Over a period of a thousand years prior to 300 c.e., several centuries before the rise of Islam, the Sabaean kings had consolidated and united all the kingdoms of the south in four different phases.

The impregnable insularity of South Arabia was not to last. The virile northern Arabs began to use the horse for the first time, and could now play a more aggressive role as valued allies or dangerous foes in the conflicts of the southern city states. An even more threatening challenge, however, came not from a Semitic power but an Indo-European one. The Greek Macedonians, especially the Ptolemies of Egypt, directly challenged South Arabian trade. Hippalus in the second century b.c.e. had discovered the secrets of the monsoon, thus permitting the Ptolemies to directly trade between Egypt and India. (The Arabs had much earlier found a way to sail to and from India and the Far East using the prevailing winds.) The Abyssinians of Axum, closely related to the South Arabians and also a Semitic people, were poised to strike across the narrow strait of the Red Sea.

At this time, around 300 c.e., Near Eastern history was being altered also by the dynamics of a newer force—religion. The capital of the Roman Empire had moved from Rome to Constantinople. With the conversion of Constantine, a newly rejuvenated Christian Byzantium emerged and struggled with Zoroastrian Persia for supremacy across the arc of the Fertile Crescent. The conversion of the Abyssinian Negus, Ezana, to Christianity increased the influence and effectiveness of Byzantium. Arabia was now surrounded by these newer and more powerful threats.

Another monotheistic religion, Judaism, also began to spread south, after the sack of Jerusalem and the destruction of the Temple in 70 c.e. In the fifth century the kings of South Arabia, ill-disposed toward their traditional enemies, Byzantium and Abyssinia, both Christian states, adopted some indigenous forms of Judaism. The royal house of Himyar was Jewish in any event. Meanwhile, Christianity, with its universalistic claims and evangelical mission, established churches in the cities of the south and at Najran, an Arabized city with strong links to Monophysite Syriac Christianity.

In the first quarter of the sixth century the struggle for Arabia between the two religions of the Old and New Testament became critical. Yusuf Asar, the Judaizing king of Himyar, an important southern state, tried to spread Judaism. The turning point in the ensuing clashes with Christianity came after the famous massacre of Christians at Najran. In 520 c.e., with the blessings of the Christian world, an Abyssinian expedition crossed the straits of Bab al-Mandab, and invaded Arabia, crushing the last Judaizing king of Himyar.

South Arabia now entered a century or more of chaos and anarchy. As an Abyssinian protectorate for over half a century, it lived through a period when an Abyssinian soldier of fortune killed the Abyssinian Negus' viceroy and declared virtual independence from Abyssinia; he may have led the historically uncertain but celebrated expedition to Mecca. In the last quarter of the sixth century the Persians invaded the Yemen at the invitation of the *qayl* of the important Dhu Yazan family. The Persian occupation lasted for half a century and was ended by a final Arab invasion, flying the banner of a new religion: Islam.

Religion stimulated a cultural awakening in the politically prostrate land. Arabia of fragrance and happiness *(Felix)* was torn by religious passion. Arabia Petraea (Provincia Arabia) from the Hijaz to Syria became the "breeding ground of heresies" *Arabia haeresium ferax* (Holt et al., 1970, p. 13).

After the council of Chalcedon (451 c.e.) the Western churches and the "imperial" church in Constantinople defined a view about Jesus' divinity and humanity. The national churches of Egypt, Abyssinia, and Syria did not accept this dogmatic definition and took what is called the Monophysite position in this debate, whereas the Christian churches of Iraq and Persia accepted the Nestorian view.

Monophysite Christianity, which was the Abyssinian version of the religion, clashed with Judaism, Nestorian (Persian) Christianity, and an Indo-European religion, Iranian Zoroastrianism. These religious currents played an important role in the south and were to have an impact on the later history of ideas in the rise of Islam to the north.

The South Arabians left a mark on world history. They were dominant for over a millennium in the southern part of the Near East and were responsible for a commercial revolution that joined the Indian Ocean and the East to the Mediterranean, another trade route first developed by an earlier Semitic people, the Phoenicians. This route was the longest, and possibly the oldest and richest, of the trade routes in world history and lasted until the arrival of ocean-going vessels. The advertising of South Arabia's wares added to the centuries-old allure of India and the East.

South Arabia "opened up the deserts of the north. The north ceases to be only an arid expanse, but becomes a transit area through which pass the commercial arteries of world trade" (Holt et al., 1970, p. 17). It was this impetus to the urbanization of oases in western Arabia that was to play a decisive role in Arabia's future. The oases became way stations, caravan cities on a trade route traveled by the "ship of the desert," the camel, in a caravan train. The Bedouin and the horse were now more than auxiliary supports for southern armies; they provided guardians and guides for the large caravan trade. The oases, now with urban and caravan cities, developed a new community of traders on the "incense route" who significantly contributed to the later development of Arabs and Islam.

The Arab settlements' fortunes could rise or fall, depending on the prosperity of the Mesopotamian or the West Arabian trade route. These caravan routes through the arid north were the setting for the rise of Islam. The vast area was not the homogeneous society of the south but a heterogeneous society primarily composed of desert nomads and the settled or sedentary Bedouin tribes of the oases.

Life in the oases throughout the earliest recorded history depended upon events in the ancient Near East at the frontiers of the desert. In the first millennium before the Christian era, the Arabs faced the political might of the Assyrians in a united Fertile Crescent; later they confronted the neo-Babylonians and Persians, but after the second century c.e., they had encountered a divided Fertile Crescent. The Fertile Crescent was separated for several centuries by hostilities between the Seleucids (and later the Romans) on the west and the Parthians on the east. In the third century of the Christian era, the conflicts were now between a Christian Byzantine empire and the Persian Sasanids.

The Arabs' settlements had many similarities but different circumstances. Yathrib (later known as Medina) and Najran had an agricultural basis. In the northeast, Arab cities such as Hira were under Persian influence; on the northwest Petra was under Hellenized Arabs and later Roman influence; and intermediate between the two powers and influenced by both was Palmyra, under Greco-Aramaicized Arabs. All these cities on the borders of the desert were heavily influenced by and dependent on the surrounding empires. For a brief period when the Seleucids had weakened, the Palmyrene Arabs conquered Syria until the Romans arrived to annex the desert kingdom. In 106 c.e. the Romans under Trajan created *Provincia Arabia* after their annexation of Petra. The climax of Arab power was seen in the third century when, under its ruler Odenathus and his famous widow queen Zenobia, Palmyra conquered Egypt and Asia Minor. However, in 272 c.e., Aurelian destroyed Palmyra, closing the most powerful military chapter of the pre-Islamic Arabs.

For the next three centuries, the most celebrated Arab states were the Lakhmids, clients of the Persians, and the Ghassanids, clients of Byzantium and Himyar in the south. Religion now played a very significant role in the conflicts of the region.

The Lakhmid and Ghassanid dynasties are vividly remembered by the Arab poets they patronized. It was these pre-Islamic Arab poets who curiously perfected a "literary *koinê,* classical Arabic, the elaboration of a complex metrical system, and the composition of a highly artistic poetry, unique in the literary history of the Semites"(Holt et al., 1970, p. 23). This achievement gave impetus to the further development of an Arab identity and a strong natural sentiment through the Arabic language *arabiyya.*

In the world of inner Arabia, however, the next and most significant of events for the Arabs takes place in the caravan city of Mecca, in the Hijaz on the trade routes, where the religious and the commercial currents meet. Mecca was halfway between Jewish Yathrib (Medina) and Christian Najran. Arabs came to Mecca annually during the sacred months to visit the Holy City with its *Haram,* the sacred precinct, and its *Ka'ba,* the temple. They also visited nearby Arafat, on a pilgrimage to the Holy Mountain, and Ukaz, the site of a fair and poetry contests.

The role of Muhammad and the rise of Islam cannot be fully understood without an examination as to why and how the universal religions developed in the Fertile Crescent and the surrounding lands in the centuries before Christ.

As we have seen, the Fertile Crescent was for almost two millennia the center of more long-distance trade routes than any other region. It stood at the crossroads of both land and sea routes to China and India to the east, Africa to the south, and the Mediterranean lands and Europe to the west. Merchants thus had the opportunity to prosper from this new, ever expanding trade and from the old agrarian economy base of the rich Mesopotamian alluvial plains and the Nile Valley. The early rise of agriculture in this region had already supported the growth of cities and centralized imperial powers. The economy of the region spurred the accumulation of relative wealth and allowed higher cultural forms to develop in the cosmopolitan areas. Relative peace and prosperity, supported by powerful empires, over time brought the growth and tolerance of new ideas, and contributed to the birth of the first universalist religions.

Earlier religious traditions of clans and tribes often involved the worship of deities that placated nature, ensured regular seasons, and therefore survival, or assured fertility. Magic and ritualistic elements were practiced to appease these gods. As a clan or tribe collectively attended to most of its members' needs, sexual and aggressive drives within the group were permitted freer expression; these drives did not threaten the group. The main threats were external. The expression of aggression in fact would be encouraged so every able-bodied male could be called upon to defend the tribe at any time against its enemies—other tribes. In a tribal setting the basic group, the family, did not have to be strong.[1] Over time a large group of tribes sharing geography, such as the Bedouin tribes in Arabia, could develop some elements of a common culture.

Large towns and cities emerged in the kingdoms and empires of the Fertile Crescent and surrounding areas. Opportunities offered in these new towns and cities would attract the gathering of individuals from many surrounding clans, tribes, and distant cultures. These groups brought their own religious beliefs and practices and they often spoke different languages. The separate tribal traditions would subsequently break down in the shared environment of the cities where each tribe's unique traditions and religious values became one of many. Confrontation with alternative belief systems posed an obvious threat to a person's own beliefs and worldviews, and the breakdown of accepted traditional views would force and accelerate change.

Thus, traditions and tribal identifications would not be easily sustained in the relative anonymity of a large city where neighbors were not only from different tribes but held other beliefs. (For a review of how value and belief systems are "legitimated" and "maintained" [see Berger and Luckmann (1967) pp. 107–125]. Though "culture contact" and "culture shock" are mentioned, their role in the erosion of social constructs is not elaborated.) As the tribal structure deteriorated, the individual initially depended

---

[1] The survival of tribes in relatively isolated areas of Asia, Africa, and South America with similar patterns well into the twentieth century, suggests how stable culture patterns can be and that the expressions of aggression and sexuality can only be understood when they are supported and sanctioned by the meaning, function, and structure of the family within clan and tribe.

mainly on his family and extended kin. As the surviving tribal belief system declined further over time, the mechanisms that sustained and enforced a mutual reciprocity of kinship support collapsed leaving the individual alone and vulnerable in a city.[2] The failure of tribal values in a city, with the decreased support systems, heightened overall insecurity and affected a city's peace. The resulting disorder and the increased group conflicts, unmanageable by power or force alone, probably contributed significantly to the rise of the new synthesizing religions.[3]

For our present purposes religion as I understand it is "a shared system of theistic beliefs and sacral practices." One might make a further distinction between universalist and local religions. The former transcends and dissolves (or at least significantly weakens) other loyalties; even the most basic one of kinship. Local or parochial religions do not transcend but rather reinforce bonds like kinship or territoriality.

A religion claiming divine origin and joining diverse tribes and cultures and languages could ensure peace and restore order among the groups. The new religion would embody a unified ethics and define the individual's aggression and sexuality. With the clan and tribe's demise the "locus of control" would shift from many distinct older beliefs and values controlled by the group to control vested in the individual. The emergence of cities thus contributed to the breakdown of clan beliefs and tribal religions[4] and led to the formation of one large group based on a new religion. This new religion eroded the old unnecessary tribal ties, but still needed to strengthen the most basic group previously supporting the tribe—the family. Separate tribal identities were merged to form a new religious identity often linked to ties with the city, state, and ruler.

Cities also strengthened the formation of a new class of prosperous merchants. Max Weber linked the needs of the entrepreneurial merchant class to a new morality that guaranteed more

---

[2] The decline of tribal values in the city of Mecca in seventh century Arabia was the basis for Muhammad's concern for neglected orphans and the destitute. It is a bigger problem today in large megacities as support systems collapse.

[3] While Weber (1963) has written of the possibilities of religious change when certain social phenomena occur, he has not defined universal rules, nor the role of cities, with large groups of people living together, in fostering new religions.

[4] This process of group breakdown and resynthesis in urban settings continues to the present and is reflected in terms such as *melting pot* or *mosaic*.

peace and included fair dealing in trade and contracts. Christianity, Manichaeism, Judaism, and Zoroastrian Mazdeism, the new universalist religions that were born in this region, made demands on a personal level rather than on a group or tribal level. These religions expected individual support of a moral and cosmological belief system as defined by a body of sacred scripture. They claimed universal validity and "a comprehensive solution of human problems in terms which involved a world beyond death" (Hodgson, 1974, p. 125). Every individual was expected to acknowledge attachment to a universal religious tradition: doctrines and morals were not for the privileged alone, but were made intelligible for the ordinary person. Behavior was no longer defined and controlled externally by the small clan or tribe; ethical values and standards were now "internalized." God's law brought inner spiritual transformation and became an interior law written in the heart of every believer. Thus, the individual was to be responsible for his or her own ethical conduct. The formation of a universal religious identity would reduce the level of group conflicts and make life more viable in the city. The Judeo-Christian and the Zoroastrian traditions emphasized interpersonal justice within the community. Peace, stability, and cohesiveness were welcomed by the merchant class because this allowed commerce to flourish. Thus the merchants were often the first converts to the new peacemaking religions (Weber, 1958).

These universalist faiths were "monotheistic" because they worshipped a single god. The worship of images and idols of the old nature gods yielded now to transcendent symbols, such as fire among the Zoroastrians. The real symbol of divine grace, however, became the community of worshippers itself. Monotheism demanded the creation of one exclusive group—a righteous community—that defined its values and moral universe as superior. The righteous community became uncompromising over time and even more rigid in its demands on the individual members: there was only one true belief and all else was false. A monotheistic religion by definition had to be universalist and fiercely responsive or lose its status as the sole claimant to a revealed truth; it would need a proselytizing mission to support and further this claim to the truth. Inevitably, then monotheistic religions would have a natural tendency to clash with rivals who made similar claims.[5]

A polytheistic religious community that tolerated a multitude of practices, allowed differences and conflict, by comparison, could not claim to be universal nor wish to aggressively proselytize. There would be enough conflicting claims within its own pantheon of gods and goddesses to permit easy, uniform, or assertive universal spread.[6] Such religions would accept multiple beliefs, and a changing, fluid, imprecise, and at times uneasy harmony would prevail. Religious rivals from outside would be welcome initially as just one more claimant to the truth and would easily seem just like the petty rivals within.

Polytheism, with its liberal approaches, allowed the individual the freedom and choice to develop superstition, magic, idiosyncratic belief and practice, with concrete representations of the Divine in the form of idols. There emerges later a stage, Henotheism, with a belief in one Supreme God, with the other gods reduced to representations or subordinate deities. There was thus a form of monotheism common to all religions and philosophies including atheism itself, since it was one Supreme God, not one or all of the gods of polytheism that atheism negated.

As a reaction to the confusing array of divine options available there was eventually a reaction—there was to be only one God. Abstract representations of this God were a threat and danger because they could multiply. It was this fear of multiple representations that resulted in a concrete insistence on the banning of all image and representation. This demand for only one form of belief and its aniconic representation, however, could be based

---

[5] In the early Christian world, for quite some time, there were only two kinds of people, those belonging to the Kingdom of God, and those who were subjects of Satan. This is probably an early example of the defense mechanisms of splitting and projection used by a group. "We" are all good on the side of God, the "others" are all bad and Satan personified (see Pagels [1995] for a history first of demonization of outsiders, i.e., nongroup members, and then of insiders—those recognized as group members—as heretics).

[6] The limited spread, for instance, of Greek religion (and its ultimate decline) and the limited range of Hinduism supports such a view. Hinduism has spread "tolerance" and a multitude of beliefs over a large but geographically linked area. It has both a powerful synthesizing belief system and a multitude of practices. It does not proselytize nor have a universal mission. The increase in the number of Protestant confessions and the wars over religion over time also necessitated the slow acceptance of tolerance and the rise of secular views.

only on a decision by a group that every other approach was unacceptable and therefore forbidden. Monotheism could only be defined by a group and maintained by a group. Monotheism became a group religion par excellence.

Polytheism, in fact, did not pose a direct threat to other religions and conversion, in this context, was by definition absurd. Gods had similar characteristics across cultures and were translatable. "The conviction that God or the gods were international was a characteristic of the polytheistic religions of the ancient Near East" (Assman, 1997, p. 45). These religions were not "something primitive or tribal" but "highly developed cultural achievements."

Assmann traces the monotheism of Moses to the short-lived monotheism of the Egyptian king Akhenaten (1360–1340 b.c.e.). It was "the first conflict between two fundamentally different and mutually exclusive religions in recorded history . . . " and "the most radical and violent eruption of a counter-religion in the history of mankind. The temples were closed, the images of the gods were destroyed, their names were erased and their cults were discontinued" (pp. 24–25). Tradition was opposed "in the most violent forms of negation, intolerance and persecution" (p. 210).

Moses' followers in turn denied the Egyptians any part in the origins of their beliefs and condemned them as polytheistic idolaters. This began a cycle in which every counterreligion denounced the others as false. The Bible preserved the image of Egypt, with its idolatry, as its own counterimage.

The biblical influence over Western secular notions of identity has been linked to notions of identity that tragically are violently exclusionary. These identities negatively define "us" against "them" in ethnic, religious, racial, gender, and nationalistic terms. Schwartz (1997) contends that it is the very concept of monotheism and its several paradigms of oneness that infuse collective or group identity founded in violence against the other.

Monotheistic religions can increase in numbers, power, and influence very rapidly. Political power has always been attractive, and political power groups in turn are attracted to a group that offers uniformity, peace, and stability. It is easier to govern a unified and more promising group than deal with a multitude of groups with varied and often conflicting claims.

In fact, the universalist religious communities became so powerful by the fourth and fifth century c.e., that they were able to gain political power. In the Roman Empire a form of Christianity attained official status and then officially defined itself as "universal" (Catholic); in the Sasanian (Persian) Empire, Zoroastrian-Mazdeism gained a similar status.

The rise of universalist religions in the big cities was significant for another reason. Before the advent of universalist religions, beliefs and values were local, limited to a small group or tribes that spoke a common language. Beliefs and values represented the collective wisdom of the group; they were spread by myths and rituals or signs and symbols and were built into the language by maxims, proverbs, and sayings. Language has been defined as a carrier of an enormous "edifice of symbolic representations" of everyday life and abstract constructs that accumulated as the "social stock of knowledge" (Berger & Luckmann, 1967, pp. 40–41). These constructs were transmitted across generations, mainly by child-rearing practices of the group, including traditions passed from mother to child. Knowledge carried across generations by learned priests and bards was largely limited by the range and extent of oral tradition or scribal practice. With the aid of mnemonic devices, prodigious feats of memorization could carry a vast lore of religious learning.

Universalist religions in the Fertile Crescent changed the pattern of transmission of the culture and its values by combining large segments of approved and accepted religious belief into sacred books such as the Old Testament. Sacred books lent stability to belief systems in the new *sacra lingua*.

These religions were a response to the breakdown of values of the cities' inhabitants and an attempt to unify many tribes and cultures, often speaking diverse languages (the tower of Babel) and holding divergent beliefs and values. More important, universalist religions were critical to the spread of ideas and values outside the purely religious beliefs. Languages changed or evolved slowly as the maximum size of a language group was confined to a limited geographical range, often within a radius of a few days of travel on foot or animal-based transport. Thus, ideas, beliefs, and value systems were restricted for millennia to the geographical range of a tribe and its language or the *lingua franca* of a tribe and its neighbors. (The range of cultural influence, for example, of an Amazonian tribe is even today limited by its language and geography.)

War and conquest often broadened the sway of an imposed language and its culture. The death of a new ruler, or the decline of the regime, however, returned the old boundaries, and overturned the imposed language and culture. In his sweeping conquests from Greece to India, Alexander left behind one of the longer lasting civilizations, the Hellenic. For several centuries Greek culture held dominance throughout much of the region, and the Greek cities flourished, together with Iranian and Aramaic cultures. The "Hellenistic" age, from the Mediterranean basin to the Oxus in the Far East, lasted for almost five centuries, but "the eventual results of this superimposition of Hellenic culture upon the Iran-Semitic and Egyptian are still in debate" (Hodgson, 1974, p. 119). Perhaps the impact of a culture alone is not as long lasting as a culture intertwined with a universal religion. And although subsequently Greek theology had a brilliant career, the advent of Christianity brought the decline of the Greek religion and the diminution of older Hellenic influences.

Universalist religions would change the course of history in a more lasting manner.[7] The religions and the new sacred languages vastly increased the range of values of the regions of the Fertile Crescent. These values were no longer bound by geography, by the range of the tribe and its language: the range was as vast as the reach of the religion. The new religions carried religious values and a vast corpus of views that prescribed an ideal role for the individual and the society. It included a sweeping view of the past, present, and future, with ideas that ranged from family structures to legal systems, and an overall worldview toward believers and unbelievers. The transformation of the societies that the religions confronted, and converted, was sudden and immense.[8]

---

[7] The European imperial expansion from the fifteenth century to well into the twentieth was linked to religion. The Bible preceded or often accompanied the gun.

[8] Christianity brought together the barbarian tribes of Northern Europe (as late as the 11th century) and transformed and unified them as no other influence could. The decline of religion in a secular age is likely to make a similar type of unification of tribes in the new national structures in Africa a far more complex task.

Religion was not just a message but a medium for a whole culture, a whole way of life in the new sacred languages (see McLuhan and Fiore [1967], for the massive impact on societies of the nature of the medium rather than the content of the message). Religion carried with its language the imperium of a well-defined representational world of its own culture and the quickest manner then known for its dissemination.

Religion was thus the best medium for the transmission of ideas and values across tribes, cultures, and nations. The holy texts maintained by scribes and priests permitted a stable and fairly immutable set of beliefs capable of transmission, often hundreds and thousands of miles apart and for generation after generation. Universalist religions had transcended language alone as the best and most extensive carrier of ideas across both space and time.[9]

It would seem obvious by the sixth century, when universalist religions had spread almost completely over the Fertile Crescent, that no king or emperor could dominate the minds of so many, over such vast distances, and over mortal time. Not even a dynasty could have a powerful impact unless it had the universalist religion's sanction and support. A universalist religion alone provided a medium capable of influencing millions with its ideas and values and offering immortality over space and time.

It was in this setting, less than 750 miles from the birthplace of two universalist religions, Judaism and Christianity, that Muhammad received revelations which gave birth to a new universalist faith that united the strife-torn tribal world of the Bedouin and soon a great part of the known world.

---

[9] It was after a millennium and a half, beginning in the fifteenth century, that the arrival of a new medium, printing, reinvigorated Europe and Christianity. God's words could be spread further by "printing than preaching" with a new "formidable weapon." The advent of print encouraged the growth spurt of the Protestant Church, and the rapid transformation of Europe. Islam was offered its first and most dangerous challenge (Eisenstein, 1968). The decline of print and the advent of the electronic media will threaten, impact, and transform cultures in ways as yet unclear.

5

The Early History of Mecca and Muhammad's Ancestors

MECCA, the holiest city of Islam and the birthplace of its founding Prophet, Muhammad, lies on the western side of the Arabian peninsula. At the time of Muhammad's birth it had been a city in which those following the traditional religions lived, but it was also the "Sacred House" (Quran 5:97) of the "religion of Abraham" (Quran 2:130).

Islamic tradition teaches that the Arabs were descended from Ishmael, the son of Abraham and Hagar. Isaac, from whom the Jews descended, the son of Abraham and Sarah, fought often with Ishmael, his half-brother; and Sarah, overcome with jealous anger towards Hagar, sought to have her banished. Abraham was therefore commanded by God to take Hagar and her son Ishmael to Mecca and to construct the holiest of shrines, the *Ka'ba*.

The historian Tabari (d. 923 c.e.) brings together different versions of the traditions as Abraham travels toward Mecca. In his view:

> When God pointed out to Abraham the place of the House and told him how to build the sanctuary, he set out to do the job and Gabriel went with him. It was said that whenever he passed a town he would ask, "Is this the town which God's command meant, O Gabriel?" And Gabriel would say: "Pass it by." At last they reached Mecca, which at that time was nothing but acacia trees, mimosa, and thorn trees, and there was a people called Amalekites outside Mecca and its surroundings. The House at that time was but a hill of red clay. Abraham said to Gabriel, "Was it here that I was ordered to leave them?" Gabriel said, "Yes." Abraham directed Hagar and Ishmael to go to the Hijr, and settled them down there. He commanded Hagar, the mother of Ishmael, to find shelter there. Then he said "My Lord, I have settled some of my posterity in an

uncultivable valley near Your Holy House . . . " with the quote continuing until " . . . that they may be thankful" (Quran 14:37). Then he journeyed back to his family in Syria, leaving the two of them at the House. (Quoted in Peters [1994, p. 3])

The Quran describes too that Abraham was the builder of God's House.

Remember We made the House a place of assembly *(mathaba)* for the people and a secure place; and take the station *(maqam)* of Abraham as a prayer-place *(musalla);* and We have made a pact with Abraham and Ishmael that they should sanctify My House for those who circumambulate it, those using it as a retreat *('aqifun)*, who bow or prostrate themselves there.

And remember Abraham said: My Lord, make this land a secure one, and feed its people with fruits, those of them who believe in God and the Last Day. . . .

And remember Abraham raised the foundations of the House, yes and Ishmael too, (saying) accept (this) from us, for indeed You are All-hearing and All-Knowing. (Quran 2:125–127, quoted in Peters [1994, p. 4])

Muslims, who in later generations were curious about the antiquity of the most sacred buildings in their world, found this information on the authority of Zamakhshari (d. 1144 c.e.). In a comment on the above passages of the Quran, he added:

Then, God commanded Abraham to build it, and Gabriel showed him its location. It is said that God sent a cloud to shade him, and he was told to build on its shadow, not to exceed or diminish (its dimensions). It is said that he built it from five mountains: Mount Sinai, the Mount of Olives, Lebanon, al-Judi, and its foundation is from Hira. Gabriel brought him the Black Stone [that is, the stone embedded in the southeast corner of the Ka'ba] from Heaven.

It is said that Abu Qubays brought it [that is, the Black Stone] forth, and it was drawn from inside it, where it had been hidden during the days of the Flood. It was a white sapphire from the Garden, but when menstruating women touched it during the pre-Islamic period, it turned black.

It is said that Abraham would build it as Ishmael handed him the stones. (Quoted in Peters [1994, p. 5])

Mecca was uninhabited at the time of Abraham and Ishmael, and the *Ka'ba* was an isolated structure. The Arab historians who had already linked the biblical patriarch with Mecca now linked

Muhammad to his biblical ancestor by an appearance in the Tabari account of an Arab people, the Jurham, who replaced the Banu Ishmael.

> [A]nd God commanded his friend Abraham and Abraham's son Ishmael to rebuild it [the Ka'ba] on its original foundations. This they did, as is stated in the Quran: And when Abraham and Ishmael were raising the foundations of the House (Abraham prayed): Our Lord! Accept from us (this duty). Only You are the Hearer, the Knower.
>
> It had not had any custodians since its destruction in the time of Noah.[1] Then God commanded Abraham to settle his son by the Ka'ba, wishing thereby to show a mark of esteem to one whom he later ennobled by means of his Prophet Muhammad. Abraham, the Friend of the Compassionate, and his son Ishmael were custodians of the Ka'ba after the time of Noah. At that time, Mecca was uninhabited, and the surrounding country was inhabited by the Jurhum and Amalekites. Ishmael married a woman of the Jurhum. (Tabari, 1988, pp. 51–52)

Genealogy was an important facet of Arab cultural tradition. Every individual wanted to be certain that his tribe was honorable, and this honor was linked by traditional lore to the greatness of the tribe's ancestors. To the desert Arabs, every action taken had to honor their tribe and its past glory. Arab tribes were descendants of two distinct ancestors: the northern Arabs were descendants of Adnan, and the southern Arabs or Yemenites were descendants of Qahtan. After the breaking of the famous dam of Marib, mentioned in the Quran (34:16), the Southern Arabs moved north. It was the general economic and social decline of South Arabia, however, and not the breaking of the dam, that had been important to agriculture, that precipitated this northern migration.

Muslim scholars claim Adnan is a descendant of Ishmael through either his son Nabit or Qaydar. The statement by Tabari that Ishmael married a woman from the Jurhum is possibly an attempt to cover the considerable time gap between Ishmael and Jurhum (scholars believe that Ishmael lived circa 1800 b.c.e. [see Tabari, 1988, p. xxviii]). The control of the Ka'ba passed to the Khuza'a from the Jurhum after the Khuza'a came from Yemen in the fifth or sixth century c.e. It was one of the descendants of

---
[1] There is nothing in the Quran to connect Noah with the Ka'ba, so this must be a deduction by later Muslim scholars from the statement that the whole world was destroyed by the flood in the time of Noah.

Ishmael, Qusayy, from the Quraysh clan who ultimately returned to power in Mecca.

The Arab historian Tabari recorded the transition as follows:

> At Abraham's death Ishmael became the sole master of the Ka'ba, and when he too died aged 130, his son Nabat succeeded him, apparently without difficulty. The difficulty arose in the next generation: at the death of Nabat, whose mother was a Jurhumite, as we have seen, his sons and grandsons were too few to compete with the powerful Jurhum, who took over the sanctuary. (Quoted in Peters [1994, p. 8])

Ibn Ishaq goes on to describe the early years of the Jurhum.

> The sons of Ishmael and the sons of Nabat were with their grandfather Mudad ibn 'Amr and their maternal uncles of Jurhum-Jurhum and Qatura who were cousins being at that time the people of Mecca. They had come forth from the Yemen and travelled together and Mudad was over Jurhum Samayda', one of their men, over Qatura. . . . When they came to Mecca they saw a town blessed with water and trees and, delighted with it, they settled there. Mudad ibn 'Amr, with the men of Jurhum settled in the upper part of Mecca in Qa'ayaqi'an and went no farther.
>
> Then God multiplied the offspring of Ishmael in Mecca and their uncles from Jurhum were rulers of the temple and judges in Mecca. The sons of Ishmael did not dispute their authority because of their ties of kindred and their respect for the sanctuary lest there should be quarreling or fighting therein. When Mecca became too confined for the sons of Ishmael they spread abroad in the land, and whenever they had to fight a people, God gave them the victory through their religion and they subdued them. (Ibn Ishaq, 1955, pp. 45–46)

Coming from the south the Khuza'a tribe wrested power from the Jurhum and took over Mecca. How this happened is unclear. Tabari suggested forms of divine vengeance, whereas Ibn Ishaq offered political reasons.

> Afterwards Jurhum behaved high-handedly in Mecca and made lawful that which was taboo. Those who entered the town who were not of their tribe they treated badly and they appropriated gifts which had been made to the Ka'ba so that their authority weakened. When Banu Bakr ibn Abd Manat of the Kinana and Ghubshan of Khuza'a perceived that, they came together to do battle and drive them out of Mecca. War was declared and in the fighting Banu Bakr and Ghubshan got the upper hand and expelled them from Mecca. (Ibn Ishaq, 1955, pp. 46–47)

Meanwhile the sons of Ishmael had turned to paganism before they returned to Mecca as the Quraysh. In the period of the

Muhammad's Ancestors

Barbarism *(al-jahiliyya)*, or the "Era of Ignorance" as the pre-Islamic days were called, the worship of stones was widespread. Muslim historians traced the practice to the sons of Ishmael. The pre-Islamic past was studied extensively by Ibn al-Kalbi (d. 821) in his *Book of Idols* (1952).

> They say that the beginning of stone worship among the sons of Ishmael was when Mecca became too small for them and they wanted more room in the country. Everyone who left the town took with him a stone from the sacred area to do honour to it. Wherever they settled they set it up and walked round it as they went round the Ka'ba. This led them to worship what stones they pleased and those which made an impression on them. Thus as generations passed they forgot their primitive faith and adopted another religion for that of Abraham and Ishmael. They worshipped idols and adopted the same errors as the peoples before them. Yet they retained and held fast practices going back to the time of Abraham, such as honouring the temple and going round it, the great and little pilgrimage.... (Ibn Ishaq, 1955, pp. 35–36)

Ibn Ishaq also had a list of tribes and the idols they worshipped. Some are even mentioned in the Quran, as he observes:

> The people of Noah had images to which they were devoted. God told His Apostle about them when He said: "And they said, 'Forsake not your gods; forsake not Wudd and Suwa and Yaghuth and Ya'uq and Nasr.'" And they had led many astray. (Quran 71:23, quoted in Ibn Ishaq, 1955, p. 36)

Ibn Ishaq's text continues:

> Every household had an idol in their house which they used to worship. When a man was about to set out on a journey he would rub himself against it as he was about to ride off: indeed that was the last thing he used to do before his journey; and when he returned from his journey the first thing he did was to rub himself against it before he went in to his family....
>
> Now along with the Ka'ba the Arabs had adopted Tawaghit, which were temples which they venerated as they venerated the Ka'ba. They had their guardians and overseers and they used to make offerings to them as they did to the Ka'ba and to circumambulate them and sacrifice at them. Yet they recognized the superiority of the Ka'ba because it was the temple and mosque of Abraham the friend (of God). (Ibn Ishaq, 1955, p. 38)

Two idols, the result of waywardness of the Jurhum, were adopted by the Quraysh who also had other idols.

> Quraysh had an idol by a well in the middle of the Ka'ba called Hubal. And they adopted Isaf (or Asaf) and Na'ila by the place of Zamzam, sacrificing beside them. They were a man and a woman of Jurhum—Isaf ibn Baghy and Na'ila bint Dik—who were guilty of sexual relations in the Ka'ba and so God transformed them into two stones.
>
> Abdullah ibn Abu Bakr . . . on the authority of 'Amra bint 'Abdu'l-Rahman . . . that she said, "I heard Aisha (one of the wives of Muhammad) say, 'We always heard that Isaf and Na'ila were a man and a woman of Jurham who copulated in the Ka'ba so God transformed them into two stones.' But God alone knows if this is the truth." (Ibn Ishaq, 1955, pp. 37–38)
>
> [Two goddesses were particularly well known.] Al-Lat [was a goddess who] belonged to the Thaqif in Ta'if, her overseers and guardians being Banu Mu'attib of Thaqif. Manat was worshipped by al-Aus and al-Khazraj and such of the people of Yathrib as followed their religion by the seashore in the direction of al-Mushallal in Qudayd. (Ibn Ishaq, 1955, pp. 38–39)

According to the traditional calculations, the descendants of Ishmael, now called Quraysh, returned to Mecca seven centuries after Abraham had built the Ka'ba.

> The Quraysh at that time were in scattered settlements and tents [or "houses"] dispersed among their people, the Banu Kinana. So the Khuza'a possessed the temple, passing it on from son to son until the last of them, Hulayl ibn Habashiyya . . . (the "King" of Mecca). . . . (Ibn Ishaq, 1955, p. 48)

A leading figure among the Banu Kinana was Qusayy who united his tribe, the Quraysh. Tabari describes what happened after the arrival of Qusayy in Mecca.

> Qusayy . . . was a strong man of good lineage, and when he asked Hulayl ibn Habashiyya al-Khuza'i for the hand of his daughter Hubba, Hulayl, recognizing his lineage and regarding him as a desirable match, gave his consent and married her to him. At that time, it is claimed, Hulayl was in charge of the Ka'ba and ruled in Mecca. [According to] Ibn Ishaq: Qusayy stayed with him [that is, Hulayl] and Hubba bore him Abd al-Dar, Abd Manaf, Abd Uzza and Abd. His progency increased, his wealth multiplied and he became greatly honored, and when Hulayl al-Habashiyya died Qusayy thought he had a better right to the Ka'ba and to rule over Mecca than the Khuza'a and the Banu Bakr, since the Quraysh were the noblest and purest of the descendants of Ishmael, son of Abraham. He spoke to some men of the Quraysh and Banu Kinana and called upon them to expel the Khuza'a and the Banu Bakr from Mecca. They accepted his proposal and swore an oath of allegiance to him to do this. (Tabari, 1988, p. 20)

Ibn Ishaq adds a tradition as to how Qusayy made the decision to battle the Khuza'a, but then proceeds in his fashion to discount it.

> Khuza'a allege that Hulayl ibn Habashiyya had enjoined this on Qusayy when he saw how his daughter's children had multiplied, saying: "You have a better right to the Ka'ba and to rule in Mecca than Khuza'a," so that this was the reason why Qusayy acted as he did. But this is a story which we have not heard from any other source, and only God knows the truth. (Ibn Ishaq, 1955, p. 49)

The casualties were heavy on both sides in the battle between the Quraysh and the Khuza'a, so they sought arbitration. The arbitrator's verdict favored Qusayy's right to Mecca. Tabari added other versions to this transfer of power. In one version, Hulayl gave the custodianship of the Ka'ba to his daughter, Hubba. When she pleaded that she was not strong enough to open the door, he gave her an assistant, Abu Ghubshan. Qusayy purchased the custodianship of the Ka'ba from him for a skin full of wine and a lute. This act disturbed the Khuza'a, who went to war. In another version, Tabari relates "I have heard, and God knows best, that the Khuza'a were seized by an outbreak of pustules which was likely to wipe them out and that seeing this, they abandoned Mecca" (1988, p. 21).

Both Tabari and Ibn Ishaq detail the events that occurred next. In Ibn Ishaq's account:

> Thus Qusayy gained authority over the temple and Mecca and brought in his people from their dwellings to Mecca. He behaved as a king over his tribe and the people of Mecca, and so they made him King; but he had guaranteed to the Arabs their customary rights because he felt that it was a duty upon himself which he had not the right to alter ... until the coming of Islam when God put an end thereby to them all. Qusayy was the first of Banu Ka'b ibn Lu'ayy to assume kingship and to be obeyed by his people as king. He held the keys of the temple, the right to water the pilgrims from the well of Zamzam, to feed the pilgrims, to preside at assemblies, and to hand out the war banners. In his hands lay all the dignities of Mecca; he divided the town into quarters among his people and he settled all the Quraysh into their houses in Mecca which they held.
>
> People assert that the Quraysh were afraid to cut down the trees of the sanctuary in their quarters, but Qusayy cut them down with his own hand or through his assistants. Quraysh called him the "uniter" because he had brought them together and they drew a happy omen from his

rule. So far as Quraysh were concerned no woman was given in marriage, no man married, no discussion about public affairs was held, and no banner of war was entrusted to anyone except in his house, where one of his sons would hand it over.... His authority among the Quraysh during his life and after his death was like a religious law which could not be infringed. He chose for himself the house of meeting *(dar-al Nadwa)* and made a door which led to the mosque of the Ka'ba; in it the Quraysh used to settle their affairs. (Ibn Ishaq, 1955, pp. 52–53)

Qusayy and the Quraysh were now the masters of the Meccan holy site *(Haram)*. The origins of the Quraysh were still somewhat unclear, as there was no eponymous "Quraysh" in the genealogy of the tribe.

> Ibn al-Kalbi (maintains that) Quraysh is a collective name, and cannot be traced back to a father or mother, or to a male or female guardian.... Others say that Quraysh were so called after a creature which lives in the sea and eats other sea creatures, namely, the shark *(qirsh)*. The descendants of al-Nadr ibn Kinana were named after the *qirsh* because it is the most powerful of sea creatures.... yet another account is that they were called Quraysh because they made a profit *(taqarrasha)* from raiding. (Tabari, 1988, pp. 29–30)

It is clear from the varied etymological attempts that there is no clear conviction among Arabs as to the identity of the Quraysh or their origins.

Qusayy is regarded as the founder of Mecca as a city. It was previously just a settlement around the holy sanctuary. He had brought together the Quraysh who had little or no influence and were disunited. It is likely that his assignment of districts in the building of the city later led to friction and bitter hostilities. Those who inhabited the area around the Ka'ba were called the Quraysh al-Bitah, and those who were assigned the outskirts were called Quraysh al-Zawahir. There were further divisions among the Quraysh al-Bitah. Abd al-Dar had succeeded Qusayy, but his family in the course of time, was challenged by that of Abd Manaf, another son of Qusayy. Mecca was split further into two hostile camps. These divisions led to fighting, although in a timely compromise Abd al-Dar retained some nominal privileges while Abd Manaf maintained power. As the numbers of the Quraysh increased, power was further divided. Mecca had strife not only between individuals struggling for power but their extended families too.

Abd Manaf's four principal sons did much to develop trade in Mecca and became prosperous. Hashim, the great grandfather of Muhammad, acquired from his brother Abd Shams, the right of supplying food and water to the pilgrims. He and his brothers even concluded some commercial treaties with the rulers of the north and possibly with the Ghassanids, allies of the Byzantine Empire. It is alleged that he also began the tradition of two caravan journeys a year, in summer and in winter. While the extent of the international trade in incense and spices through Mecca has been recently questioned (Peters, 1994, p. 75), the Quraysh did trade in leather and raisins, as the sources mention. The influence and revenues from the shrine, with Hashim's trade initiatives, may have allowed a trading zone of barter and exchange between Mecca and the ill-defined frontiers of Syria and Iraq.

It is evident that Muhammad's ancestors were important in the politics of Mecca, that their importance was not exaggerated, as some Western scholars have suggested. The early death of Hashim in Gaza on a trading journey to Syria weakened the clan to some extent until his son Abd al-Muttalib improved its status once again. Abd al-Muttalib took the initiative to dig the well, Zamzam, beside the Ka'ba, which became the central well of Mecca and shared in the sanctuary's prestige. As he had already inherited the right to provide water for pilgrims, this well, Zamzam, enhanced the esteem of his clan. That Abd al-Muttalib was also able to marry his daughters into the most powerful families in Mecca indicates his standing. After his death, however, the clan's fortunes waned and they became one of the weaker and poorer clans. Muhammad's father, Abdullah, did not share in the trade with Syria on the same scale as other Meccan clans.

Social and Ethical Structures in Mecca

The pre-Islamic world was a world of groups. History reveals a world of clans and tribes and skilled or unique leaders. Watt describes a:

> [B]ewildering multiplicity of groups within groups. The Arabs have half a dozen or more words for groups of different sizes, which later writers

arranged in precise hierarchical order; but the usual practice was to call any group, whatever its size, "Banu Fulan," the sons of so-and-so. (Watt, 1956, p. 78)

The words *tribe* and *clan* are often used arbitrarily. The division and subdivision of a tribe was not a nomenclatural issue but a political fact. Within each group were smaller groups that were rivals and pursued contrary policies.

The only governing organization in Mecca was the *mala*, or senate. It was an assembly of all the leading men or chiefs of the varied clans. The main function of this council was to deliberate on issues. It had no executive authority, as each clan was independent. Only unanimous decisions could be made in the *mala*. Troublesome minorities were dealt with by a group boycott. The *mala* thus served mainly as a forum for building relationships and mediating petty conflict. There were some offices that the sources and tradition mention. Among these were the *siqaya* (superintendence of the water supply, especially for pilgrims), the *rifada* (provisioning of pilgrims), the *liwa* (arranging and carrying the standard of war), and the *nasi* (the privilege of deciding when a month was to be intercalated in the lunar year to allow correspondence with the solar year).

The individual's status in this setting was linked to that of the clan's, as well his own skills and personal qualities. To persuade his clan and others to follow him, he needed diplomacy and financial shrewdness. But the defining characteristic for prestige for the desert Arab nobility was military power: a leader needed to protect his clients and avenge any insults or injuries.

The Quraysh had built trading relationships with other tribes that were attracted to Mecca as *hulafa* or confederates. The secret of Quraysh strength as warriors was the numbers of confederates they could muster to fight against any rival. Some of these nomadic tribes had entered into safe-conduct agreements for traders from Mecca and their prosperity was closely linked to Meccan commerce.

Groups and how they related were a major fact of life in Arabia. The very survival of an individual depended on ties of loyalty to family, clan, and tribe. In turn, the solidarity of tribes was vital for their own survival as groups. Tribes were often at war

Muhammad's Ancestors

with neighboring tribes and needed military power to survive. Tribal solidarity was maintained by the system of blood-feuds. To harm someone would invite a feud. Security of a person or property depended on the tribe's readiness to avenge theft and murder. There was no supreme law; each tribe was sovereign and independent. Justice took the form of "an eye for an eye." A murderer's tribe was held responsible for his actions and the offending tribe's demand was a "life for a life," often creating a chain of reactions sometimes stretching through generations.

Even though a tribe or a confederation was considered a single "political" unit, Arabs did share a sense of identity based on their common descent through Ishmael, a common language, and shared ideas and views of tribal life and conventions.

The moral ideal in the desert was based on *muruwah* or manliness, described as "bravery in battle, patience in misfortune, persistence in revenge, protection of the weak, defiance of the strong" (Watt, 1953, p. 20, attributed to R. A. Nicholson). Generosity and hospitality were admired by desert Arabs as much as loyalty and fidelity were held as virtues. A man's authority and respect depended upon his degree of *muruwah*. Tribe succession also depended on these values, a tribal leader was no more than a first among equals. The eldest son inherited his father's position only if he qualified as a man of wisdom and good judgment. A tribe risked its survival if it ignored this custom; the leader chosen was a well-respected male from a leading family.

Pre-Islamic Religions in Arabia

The religious practices of the people of Arabia evolved over a considerable period. Deities were everywhere; they dwelled in stones—sculpted, shaped, or in their natural state—trees, springs, or the heavenly bodies. The oasis dwellers had their gods and the Bedouin theirs, the latter often carried about on the nomads' search for pasturage. Each tribe or confederation of tribes had its patron deity which gave the group a focus based on religious solidarity. Worship included pilgrimage *(hajj)*, and at Mecca the Bedouin came to the town annually under the protection of a sacred truce to offer sacrifice in the sacred enclosure called the *Haram* and at other sites in the vicinity. Muhammad adopted, and adapted, some of these local rites into Islam on the assumption that Abraham had once been in Mecca and that Ishmael and Hagar had lived and died there. The Quran says merely that Abraham and Ishmael had built the Ka'ba (2:124–127), the cube-shaped stone house-shrine that stood in the midst of the *Haram*, but Muslim tradition later supplied the details (from Jewish converts?) of how he had gotten there from the distant Negev. So by incorporating a purified form of these rituals connected with the Ka'ba and the *hajj* into Islam, Muhammad was convinced that he was doing nothing less than restoring the pristine "religion of Abraham" (Quran 2:135).

For all Muslims the Quran is a divine revelation and the very words of God, and it has some harsh and direct things to say about the beliefs of the polytheist Meccans. The earliest passages in the Quran, which are directed toward weaning them away from their idolatry, appeals to the Meccans' worship of Allah, whom they recognized as the supreme God, even though they continued to worship what the Quran derisively calls his "daughters." Allah—the name is a contraction of al-ilah, "the god"—was a deity whose worship was widespread among the Arabs of the Fertile Crescent in pre-Islamic days. He appears to have had a special cult in Mecca, however, where the Ka'ba, Mecca's chief shrine, was regarded as his "house," although there was no effigy or idol within. But whatever the Meccans thought of Allah, for Muhammad he was the *only* God, without peer or associate, the same One True God first worshipped by Abraham and then by the Jews and Christians, and a good part of the early Quran is dedicated to attempting to convince his fellow Meccans of that truth.

6

The Early Years of Muhammad and the Prophetic Call

ERNEST RENAN has remarked that unlike other religions which were created in mystery, Islam was born in the full light of history (quoted in Lewis, 1958, p. 16) and that the life of Islam's founder, Muhammad, was as well known as the lives of the founders of the Protestant Reformation a thousand years later. More details are documented about Muhammad than about the founder of Christianity. The life of Muhammad had been copiously recorded in early biographies, notably in the *Sira* or Life by Ibn Ishaq (d. 767) (Ibn Ishaq, 1955). The biography of al-Tabari "is full of graphic details and vivid descriptions which make it delightful to read . . . as though it must have been experienced directly. The animated dialogues, turns of phrases in reported speech, moments of humor . . . " (quoted in Tabari, 1990, p. xi) are not lost even in translation. Besides providing general outlines, these early biographies contain many stories about Muhammad himself and his associates. There are also large collections of "Traditions," or *hadith,* that are anecdotal accounts of the sayings and actions of Muhammad.

Each individual *hadith* is attested to by a chain of authorities, in the form, "I heard from . . . who heard from . . . who heard from . . . who heard the Prophet say. . . . " The careful listing of authorities in each case, tracing back to an eyewitness, would seem to be an absolutely credible historical record. Unfortunately this is not so, as the *hadith* were collected and recorded several generations after the death of the Prophet and are thus to be treated with caution. They are mainly of legal or theological interest.

The generally accepted source, however, for the life of the Prophet is the Quran. It is a contemporary and authentic record of the direct revelations of the word of God given by Muhammad to the people of Mecca and Medina. The Quran in many ways might be considered autobiographical.[1] A number of major events in the life of Muhammad are recollected through him and by him in the revelations.

In fact, the revelations also reveal critical moments in the life of Muhammad. With the Quran and evidence from other sources, it is possible to reconstruct a biography of Muhammad that brings out the most significant events of his career. No further information about his life is likely to appear.

Muhammad, son of Abdullah, and the grandson of Abd al-Multalib, was born in the Year of the Elephant, usually said to be 570 c.e. This was the year when an Abyssinian Abraha, once the viceroy of the Abyssinian Negus for Yemen and later an independent ruler there, who had invaded Yemen, sent an expedition towards Mecca. This unsuccessful campaign against Mecca was recalled a half-century later and gave its name to the year of the birth of Muhammad. At about this time the Persians had invaded Yemen, massacred all the Abyssinians, and stayed to rule. South Arabia lay in political and economic ruin with its Arab tribes moving back to a nomadic existence.

The Birth of Muhammad

It is alleged in popular stories (and only God knows the truth) that Amina, daughter of Wahb, the mother of God's Apostle, used to say when she was pregnant with God's Apostle that a voice said to her, "You are pregnant with the lord of this people and when he is born say, 'I put him in the care of the One from the evil of every envier; then call him Muhammad. . . . ' Shortly afterwards 'Abdullah the Apostle's father died while his mother was still pregnant. (Ibn Ishaq, 1955, p. 69)

---

[1] Many other *homines Religiosi* such as St. Augustine and Gandhi have also left autobiographical writings. Nietzsche thought that all philosophical writing reflects "involuntary and unconscious autobiography" (quoted in Vaillant, 1993, p. 248).

The Early Years of Muhammad

Muhammad was a posthumous child and was brought up by his grandfather Abd al-Muttalib. It was the custom among the leading families of Mecca to send their children to wet-nurses or foster mothers among the nomadic tribes of the desert. The belief was that this allowed the children to grow up in the healthier desert air. Muhammad's wet-nurse for 2 years or more was Halimah of the clan of Sa'd ibn Bakr of the great tribe of the Hawazin.

Ibn Ishaq's account of the early years of Muhammad recounts the miracles and auguries of the future similar to those found in the New Testament regarding the birth and childhood of Jesus. The period with the foster mother is extraordinarily eventful:

> Thaur ibn Yazid from a learned person who I think was Khalid ibn Ma'dan al Kala'i told me that some of the Apostle's companions asked him to tell them about himself. He said: "I am what Abraham my father prayed for and the good news of (my brother) Jesus. When my mother was carrying me she saw a light proceeding from her which showed her the castles of Syria. I was suckled among the Banu Sa'd ibn Bakr, and while I was with a brother of mine behind our tents shepherding the lambs, two men in white raiment came to me with a gold basin full of snow. Then they seized me and opened up my belly, extracted my heart and split it; then they extracted a black drop from it and threw it away; then they washed my heart and my belly with that snow until they had thoroughly cleaned them...." A learned person told me that what urged his foster mother to return him to his mother, apart from what she told his mother, was that a number of Abyssinian Christians saw him with her when she brought him back after he had been weaned. They looked at him, asked questions about him, and studied him carefully, then they said to her, "Let us take this boy, and bring him to our king and our country; for he will have a great future. We know all about him." The person who told me this alleged that she could hardly get away from them. (Ibn Ishaq, 1955, pp. 72–73)

Misfortune abounded in young Muhammad's life. When he was 6 years old, his mother died, and 2 years later his grandfather passed away. Ibn Ishaq recounts these tragedies:

> The Apostle lived with his mother Amina daughter of Wahb and his grandfather Abd al-Muttalib in God's care and keeping like a fine plant, God wishing to honour him. When he was six years old his mother Amina died.... in Abwa, between Mecca and Medina, on her return from a visit with him to his maternal uncles.... Thus the Apostle was left to his grandfather for whom they made a bed in the shade of the Ka'ba. His sons used to sit round the bed until he came out to it, but none of them

> sat upon it out of respect for him. The Apostle, still a little boy, used to come and sit on it and his uncles would drive him away. When Abd al-Muttalib saw this he said: "Let my son alone, for by God he has a great future." Then he would make him sit beside him on his bed and would stroke his back with his hand. It used to please him to see what he did.
>
> When the Apostle was eight years of age, eight years after the "Year of the Elephant," his grandfather died.... The Apostle (then) lived with his uncle Abu Talib, for (so they allege) the former had confided him to his care because he and Abdullah, the Apostle's father, were brothers by the same mother.... It was Abu Talib who used to look after the Apostle after the death of his grandfather and he became one of his family. (Ibn Ishaq, 1955, pp. 73, 79)

The "recognition" stories that inspire the infancy narratives of Muhammad may be of questionable historicity (Peters, 1994, p. 133). One tradition claimed, as we have seen, that Muhammad was acknowledged by Abyssinian Christians as God's Apostle. Another anecdote described how Muhammad was recognized at the moment of his birth by Jews. The most famous and well-described recognition event occurs during Muhammad's adolescence on a caravan journey with his uncle to Syria.

> Abu Talib had planned to go on a merchant caravan to Syria, and when all preparations had been made for the journey, the Apostle of God, so they allege, attached himself closely to him so that he took pity on him and said that he would take him with him.... When the caravan reached Busra in Syria there was a monk there in his cell by the name of Bahira, who was well versed in the knowledge of the Christians.... When Bahira saw him ... (Muhammad) ... he stared at him closely, looking at his body and finding traces of his description (in the Christian books) ... he began to ask him about what happened in his waking and in his sleep, and his habits and affairs generally, and what the Apostle of God told him coincided with what Bahira knew of his description. Then he looked at his back and saw the seal of prophethood between his shoulders in the very place described in his book.
>
> When he had finished he went to his uncle Abu Talib ... and said "Take your nephew back to his country and guard him carefully against the Jews, for, by God! if they see him and know about him what I know, they will do him evil; a great future lies before this nephew of yours, so take him home quickly. (Ibn Ishaq, 1955, pp. 79–81)

Very few other details about Muhammad's early childhood and adolescence are known. He was reportedly involved in the so-called Sinful Wars. This may have occurred in an uncertain period before his marriage to Khadija, supposedly when he was

25 years old. Neither Ibn Ishaq nor Tabari detail events of this war in their biographies of Muhammad, nor is it clear what role he played. The hostilities were triggered by a violation of the "truce of God" during the holy months, hence the name "Sinful Wars." Even in the pre-Islamic period there were months that were considered holy when no fighting was permitted. The Quraysh were at first peacemakers in a conflict between the Kinana and the Hawazin at the fair of Ukaz but were drawn into the combat. The sources are uncertain about the age of Muhammad and what he did in these conflicts. It is likely that this was a violation of customary religious practice. If he was actively involved, this could raise questions about his freedom from sin before his call to prophecy (see Peters [1994, p. 136], for the doctrine of the Prophet's "impeccability").

The next important event in his life was his marriage to Khadija.

> Khadija was a merchant woman of dignity and wealth. She used to hire men to carry merchandise outside the country on a profit-sharing basis, for the Quraysh were a people given to commerce. Now when she heard about the prophet's truthfulness, trustworthiness and honorable character, she sent for him and proposed that he should take her goods to Syria and trade with them, while she would pay him more than she paid others. He was to take a lad of hers called Maysara. The Apostle of God accepted the proposal and the two of them set forth until they came to Syria. (Ibn Ishaq, 1955, p. 82)

On this business journey to Syria, Ibn Ishaq describes another recognition event. In this story, there is once again a Christian monk, who on this occasion is anonymous. The commercial exchange that occurs is a barter, which is very likely a typical Meccan transaction near the borders of Syria.

> The Apostle stopped in the shade of a tree near a monk's cell, when the monk came up to Maysara and asked who the man was who was resting beneath the tree. He told him that he was of Quraysh, the people who held the sanctuary; and the monk exclaimed: "None but a prophet ever sat beneath this tree."
> Then the prophet sold the goods he had brought and bought what he wanted to buy and began the return journey to Mecca. The story goes that at the height of noon when the heat was intense as he rode his beast Maysara saw two angels shading the Apostle from the sun's rays. When he brought Khadija her property she sold it and it amounted to double or

thereabouts. Maysara for his part told her about the two angels who shaded him and of the monk's words. Now Khadija was a determined, noble, and intelligent woman possessing the properties with which God willed to honour her. So when Maysara told her these things she sent to the Apostle of God and—so the story goes—said: "O son of my uncle I like you because of our relationship and your high reputation among your people, your trustworthiness and good character and truthfulness." Then she proposed marriage. Now Khadija at that time was the best born woman in Quraysh, of the greatest dignity and, too, the richest. All her people were eager to get possession of her wealth if it were possible. (Ibn Ishaq, 1955, p. 82)

The prophet went to his uncles and told them about Khadija's proposal. His uncle, Hamza ibn Abd al-Muttalib, went with him to Khadija's father, Khuwaylid ibn Asad. When the father approved the proposal Muhammad married her. She was said to have been 40 and he was 25 years old at this time. Khadija was the mother of all Muhammad's children except his son al-Qasim, the "Pure and the Good," who died very young. His daughters Zaynab, Ruqayya, Umm Kulthum, and Fatima lived to embrace Islam and migrate with him to Medina.

Muhammad was now firmly set in the direction towards worldly success. Though there is no mention of any other trading missions by Muhammad, he must have achieved some success as he was able to marry his daughter Zaynab to a promising young man of the clan of Abd Shams. That he was considered to be a promising man of the clan of Hashim can be noted from the fact that two of his other daughters were married to the sons of Abu Lahab.

Khadija played an important role at critical junctures in Muhammad's life. She encouraged him to take on the mantle of prophethood. Khadija's cousin Waraqa, a religious-minded man, who later became a Christian, had also been supportive. The early years of Muhammad's marriage were crucial in preparing for the many challenges that lay ahead of him. Very little detail has been preserved, however, of this period.

Muhammad's marriage to a wealthy widow, one of the more successful of Mecca's entrepreneurs, was providential for Muhammad. Even the Quran reflected this awareness.

> By the morning brightness, and the night when it is still,
> Your Lord has not forsaken you, nor does He hate you.

And truly, the last is better for you than the first.
And truly the Lord will give to you, so that you will be content.
Did He not find you an orphan, and He gave you refuge?
He found you wandering and guided you?
Did He not find you destitute and enrich you? (Quran 93:1–8)

According to Peters, the reading of this *sura* did not find much enthusiasm from later commentators. Later Muslims did not like the reminder that Muhammad had been orphaned and poor as well as a pagan ("wandering"). Ibn Ishaq made no mention of the Prophet's poverty. There was no place for poverty and suffering in the "legend of Muhammad" (Peters, 1994, p. 138).

Ten years after his marriage, when Muhammad was 35 years old, as both Ibn Ishaq and Tabari inform us, a significant event occurred in Mecca. The Quraysh decided to rebuild the Ka'ba. In Tabari's version

> The reason for their demolition of the Ka'ba was that as at this time it consisted of loose stones rising to somewhat above a man's height, and they wished to make it higher and roof it over, since some men, Qurashites and others, had stolen the treasure of the Ka'ba, which was kept in a well in its interior....
> A ship belonging to a Greek merchant had been driven ashore by rough seas at Jeddah and had been broken to pieces. They took its timbers and prepared them for use in roofing over the Ka'ba. There was a Copt in Mecca who was a carpenter, and thus they had both the materials for restoring it and a craftsman ready and at hand. There was a snake which used to come out of the well in the Ka'ba into which votive objects were thrown, and which would lie on top of the Ka'ba wall every day. People were afraid of it because whenever anyone went near it it would draw itself up, make a rustling noise, and open its mouth. One day, as it was lying on top of the Ka'ba as usual, God sent against it a bird which seized it and carried it off. On seeing this, the Quraysh said, "We may hope that God is pleased with what we intend to do. We have a companion who is a craftsman and we have timber, while God has dealt with the snake for us...."
> The clans then gathered stones to rebuild the Ka'ba. Each clan gathered them separately and built separately, and when the building reached the place where the Black Stone was to be put they began to dispute about it, since every clan wished to lift the Stone to its place to the exclusion of the other clans. They started to split up into factions, to form alliances, and to make agreements among themselves in preparation for battle. The Banu Abd al-Dar brought a bowl full of blood and made a compact with the Banu Adi ibn Ka'b to support one another to the death. They thrust their hands into this bowl of blood, and were called "the bloodlickers" *(laaqat al-dam)* on account of this. The Quraysh remained in this state for

four or five days, and then they gathered in the mosque to consult together and to reach an equitable agreement.

Some narrators assert that Abu Umayya ibn al-Mughira, who at that time was the oldest member of Quraysh, said "Men of Quraysh, make the first man who comes in at the door of this mosque the arbiter of your differences so that he may judge on the matter." The first man to come in was the Messenger of God, and when they saw him they said, "This is the trustworthy one *(al-Amin)* with whom we are satisfied. This is Muhammad." He came up to them, and they told him about the matter, and he said "Bring me a cloak." They brought him one and he took the Black Stone and placed it on it with his own hands. Then he said, "Let each clan take one side of the cloak, and then lift it up all together." They did so, and when they had brought it to its place he put it in position with his own hands. Then they built on top of it. Before the revelation first came to him, Quraysh used to call the Messenger of God "the trustworthy one. (Tabari, 1988, pp. 51, 56–59)

This is one of the earliest examples of the Prophet's skills in bringing warring factions together.

The Beginning of the Prophetic Mission

The years between his marriage and the summons to prophecy were uneventful. The Quran makes no mention of any major events: the Quran's interest in the real world, the context of its *suras,* and the world of Mecca is very limited. It is unclear what mark Muhammad made in Mecca until he announced his mission when he was about 40 years of age. Muhammad had known and heard stories about Abraham and the Ka'ba and he regularly prayed following the practices of the Quraysh. He was also involved in a form of solitary devotional practice called *tahannuth.* This was a pre-Islamic practice that Muhammad followed, along with some Quraysh. It was not incorporated into later Islamic practice. Troubled by the social malaise in Mecca, Muhammad may have deliberately sought a form of solitude. He went to worship and reflect on the Divine by going to Hira, a hill some distance from Mecca. Tradition suggests that he had visions during this retreat.

> The Messenger of God used to spend this month in every year in religious retreat, feeding the poor who came to him. When he had completed his

The Early Years of Muhammad

month of retreat the first thing which he would do on leaving, even before going home, was to circumambulate the Ka'ba seven times, or however many times God willed; then he would go home.

When the month came in which God willed to ennoble him, in the year in which God made him his Messenger, this being the month of Ramadan, the Messenger of God went out as usual to Hira accompanied by his family. When the night came on which God ennobled him by making him his Messenger and thereby showed mercy to his servants, Gabriel brought him the command of God. The Messenger of God said, "Gabriel came to me as I was sleeping with a brocade cloth in which was writing. He said, 'Recite!' And I said, 'I cannot recite.' He pressed me tight and almost stifled me, until I thought that I should die. The he let me go, and said, 'Recite!' I said, 'What shall I recite?' only saying that in order to free myself from him, fearing that he might repeat what he had done to me. He said:

Recite in the name of your Lord who creates! He creates man from a clot of blood. Recite: And your Lord is the Most Bountiful, He who teaches by the pen, teaches man what he knew not. [Quran 96:1–5]

I recited it, and then he desisted and departed. I woke up, and it was as though these words had been written on my heart. There was no one of God's creation more hateful to me than a poet or a madman; I could not bear to look at either of them. I said to myself, 'Your humble servant (meaning himself) is either a poet or a madman, but Quraysh shall never say this of me. I shall take myself to a mountain crag, hurl myself down from it, kill myself, and find relief in that way.' " (Tabari, 1988, pp. 70–71)

Muhammad was troubled by these visions and he wondered at first, as Tabari clearly indicates, whether he was a contemptible poet or possessed madman. He even sought relief considering hurling himself from a mountain. Khadija meanwhile had become anxious and had sent messengers out to search for him. Khadija was very supportive, as Tabari relates.

When I came to Khadija, I sat down with my thigh next to hers, and she said to me, "Abu al-Qasim, where have you been? I sent messengers to look for you all the way to Mecca and back." I said to her, "I am either a poet or a madman," but she answered, "May God save you from that, Abu al-Qasim! God would not do that to you, considering what I know of your truthfulness, your great trustworthiness, your good character, and your good treatment of your kinsfolk. It is not that, cousin. Perhaps you did see something." "Yes," I said, and then told her what I had seen. "Rejoice, cousin, and stand firm," she said. "By Him in whose hand is Khadija's soul, I hope that you may be the prophet of this community." Then she rose up, gathered her garments around her, and went to Waraqa ibn Nawfal ibn Asad, who was her paternal cousin. He had become a Christian, read the Scriptures, and learned from the people of the Torah and the Gospel. She told him what the Messenger of God had told her that he had seen and heard. Waraqa said, "Holy, Holy! By Him in whose hand is the soul of Waraqa, if what you say is true, Khadija, there has come to him the greatest Namus—meaning by Namus, Gabriel—he who came to Moses. (That means that) Muhammad is the prophet of this community. Tell him to stand firm."

Khadija went back to the Messenger of God and told him what Waraqa had said, and this relieved his anxiety somewhat. When he had completed his retreat he went back to Mecca and, as was his usual practice, went first to the Ka'ba and circumambulated it. Waraqa ibn Nawful met him as he was doing this and said, "Son of my brother, tell me what you saw or heard." The Messenger of God did so, and Waraqa said to him, "By Him in whose hand is my soul, you are the prophet of this community, and there has come to you the greatest Namus, he who came to Moses. They will call you a liar, molest you, drive you out, and fight you. If I live to see that, I will come to God's assistance in a way which he knows." Then he brought his head close and kissed the top of his head. The Messenger of God went home with his resolve strengthened by what Waraqa had said and with some of his anxiety relieved. (Tabari, 1988, pp. 72–73)

The reassurance from Khadija was associated with the warnings from Waraqa, but Tabari notes that they both helped to alleviate the anxiety that Muhammad was experiencing in the sudden revelation of his new role. How long this period of alarm and anxiety lasted, when he considered harming himself, is unclear. There was both "fear because of the appearance and presence of the Divine, and secondly despair which lead to thoughts of suicide."[2] The concerns of his comrades, however, did not diminish. Another revelation sought to reassure everyone that he was not *jinn*-possessed, insane, or possessed by the devil.

> Truly it is the speech of a noble messenger,
> One possessing power with the master of the established throne,
> Obeyed and trustworthy.
> Your comrade is not *jinn*-possessed.
> He saw Him on the clear horizon;
> He does not withhold knowledge of the unseen,
> Nor is it the word of a stoned Satan. (Quran 81:19–25)

Khadija continued to believe in Muhammad and was a major source of solace and support. He had sat with "my thigh next to

---

[2] See Watt (1953) for a discussion of fear and despair which had deep roots in the Semitic consciousness as the Old Testament bears witness. The thoughts of suicide could hardly have been attributed to Muhammad unless he had said something that would give this a basis (pp. 40–41, 49–50).

hers," as Tabari had described, indicating a need and acceptance of physical as well as emotional comfort. Ibn Ishaq, in noting that she was the first believer in Islam, goes on to describe how important this support was when Muhammad was ridiculed and accused of falsehood, as Waraqa had warned. He continued to need her comfort whenever he returned home.

> Khadija believed in him and accepted as true what he brought from God, and helped him in his work. She was the first to believe in God and His Apostle, and in the truth of his message. By her God lightened the burden of His prophet. He never met with contradiction and charges of falsehood, which saddened him, but God comforted him by her when he went home. She strengthened him, lightened his burden, proclaimed his truth, and belittled men's opposition. May God Almighty have mercy upon her! (Ibn Ishaq, 1955, p. 111)

The Meccans continued to criticize him for not showing proof of his divine nature.

> They say: "You to whom the Reminder is being sent down, truly you are *jinn*-possessed!
> Why do you not bring angels to us if you are one of those who possess the truth?"
> We do not send down the angels except when required, and if they came, there would be no respite. (Quran 15:6–8)

And again, in two other *suras*,

> If your Lord had so pleased, He would certainly have sent down angels; as it is, we disbelieve your mission. (Quran 41:14)

> They say: "We shall not believe you until you cause a spring to gush forth for us from the earth,
> Or until you have a garden of date trees and vines and cause rivers to gush forth in their midst, carrying abundant water.
> Or you cause the sky to fall to pieces, as you say, against us, or you bring God and the angels before us face to face.
> Or you have a house adorned with gold, or you mount a ladder into the skies. No, we shall not even believe in your mounting until you send down to us a book that we could read." Say: "Glory to my Lord! Am I aught but a man, an Apostle?" (Quran 17:90–93)

It is clear from the above verses that as he was ridiculed for being *jinn*-possessed, the demands for miraculous signs from God as evidence of his status as a Messenger of God intensified. Muhammad firmly replied that there would be no magical evidence and miracles to substantiate him—he was just a mere mortal and a messenger.

At this time there is finally a suggestion of a miraculous journey. A celebrated Quranic passage implies that Muhammad saw a supernatural vision.

> Glory be to Him who carried His servant by night from the sacred shrine to the distant shrine, whose surroundings We have blessed, that We might show him some of Our signs *(ayat)*. (Quran 17:1)

It is in this same *sura*, however, that the possibility of a heavenly journey is denied. The distant shrine has been considered to be Jerusalem, but the evidence suggests it is a reference to heaven (see Peters [1994, pp. 144–147] for a discussion of the heavenly journey). Even a century after the death of the Prophet, a great many questions surround this night journey and ascent to heaven. His biographer, Ibn Ishaq, continued to express reservations about this event. He comments:

> The following account reached me. . . . It is pieced together in the story that follows, each one contributing something of what he was told about what happened when he was taken on the night journey. The matter of the place (or time) of the journey and what is said about it is a searching test and a matter of God's power and authority wherein is a lesson for the intelligent; and guidance and mercy and strengthening to those who believe. (Ibn Ishaq, 1955, p. 181)

After a discussion of different traditions describing the event Ibn Ishaq states:

> Thus, as I see it, revelation from God comes to the prophets waking or sleeping . . . one of Abu Bakr's family told me that Aisha, the prophet's wife, used to say: "The Apostle's body remained where it was but God removed his spirit by night."

To add finality to his own views on this controversial subject, Ibn Ishaq says:

> I have heard that the Apostle used to say, "my eyes sleep while my heart is awake." Only God knows how revelation came and he saw what he saw. But whether he was asleep or awake, it was all true and actually happened. (Ibn Ishaq, 1955, p. 183)

In yet another version, Tabari describes the journey to heaven without any mention of Jerusalem. Muhammed travels in stages through six heavens where he meets Adam, John, Jesus, the patriarch Joseph, the prophet Idris, Aaron, and Moses; in the seventh heaven he meets Abraham. Ultimately Muhammad is given permission to enter Paradise where he meets God, who prescribes 50 daily prayers for him. On his descent, Muhammad once again meets Moses, who suggests that he ask God to reduce the number of daily prayers. Muhammad does this, five times in all, until the number of prayers is reduced by God to the traditional Muslim practice of five daily prayers.

It is unclear, based on the Quran, which was the first revelation. Some evidence suggests how the prophetic summons occurred. Two visions are described on two occasions in the Quran.

> By the star when it goes down,
> Your companion has not wandered, nor has he erred
> Nor does he speak of his own inclination.
> It was nothing less than an inspiration which inspired him.
> He was taught by one mighty in power,
> One possessed of wisdom, and he appeared while,
> In the highest part of the horizon.
> Then he approached and came closer,
> And he was at a distance of two bow lengths or closer.
> And he inspired his servant with what he inspired him.
> His heart did not falsify what it saw.
> Will you then dispute with him what he saw? (Quran 53:1–12)

The *sura* continues on:

> Indeed he saw him descending a second time,
> Near the lotus tree that marks the boundary.
> Near it is the garden of the dwelling, and behold,
> The lotus tree was shrouded in the deepest shrouding.
> His sight never swerved, nor did it exceed its limits.
> Indeed, he saw the signs of his Lord, the Greatest. (Quran 53:13–18)

It is evident that the person who received this vision was Muhammad. Muslim tradition suggests that these were visions of Gabriel. As there is no mention of Gabriel until Muhammad moved to Medina, it is very likely that it was a vision of God he saw on the high "horizon" and when he saw "the signs of his Lord."

What was the nature, then, of the prophetic experiences and revelations that Muhammad received? The above *sura* suggests that first he had visions of God himself. On neither of these occasions did Muhammad receive the words of the Quran. There are no descriptions of when or in what manner the revelations of the Quran were sent. The Quran was meant as a liturgical recitation, probably influenced by Jewish or Christian practice. The revelations were sent down gradually—a manner of delivery which became a basis of criticism. The question concerning the Quran's authenticity as based on the Jewish conviction that revelation is a singular act. Muhammad himself later came to a similar conviction (see Peters [1994, pp. 205–206] for Muhammad's choosing the "Night of Destiny" at Medina for a single and complete revelation of the Quran).

Muhammad's initial reaction to the revelations was fear and trembling. "The sensations of a supernatural presence, the vague visions and awareness of simple spoken phrases were followed by long sequences of words in intelligible order, bearing a clear meaning, a message" (Rodinson, 1980, p. 71).

The revelations continued to recur and were an agonizing experience for Muhammad. We are told that:

> Muhammad's face was covered with sweat, he was seized with a violent shuddering and lay unconscious for an hour as though in a drunken stupor. He did not hear what was said to him. He perspired copiously, even in cold weather. He heard strange noises like the sound of chains or bells or rushing wings. "Never once did I receive a revelation," he said, "without thinking that my soul had been torn away from me." (Rodinson, 1980, p. 74)

The nature of the revelations has caused considerable controversy over the ages, from Voltaire's suggestion that Muhammad had to resort to fraud to make an impression, to Grimme's view that Muhammad had invented a socialist mythology to get his religious taxes approved! (Rodinson, 1980, p. 76). His experiences have been compared to those of religious mystics, Christian and Muslim. Psychiatric and psychological reasons, including epilepsy, have also been suggested to link these experiences to psychopathology.

There were some other concerns. Buhl (1930) suggested that:

> [H]is later revelations sometimes come to the aid of his less elevated inclinations, when we observe how he becomes increasingly cautious in producing revelations to back him up, and how these, obviously enough, often contain conclusions at which he has himself arrived after reflection and meditation on the needs of the situation or even as a result of suggestions made by those close to him, it is very hard for us to believe that they appeared in the same innocent fashion as in the earlier period. (Buhl, 1930, pp. 141ff)

Muslim tradition itself has been comfortable enough to discuss these concerns. Aisha, one of Muhammad's wives, at one time had made a sarcastic remark about the Lord's willingness to accommodate her husband's wishes. Muslim tradition also tells a story of Abdallah ibn Saad, a secretary of the Prophet, who took down the revelations of the Quran as they were dictated. Muhammad had stopped at one point in his dictation and the secretary continued the sentence aloud, to the end, as he imagined it should be. Muhammad absentmindedly incorporated this suggestion in the religious text. Doubting the Prophet's inspiration, the secretary later abjured Islam and fled to Mecca. These revelations have also been considered to be the promptings of the unconscious. Muhammad, however, to the end was convinced that they were the voice of Allah, even though they corresponded at times so closely to the wishes of his servant. Despite this conviction, in the beginning he had his own doubts. As we know, he had been afraid that human inspiration could have played some part and that Satan may even have inserted his own evil whisperings at one time.

The Public Preaching of Muhammad

Muhammad's public preaching began 3 years after he received his first revelations. Until then his message remained mainly within the circle of the family.

> People began to accept Islam, both men and women, in large numbers until the fame of it was spread throughout Mecca. . . . Then God commanded His Apostle to declare the truth of what he had received and to make known His commands to men and to call them to Him. Three years elapsed from the time that the Apostle concealed his state until God

commanded him to publish his religion according to information which has reached me. Then God said, "Proclaim what you have been ordered and turn aside from the polytheists." (Ibn Ishaq, 1955, p. 117; Quran 15:94)

One of the first to "submit"—Islam means "Submission"—was Ali, Muhammad's cousin, and the son of Abu Talib, who had raised Muhammad. This was followed by the conversion of Zayd, a freedman of Muhammad, and then the illustrious Abu Bakr.

> Zayd the freedman of the Apostle was the first male to accept Islam after Ali. Then Abu Bakr ibn Abu Quhafa whose name was Atiq, became a Muslim.... When he became a Muslim he showed his faith openly and called others to God and his Apostle. He was a man whose society was desired, well liked and of easy manners. He knew more about the genealogy of the Quraysh than anyone else and of their faults and merits. He was a merchant of high character and kindliness. His people used to come to him to discuss many matters with him because of his wide knowledge, his experience in commerce and his sociable nature. (Ibn Ishaq, 1955, pp. 114–115)

In the beginning there were few converts. The Quraysh did not take to Muhammad's preaching. Muhammad, as the Quran reveals, had become a "Warner." He warned the Quraysh about the unlimited power of one God and the need to make changes in their lives because Hell was a promise for the sinner.

Muhammad's mission slowly began to have some success. His religious views had evolved in Mecca over time. At first his "Lord" had been the source of his Revelations, then al-Rahman, and finally Allah, as his beliefs were modified over time (Peters, 1994, p. 160). In the early Meccan *suras* Muhammad refers to God not as Allah but as Lord. After about two years, Muhammad began to use al-Rahman, "the merciful one" for his God. Later there is no more mention of al-Rahman as the unique name of God but only the familiar Allah of the pagan Quraysh. Rahman is reduced to a characterization of Allah. The teachings initially contained a single theme: man had to be grateful for God's providential direction and guidance. There were no "Warnings," no mention of Judgment day, no ethical prescriptions or demands for monotheistic belief. Two *suras* (105, 106) suggest he was still friendly with the Quraysh and one (108) suggests he practiced some old pagan rituals (Peters, 1994, pp. 153, 160). Opposition, however, soon appeared and later assumed formidable proportions. When and how did this opposition arise and what were the reasons for it?

The Interpolated Verses

The incident of the so-called "Satanic Verses" marks the beginning of the opposition. The goddesses al-Lat, al-Uzza, and Manat were important deities near Mecca. The most notable mention of them is in Surat an-Najm (*Sura* 53) of the Quran where they curiously appear in some verses and then disappear as the verses are abrogated.

The account which al-Tabari (who had received it from Ibn Ishaq) places first is as follows:

> Now the Apostle was anxious for the welfare of his people, wishing to attract them as far as he could. It has been mentioned that he longed for a way to attract them, and the method he adopted is what ibn Hamid told me that Salama said M.ibn Ishaq told him from Yazid ibn Ziyad of Medina from M.ibn Ka'b al-Qurazi: When the Apostle saw that his people turned their backs on him and he was pained by their estrangement from what he brought them from God he longed that there should come to him from God a message that would reconcile his people to him. Because of his love for his people and his anxiety over them it would delight him if the obstacle that made his task so difficult could be removed; so that he meditated on the project and longed for it and it was dear to him. Then God sent down "By the star when it sets your comrade errs not and is not deceived, he speaks not from his own desire," and when he reached His words "Have you thought of al-Lat and al-Uzza and Manat the third, the other," Satan, when he was meditating upon it, and desiring to bring it (reconciliation) to his people, put upon his tongue "these are the exalted Gharaniq (cranes) whose intercession is approved." When Quraysh heard that, they were delighted and greatly pleased at the way in which he spoke of their gods and they listened to him; while the believers were holding that what their prophet brought them from their Lord was true, not suspecting a mistake or a vain desire or a slip, and when he reached the prostration and the end of the Sura in which he prostrated himself the Muslims prostrated themselves when their prophet prostrated confirming what he brought and obeying his command, and the polytheists of Quraysh and others who were in the mosque prostrated when they heard the mention of their gods, so that everyone in the mosque believer and unbeliever prostrated, . . . Then the people dispersed and Quraysh went out, delighted at what had been said about their gods, saying, Muhammad has spoken of our gods in splendid fashion. . . .

Then Gabriel came to the Apostle and said, "What have you done, Muhammad? You have read to these people something I did not bring you from God and you have said what He did not say to you. The Apostle was bitterly grieved and was greatly in fear of God. So God sent down (a revelation) for He was merciful to him, comforting him and making light of the affair and telling him that every prophet and apostle before him desired as he desired and wanted what he wanted and Satan interjected something into his desires as he had on his tongue. So God annulled what Satan had suggested. (Ibn Ishaq, 1955, pp. 165–166)

What were then sent down to allay the fears of Muhammad, comfort him and relieve his grief are now the actual verses in the Quran.

These are only names which you and your fathers have invented.
No authority was sent down by God for them.
They only follow conjecture and wish fulfillment.
Even though guidance had come to them already from the Lord.
(Quran 53.23)

There are a number of other versions of the tradition as recorded by al-Tabari. In comparing the different versions and the motivations ascribed by various historians, two facts seem certain. It is obviously authentic that Muhammad had publicly recited these verses as part of the Quran; a Muslim would not have invented such a tale. Second, weeks or possibly months later—the date is unclear—Muhammad announced that these verses were to be replaced in the Quran by others of vastly different significance (Peters, 1994, p. 161; Watt, 1953, p. 103).

In one of the traditions quoted by Tabari, the Quraysh had made an offer to Muhammad that he would be admitted into their inner circles if he would mention their goddesses. Similar traditions suggest he was offered wealth, a position of importance, or as many wives as he wanted in marriage. Some offers, more general, would permit Muhammad to join the Quraysh leaders in worship and business undertakings.

They said, "You will worship our gods, al-Lat, and al-Uzza, for a year, and we shall worship your god for a year." "Let me see what revelation comes to me from Lord," he replied. Then, the following inspiration came from the Preserved Tablet:
Say: O Disbelievers! I worship not that which you worship; nor do you worship that which I worship. And I shall not worship that which you

worship, nor will you worship that which I worship. To you your religion, and to me my religion. (Tabari, 1988, p. 107; Quran 109:1–6)

The Quran mentions a "reproof" in the *sura* Banu Israil because of the "temptation" to which Muhammad almost succumbed.

Their purpose was to tempt you, O Muhammad.
From what had been revealed to you.
To substitute something different in our name.
Had you listened to them, they would certainly
Have been your friend.
And if we had not made you wholly firm.
You might almost have inclined unto them a little. (Quran 17:73–74)

The verses which are said to have rescinded the "Satanic Verses" are in the *sura* al-Hajj.

Never before did we send before you a messenger or apostle.
Who out of his desire allowed Satan to tamper with
Our revelations.
Yet God abrogates what Satan interpolates,
And confirms his own revelations,
For God is most wise, all-knowing. (Quran 22:52)

The revelations had at first allowed the three goddesses to be intercessors with God, but then these revelations were abrogated. Muslim scholars considered that Muhammad was aware of explicit orthodox dogma from the very beginning. The heterodoxy of the "Satanic Verses" was difficult to explain, though accepted by the earliest Islamic historians. Monotheism originally was vague and accepted the possibility of lesser divine beings. Just as Judaism and Christianity accepted the existence of angels, it is very probable that Muhammad regarded al-Lat, al-Uzza, and Manat as a lower order of celestial beings. The Quran took up the issue of "daughters of Allah" several times, including the occasion when the lines of the Interpolated Verses were placed and later rescinded.

Have you considered al-Lat and al-Uzza.
And another, Manat the third?
What males for you and females for him (Allah)?
That would surely be an unjust division! (Quran 53:19–22)

The "unjust division" is defined in other verses.

> Now ask them (O Muhammad): Hath thy lord daughters whereas they have sons? . . .
> Lo! It is of their falsehood that they say:
> Allah Hath begotten. And lo! Verily they tell a lie. (Quran 37:149–152)

> Is it that He chooses daughters (for Himself) from
> All He has created while He honors you with sons?
> Whenever one of them receives news that he ascribes to al-Rahman.
> (i.e. that a daughter has been born to him) his countenance
> Becomes dark and he is filled with inward grief. (Quran 43:16–17)

The Quran thus makes certain that the three goddesses were not "daughters of Allah." The progeny of God would certainly have to be male. If they were not directly related to Allah how were the Meccan goddesses related to Him? Later verses in the Quran in the Medinan period do not even allow them to be intercessors. Allah is unique, without associates, companions, or "daughters," and the Meccan goddesses "nothing but names," inventions of the ancestors of the Quraysh (Peters, 1994, p. 161).

What are the implications of the "Satanic Verses"? Since lesser divinities were accepted in the early Meccan period, these verses could not be considered a "conscious retreat from monotheism, but would simply be an expression of views which Muhammad had always held." Watt (1953, p. 104) raises the interesting possibility that the revelation would allow Muhammad a broader religious base, including Medina and Taif where two of the goddesses had adherents. A larger vision would certainly increase the number of his followers and reduce the power of his opposition. The leaders of the Quraysh in Mecca would also reduce their hostility and accept Muhammad back into the fold if he accepted their goddesses.

Muhammad, however, must have realized that accepting the Banat Allah, as the three goddesses, including other dieties were called, would reduce Allah to that level. Muhammad therefore turned down the Meccan incentives because that would undermine his monotheistic mission. The compromise would not work and it could have been fatal. The rejection of polytheism was final as *sura* 109 called, "The Unbelievers," stated.

Opposition and Persecution from the Quraysh

The warnings of Muhammad also aroused the anger of the Quraysh. The Quran had been especially critical of the rich.

> For him who gives in charity and guards against evil and believes in goodness, We shall smooth the path of salvation; but for him who neither gives nor takes and disbelieves in goodness, We shall smooth the path of affliction. When he breathes his last, his riches will not avail him. The Guidance is Ours; Ours is the Next World, Ours the present. I warn you, then, of the blazing fire, in which none shall burn save the hardened sinner, who denies the Truth and pays no heed. But the good man who purifies himself through almsgiving shall avoid it; and so shall he who does good works for the sake only of the Most High, seeking no recompense. Such men shall be content. (Quran 92:4–21)

It has been suggested that Muhammad would have altered the relationship between the religious shrine and the commerce (Watt, 1953, pp. 106–107) that the shrine at Mecca supported in the pilgrimage called *Hajj*. Muhammad, however, was only offering modifications to some of the *Hajj* rituals; he had no plans to banish commerce. He had been critical of the polytheism practiced in Mecca and the three cult goddesses, but the criticisms do not warrant the extreme reaction of the Quraysh to Muhammad. "On purely 'spiritual' grounds, the eventually violent Meccan rejection of Muhammad remains as mysterious as the kind of opposition that led to the execution of Jesus" (Peters, 1994, p. 168). Though it is unclear whether the grounds were religious or commercial, the issue of Meccan polytheism and Muhammad's preaching against it had created a furor.

Al-Tabari has preserved a document of the late seventh century that appears to be genuine. Urwah, in a letter to Caliph Abd al-Malik, noted that it was only after the incident around the worship of idols that some Quraysh with property in al-Taif took the lead in opposing Muhammad (Watt, 1953, p. 100). It is very likely that removing recognition from the shrine of al-Lat at al-Taif would threaten the commercial enterprise of these Quraysh, who then stirred up more anger in the Meccan community. The active opposition to Muhammad had begun.

Tabari describes the steady escalation of conflict between Muhammad and the leaders among the Quraysh.

> The Messenger of God proclaimed God's message openly and declared Islam publicly to his fellow tribesmen. When he did so, they did not withdraw from him or reject him in any way, as far as I have heard, until he spoke of their gods and denounced them. When he did this, they took exception to it and united in opposition and hostility to him, except for those of them whom God had protected from error by means of Islam. The latter were few in number and practiced their faith in secret. His uncle Abu Talib was friendly to him, however, and protected him and shielded him from harm. The Messenger of God continued to do God's work and to proclaim his message, undeterred by anything. When the Quraysh saw that he would not give them any satisfaction, they objected to his departing from their ways and denouncing their gods, and, seeing that Abu Talib protected him, shielded him from harm, and would not hand him over to them, a number of the nobles of Quraysh, ... went to Abu Talib and said, "Abu Talib, your nephew has reviled our gods, denounced our religion, derided our traditional values and told us that our forefathers were misguided. Either curb his attacks on us or give us a free hand to deal with him, for you are just as opposed to him as we are, and we will deal with him for you." Abu Talib gave them a mild answer and declined courteously, and they left him. The Messenger of God continued as before, proclaiming the faith of God and summoning people to it.
>
> After this, Muhammad was estranged from the Quraysh, and they withdrew from him and harbored a secret hatred for him. . . . This breach and enmity with his tribe weighed heavily on Abu Talib, but he could not reconcile himself to surrendering the Messenger of God to them or deserting him. (Tabari, 1988, pp. 93–94)

When the Quarysh could not get Abu Talib to support them and to renounce his nephew, they turned on the weaker followers of Muhammad.

> After this, the situation deteriorated, hostility became more bitter, and people withdrew from one another and showed open hatred to one another. Then the Quraysh incited one another against those in their various clans who had become Companions of the Messenger of God and had accepted Islam with him. Every clan fell upon those of its members who were Muslims, tormenting them and trying to force them to leave their religion. God protected his Messenger from them by means of his uncle Abu Talib who saw what the Quraysh were doing among the Banu Hashim and the Banu al-Muttalib and called on them to follow him in protecting and defending the Messenger of God. (Tabari, 1988, p. 97)

The violence intensified when beating and tormenting the Muslims did not persuade them to leave their new religion. Ibn Ishaq is somewhat more explicit than Tabari. Besides physical force there also were social pressures and an economic boycott.

The Early Years of Muhammad

> Then the Quraysh showed their enmity to all those who followed the Apostle; every clan which contained Muslims attacked them, imprisoning them, and beating them, allowing them no food or drink, and exposing them to the burning heat of Mecca, so as to seduce them from their religion. Some gave way under pressure of persecution, and others resisted them, being protected by God....
> It was that evil man Abu Jahl who stirred up the Meccans against them. When he heard that a man had become a Muslim, if he was a man of social importance and had relations to defend him, he reprimanded him and poured scorn on him, saying, "You have forsaken the religion of your father who was better than you. We will declare you a blockhead and brand you as a fool and destroy your reputation." If he was a merchant he said, "We will boycott your goods and reduce you to beggary." If he was a person of no social importance, he beat him and incited people against him. (Ibn Ishaq, 1955, pp. 143, 145)

As the hostilities increased, a number of the believers were sent by Muhammad to Christian Abyssinia: by one account there were 82 or 83 men, by another, only 11 men and four women who emigrated. We return to Tabari's account of the emigration across the Red Sea.

> It was a trial which severely shook the people of Islam who had followed the Messenger of God. Some were seduced, but God protected from error those whom He wished to protect. When the Muslims were treated in this way, the Messenger of God commanded them to emigrate to Abyssinia. In Abyssinia there was a righteous king called the Negus in whose land no one was oppressed and who was praised for his righteousness.
> Abyssinia was a land with which the Quraysh traded and in which they found an ample living, security, and a good market. When the Messenger of God commanded them to do this, the main body of them went to Abyssinia because of the coercion they were being subjected to in Mecca. His fear was that they would be seduced from their religion. He himself remained, and did not leave Mecca. Several years passed in this way, during which the Quraysh pressed hard upon those of them who had become Muslims.... (Tabari, 1988, pp. 98-99)

There were several reasons for the emigration. Many had to leave because of the persecution and hardship they faced in Mecca. The sources suggest that Muhammad feared for the faith of the weakest, who would have been easily intimidated. Some Western scholars have suggested other reasons. Noting that the early accounts indicated that this move was initiated by Muhammad, they suggest that his concern was not the physical hardships his followers faced but the risk of apostasy; if they stayed in Mecca they might deny their faith under pressure. Other reasons suggested by Watt are that some Meccans emigrated to trade or to form a military alliance with the Abyssinians, or possibly because of early schisms in the Muslim community (Watt, 1953, pp. 114–115). In an interesting aside regarding the schisms, Watt suggests that, "It is in accordance with Muhammad's character that he should quickly have become aware of the incipient schism and taken steps to heal it by suggesting the journey to Abyssinia in furtherance of some plan to promote the interests of Islam . . . " (Watt, 1953, p. 117).

The Quraysh, threatened by the possible loss of trade with Abyssinia, took action: they sent two men to the Negus with gifts of leatherwork for all the generals. They were to insist that the Negus surrender and return the exiles to Mecca, but the Negus refused to give them up or betray them.

The Boycott

At the time of the migration to Abyssinia, Muhammad won two influential and vigorous converts from his own clan: Hamzah and Umar. This conversion engendered a powerful response from the Quraysh leadership.

> Umar ibn al-Khattab, who was a staunch, sturdy, and mighty warrior, had accepted Islam, as had Hamzah ibn Abd al-Muttalib before him, and the Messenger of God's Companions began to feel stronger. Islam had begun to spread among the clans, and the Negus had given protection to those Muslims who had taken refuge in his country. When all of these things happened, the Quraysh gathered together to confer and decided to draw up a document in which they undertook not to marry women from the Banu Hashim and the Banu al-Muttalib, or to give them women in marriage, or to sell anything to them or buy anything from them. They drew up a written contract to that effect and solemnly pledged themselves to observe it. Then they hung up the document in the interior of the Ka'ba to make it even more binding upon themselves. (Tabari, 1988, p. 105)

During this period, Muhammad fearlessly continued to proclaim God's commands and to encourage his people day and night, in public and in private. His clan, the Banu Hashim, including his uncle Abu Talib, gathered support around him and protected him from the Quraysh attacks.

The Early Years of Muhammad 125

The Quraysh, unable to reach Muhammad, mocked him and laughed at him. The boycott was an attempt to isolate Muhammad and his clan from the city's commerce. The clan's protracted struggle continued for 2 or 3 years until both sides became exhausted. No supplies reached either side except what was secretly delivered by those Quraysh who had maintained relations.

> Then a number of the Quraysh took steps to repeal the agreement which the Quraysh had drawn up amongst themselves directed against the Banu Hashim and the Banu al-Muttalib. The most creditable part in this was played by Hisham ibn Amr. (Tabari, 1988, p. 112)

Hisham went around the city to get further support to annul the boycott. One of the first to support him was Zuhayr.

> They promised to meet him [Hisham] at Khatm al-Hajun, which is in the high ground above Mecca. When they gathered there, they agreed upon their course of action, and pledged themselves to deal with the document and to have it repealed. Zuhayr said, "I will be the first to begin and will be the first to speak." The next morning they went to their groups, and Zuhayr appeared in a gown, circumambulated the Ka'ba seven times, and then went up to the people and said, "People of Mecca, shall we eat food, drink drink, and wear clothes while the Banu Hashim are perishing, neither buying nor selling? By God, I shall not sit down until this unjust document which severs relationships is torn up." Abu Jahl, who was at one side of the mosque, said, "You lie, by God. It shall not be torn up." Zam'ah ibn al-Aswad said, "By God, you are a greater liar. We did not approve of its being written when it was written." (Tabari, 1988, p. 113)

Abu Jahl was apparently also challenged by others and the boycott was repealed. Unfortunately, just as the opposition to Muhammad was reduced and the boycott was crumbling, Muhammad received two devastating blows: his main psychological support, his wife, Khadija, and his legal protector, his uncle Abu Talib, died in the same year, leaving him in an even more vulnerable position in Mecca.

Tabari makes a very brief and terse comment on the losses.

> This was three years before his emigration to al-Madinah. Their death was a great affliction to the Messenger of God. This is because after the death of Abu Talib, the Quraysh went to greater lengths in molesting him than they had ever done during his lifetime.... (Tabari, 1988, p. 115)

Ibn Ishaq, while brief, has a little more to say before he goes on to the major changes Muhammad must make now in his life.

> Khadija and Abu Talib died in the same year, and with Khadija's death troubles followed fast on each other's heels, for she had been a faithful support to him in Islam, and he used to tell her of his troubles. With the death of Abu Talib he lost a strength and stay in his personal life and a defense and protection against his tribe. Abu Talib died some three years before he migrated to Medina, and it was then that the Quraysh began to treat him in an offensive way which they would not have dared to follow in his uncle's lifetime. (Ibn Ishaq, 1955, p. 191)

Without the protection of Abu Talib and his clan, Muhammad's life was in danger. He had to urgently seek other support, even if it was conditional. Desperately, he went first to Taif, long-standing rivals of Mecca. "When Abu Talib died, the Messenger of God went to al-Ta'if to seek support and protection against his own people from Thaqif. It is said that he went to them alone" (Tabari, 1988, p. 115).

He approached the leaders and nobles of the Thaqif tribe, who after hearing his plea for help in his defense and the defense of Islam, mocked him. Tabari describes the humiliating experience and his return to Mecca to continue his urgent search for succor.

> The Messenger of God rose up and left them, despairing of getting any good out of Thaqif. I have been told that he said to them, "If that is your decision, do not tell anyone about it," for he did not want his tribe to hear about this matter and be emboldened against him. However, they did not comply with his request, but incited against him their ignorant rabble and their slaves, who reviled him and shouted at him until a crowd gathered and forced him to take refuge in a garden.... (Tabari, 1988, p. 116)
>
> Then the Messenger of God came back to Mecca, and found that its people were even more determined to oppose him and to abandon his religion, except for a few weak people who believed in him....
> The Messenger of God continued in this manner. Whenever people gathered for the pilgrimage, he would go to them, summon the tribes to God and to Islam, and offer them himself together with the right guidance and mercy which he had brought to them from God. Whenever he heard of an arrival who had name and nobility among the Arabs, he would give special attention to him, summon him to God, and offer him his message. (Tabari, 1988, pp. 118, 121–122)

The pleas were finally heard by visitors from Medina, an oasis about 275 miles north of Mecca. *Medina,* the term for al-Madinah, a short form of Madinat an-Nabi, the city of the Prophet, had earlier been known as Yathrib, a collection of hamlets in a 20-square-mile oasis. This meeting was providential and fateful, as both Ibn Ishaq and Tabari recall.

> When God wished to make His religion victorious, to render His Prophet mighty, and to fulfil His promise to him, the Messenger of God went out during that pilgrimage in which he met the group of the Ansar [Helpers—the future converts from Medina], and appeared before the Arab tribes as he had been doing in every pilgrimage season. . . .
> One of the things which God had done for them [the "Helpers" who were from the tribe of Khazraj] in order to prepare them for Islam was that the Jews lived with them in their land. The Jews were people of scripture and knowledge, while the Khazraj were polytheists and idolators. They had gained the mastery over the Jews in their land, and whenever any dispute arose among them the Jews would say to them, "A prophet will be sent soon. His time is at hand. We shall follow him, and with him as our leader we shall kill you as 'Ad and Iram were killed." When the Messenger of God spoke to this group of people and called them to God, they said to one another, "Take note! This, by God, is the prophet with whom the Jews are menacing you. Do not let them be before you in accepting him." They responded to his call, believed in the truth of his message, and accepted the Islam which he expounded to them, saying, "We have left our people behind us, and no people is as divided by enmity and malice as they are. Perhaps God will reunite them by means of you; we shall go to them, summon them to your proposals, and expound to them this religion which we have accepted from you. If God reunites them in it, there will be no man mightier than you."
> Then they left the Messenger of God to go back to their country, believing and accepting the truth of his message. (Tabari, 1988, pp. 124–125)

These are the first hints of an Arab–Jewish conflict in Medina. These were minor, however, compared to the severe civil strife among the Arabs. The oasis of Yathrib had been torn by war for over a century, and the real reason for Muhammad's attractiveness as the holy Meccan prophet was the hope that he might bring peace. The following pilgrimage season another Medinan group returned to Mecca, ready to convert and to pledge allegiance to the new faith.

> The following year, 12 of the Ansar came on the pilgrimage and met the Messenger of God at al-Aqabah, this being the first al-Aqabah, and took an oath of allegiance to him according to the terms of the "pledge of women." This was before the duty of making war was laid upon them. . . .
> I was among those who were present at the first al-Aqabah [one of the pilgrims reported]. There were twelve of us, and we took an oath of

allegiance to him according to the terms of the "pledge of women," this being before the duty of making war was laid upon us. The terms were that we should not associate anything with God, should not steal, should not commit adultery, should not kill our children, should not produce any lie we have devised between our hands and feet, and should not disobey him in what was proper. If we fulfilled this, we should have paradise.... When they left the Messenger of God he sent with them Mus'ab ibn Umayr commanding him to teach them to recite the Qur'an, to teach them Islam, and to instruct them in their religion. (Tabari, 1988, pp. 126–127)[3]

A year later a larger group of the new Muslim converts, the Helpers, came to the faith at Mecca and offered allegiance at al-Aqaba, a place near Mecca. Muhammad insisted on a more representative group; trusting himself to one clan would have alienated other rival clans. This pledge of allegiance was very different from the previous pledge of women, for it introduced a totally new element to the Muslim community: it accepted aggression and the use of force to settle persecution. When the Helpers gathered to give the oath of allegiance they were asked:

People of the Khazraj, do you know what you are pledging yourselves to in swearing allegiance to this man?" "Yes," they said. He continued, "In swearing allegiance to him you are pledging yourselves to wage war against all mankind. If you think that when your wealth is exhausted by misfortune and your nobles are depleted by death you will give him up, then stop now, for, by God, it is disgrace in this world and the next if you later give him up. But if you think that you will be faithful to the promises which you made in inviting him, even if your wealth is exhausted and your nobles killed, then take him, for, by God, he is the best thing for you in this world and the next." They answered, "We shall take him even if it brings the loss of our wealth and the killing of our nobles. What shall we gain for this, O Messenger of God, if we are faithful?" He answered, "Paradise." "Stretch out your hand," they said. He stretched out his hand, and they swore allegiance to him. (Tabari, 1988, p. 134)

In another version, this time from Urwah, Tabari relates the event as follows:

The seventy representatives, chiefs those who had accepted Islam, came to the Messenger of God from al-Madinah, met him during the pilgrimage, and swore an oath of allegiance to him at al-Aqabah. They gave him their pledge in the following words: "We are of you and you are of us;

---

[3] It was called "the pledge of women" because in *sura* 60:12 Muhammad is told to require women, who wanted to be Muslims, to make such a pledge.

> whoever comes to us of your Companions, or you yourself if you come to us, we shall defend you as we would defend ourselves." After this the Quraysh began to treat them harshly, and the Messenger of God commanded his Companions to go to al-Madinah. This was the second trial, during which the Messenger of God told his Companions to emigrate and himself emigrated. It was concerning this that God revealed, "And fight them until persecution is no more, and religion is all for God." (Tabari, 1988, pp. 136–137)[4]

It is very unlikely that the occasion of the revelation was at this early date. Muhammad had very little support in Mecca to fight the Quraysh. He did not even have protection for his own life. It was much later after his emigration to Medina, that the use of force was even possible, but it is likely that some sort of a pledge of war was accepted at this meeting. The extent to which the Medinans committed themselves to hostility is unclear, but they did agree to accept the emigrants to Medina (Watt, 1953, p. 148).

Other verses from the Quran are also questionably positioned by Ibn Ishaq to explain events at this time.

> The first verse which was sent down on this subject from what I have heard from 'Urwa ibn al-Zubayr and other learned persons was: "Permission is given to those who fight because they have been wronged. God is well able to help them,—those who have been driven out of their houses without right only because they said God is our Lord. . . . " The meaning is: "I have allowed them to fight only because they have been unjustly treated while their sole offence against men has been that they worship God. When they are in the ascendant they will establish prayer, pay the poor-tax, enjoin kindness, and forbid iniquity, i.e. the prophet and his companions all of them." Then God sent down to him: "Fight them so that there be no more seduction," i.e. until no believer is seduced from his religion. "And the religion is God's", i.e. Until God alone is worshipped. (Ibn Ishaq, 1955, pp. 212–213; verses from Quran 22:39–41 and 2:193)

---

[4] This Quran (8:39) verse was probably not revealed until much later (after the battle of Badr); an almost identical verse 2:193 may have been revealed even later (cf., Peters, 1994, p. 184).

Part IV

The Rise of Islam

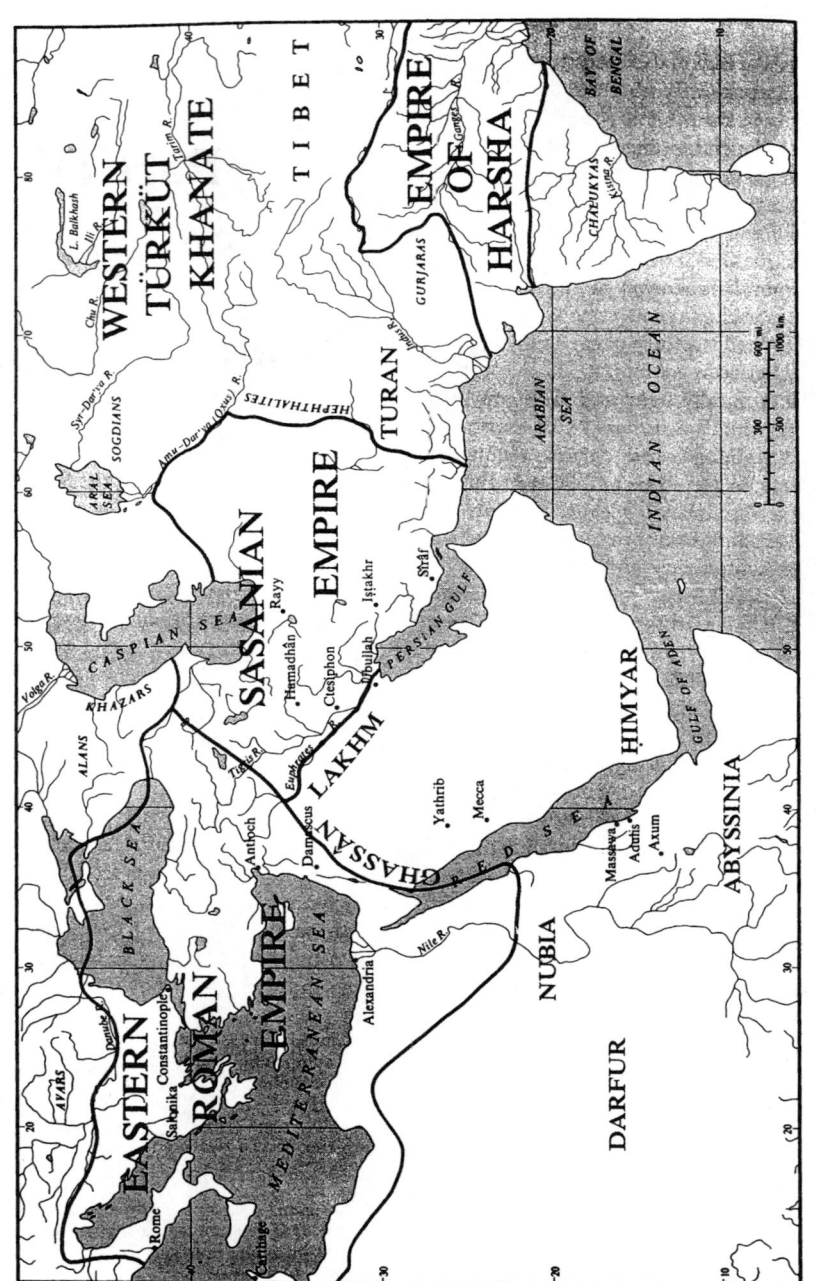

The central Mediterranean through India, c. 600 CE

7

Migration to Medina—The *Hijra*

THE arrangements with the Medinans were almost complete as the persecution by the Quraysh intensified. The migration to Medina, or the *Hijra*, as the believers call it, was about to begin.

> After God had given his Messenger permission to fight... and the Ansar [Helpers] had pledged themselves to support him according to the terms which I have described, the Messenger of God commanded those of his Companions from among the Muslims who were with him at Mecca to emigrate, go to al-Madinah, and join their brethren, the Ansar. He told them, "God has made for you brethren and an abode in which you will be safe." They went in groups. The Messenger of God remained in Mecca waiting for his Lord to give him permission to leave Mecca and go to al-Madinah. (Tabari, 1988, p. 139)

Muhammad's reason for waiting until all his followers reached Medina was to ensure that those who wavered did not give up the plan to emigrate. This also ensured that he would have strong support in Medina and not be dependent only on Medinan Muslims. These moves aroused the suspicions of the Quraysh leaders, however.

> When the Quraysh saw that the Messenger of God had acquired a following and Companions from a tribe other than themselves in a region other than theirs, and when they saw his Emigrant Companions going to join them, they realized that these had found a home and were safe from their attacks. The Quraysh were now anxious about the Messenger of God going to the people of al-Madinah as they knew that he had decided to join the Medinans in order to make war on the Quraysh.[1] They therefore met

---

[1] This benefited from "historical hindsight" (Peters, 1994, p. 186).

> together about this matter in the House of Assembly, formerly the house of Qusayy ibn Kilab, where the Quraysh had always made their decisions, and there they deliberated what to do about the Messenger of God, since they had come to be afraid of him. (Tabari, 1988, p. 140)

The Quraysh seem to have discussed various suggestions, including banishing Muhammad from the land to keeping him in fetters, locked up until his death. Muhammad's implacable foe, Abu Jahl, had a better plan.

> Abu Jahl . . . said "By God, I have an idea about him, which I do not think you have hit upon yet." "I think that you should take one young, strong, well-born, noble young man from each clan; then we should give each young man a sharp sword; then they should make for him and strike him with their swords as one man and kill him. Thus we shall be relieved of him, and if they do this, the responsibility for shedding his blood will be divided up among all the clans, and the Banu 'Abd Manaf will not be able to wage war against the whole of their tribe, and will be content to take blood money from us, which we can pay them." The old man from the Najd was saying, "What this man says is right. This is the correct decision; you have no other." Thereupon they dispersed, having agreed upon this. Then Gabriel came to the Messenger of God and said, "Do not spend this night in the bed in which you usually sleep." When the first third of the night had gone past, the young men gathered at his door and waited for him to go to sleep so that they could fall upon him. When the Messenger of God saw them there he said to 'Ali ibn Abi Talib, "Sleep on my bed and wrap yourself up in my green Hadrami cloak; nothing unpleasant will befall you from them." The Messenger of God used to sleep in that cloak when he went to bed. (Tabari, 1988, p. 142)

While the young men were gathered at the door, Muhammad slipped away to the house of Abu Bakr. It is then that the would-be assassins discovered Ali, who had been sleeping in Muhammad's bed.

> When morning came the group of people who were lying in wait for the Messenger of God went into his house. 'Ali rose from his bed, and when they came close to him they recognized him and said, "Where is your companion?" He replied, "I do not know. Do you expect me to keep watch over him? You told him to leave and he has left." They scolded him and beat him. Then they took him to the mosque and imprisoned him for a while, but after this they left him alone. Thus God delivered his Messenger from their plotting. About this event God revealed: "and when those who disbelieve plot against you to wound you fatally or to kill you or to drive you out; they plot, but God plots; and God is the best of plotters." (Tabari, 1988, p. 144; verse from Quran 8:30)

This incident requires extended discussion. As we noted earlier, the "scientific myth" of the primal horde has been elaborated by Freud (1921/1955b) as a mythic stage in human development followed by another stage "the totemic community of brothers, all with equal rights and united by the totem prohibitions which were to preserve and to expiate the memory of the murder" (p. 135) of the primal father. Freud's Lamarckian model of subsequent group solidarity was based on "complicity in the common crime" from this bygone age (1913/1955a, p. 146). This model, however, provides no understanding of how and why common guilt should bring individuals together to form a group. Balter (1978) provides an interesting example from Herodotus that suggests essential mechanisms of what he calls the "Cypselian paradigm."

In Herodotus' monumental history the birth of the Corinthian tyrant, Cypselas, was preceded by prophecies that he would overthrow the ruling family and take its place. The ruling family therefore sent 10 men to kill him as soon as he was born. On arriving at the home, they asked the mother, Labda, to show them the baby.

> Now they had agreed by the way that whoever first got hold of the child should dash it against the ground. It happened, however, by a providential chance, that the babe, just as Labda put him into the man's arms, smiled in his face. The man saw the smile, and was touched with pity, so that he could not kill it; he therefore passed it on to his next neighbor, who gave it to a third; and so it went through all the ten without any one choosing to be the murderer. The mother received her child back, and the men went out of the house, and stood near the door, and there blamed and reproached one another; chiefly however accusing the man who had first had the child in his arms, because he had not done as had been agreed upon. At last, after much time had been thus spent, *they resolved to go into the house again and all take part in the murder.* (Herodotus, quoted in Balter [1978, p. 333])

Their plan was thwarted, as the mother overheard the plot and hid the child. These men's defense maneuvers could be considered externalization of the guilt onto another person, or "the alter ego," in an attempt to resolve inner conflict. This myth suggests there may be conscious as well as unconscious elements. Each member accepts the guilt for the other members, so that all the others do the same for him.

The "Cypselian paradigm" suggests that the 10 assassins attempted to alleviate their individual guilt by externalization of the guilt onto an "alter ego." In the Meccan attempt to kill Muhammad, there is no suggestion that the young men felt any guilt. It was presumed that their clans would assume responsibility. It is unclear whether there was guilt experienced by any individual or even by the members as a group. In pre-Islamic Arabia there were no obligations towards those with whom one had no treaty—Muhammad's "protection" by his clan was almost nonexistent. The guilt of individuals for action taken in a group or sanctioned by a group is assumed by the "group ego."[2]

We continue with the Tabari's account of the Prophet's escape from his assassins.

> When the Messenger of God decided upon departure, he went to Abu Bakr, and the two of them left by a window in the back of Abu Bakr's house and went to a cave in Thawr, a mountain below Mecca, and entered it. Abu Bakr told his son 'Abdallah to listen to what people were saying about them during the day and to bring them the day's news in the evening. . . .
> The Messenger of God and Abu Bakr spent three days in the cave. When the Quraysh realized that he was missing, they offered a hundred she-camels for whoever would bring him back to them. Abdallah ibn Abi Bakr spent his time among the Quraysh listening to what they were plotting and to what they were saying about the Messenger of God and Abu Bakr. Then he would come to them in the evening and give them the news. (Tabari, 1988, p. 148)

When the search had slackened, the two set out on camels for Medina accompanied by Abu Bakr's freedman and a guide. They took a circuitous route for the first part of their travel and were forced to use ruse and guile until they were close to the haven of Medina, which they reached in September 622. This strategy was necessary as they were in real danger. By tribal tradition Muhammad's blood could be shed with impunity as he had no protection until he reached Medina. A verse in the Quran (9.40) confirms part of the story.

---

[2] The concept of shared guilt for atrocities committed by large groups and the demands for atonement and apology by groups victimized, for instance, in the Second World War, is relatively recent. Groups have often not accepted responsibility for their actions. The reluctance of Japan and the United States to apologize for bombing each other are the most evident examples of such group phenomena.

> If ye (the Medinans) do not aid him, God hath already aided him, when the unbelievers (the Meccans) expelled him with only one companion; the two of them were in the cave, and he was saying to his companion: "Grieve not, verily God is with us." . . .

With this arrival the second or Medinan period of Muhammad's career began.

Arrival in Medina

Muhammad reached Medina in the year 622 c.e. Unlike Mecca, where no agriculture was possible, Medina grew dates and cereals. It had originally been settled by Jewish clans from the north, the al-Nadir and Qurayzah. The richness of the oasis had attracted pre-Islamic Arabs who came at first as clients of the Jews but later dominated them. The eight Arab clans were mainly grouped into two tribes, the Aws and the Khajraj, which often fought each other.

A fierce battle in 618 c.e. between the Arab clans had led to heavy slaughter. When the two sides were exhausted, hostilities ended, but peace was not declared. Feuds continued to tear apart the Arab clans and the Jewish groups maintained an uneasy balance of power.

The nomadic background of the settlers, who were unaccustomed to agricultural life in an oasis, was a source of tension at Medina. When blood was shed in some of the many conflicts, the only manner in which nomadic custom would resolve this was the blood feud or vendetta. If a man was killed or injured in a fight, his clansmen would demand an exact equivalent from the responsible person, family, or clan. In some instances, 100 camels for the life of an adult male was considered equivalent and just compensation. In an oasis, however, where contacts between people were much more frequent than in the wide desert, conflicts were not easily given up, and what constituted a fair equivalent was arguable. In one celebrated instance where a chief was killed, even the killing of a youth in revenge was considered not equivalent and war went on for years.

In this pre-Islamic setting, arbitration was often resorted to by the sides in a conflict and men of wisdom were chosen to play such a role. While arbitrators had no power to execute a judgment, the parties were bound by oath to accept their decisions. However, Medina, being a large oasis with frequent disputes, needed more than the ad hoc settling of conflicts; it needed a permanent and consistent answer to its recurrent strife.

The warring factions of Medina, therefore, looked to Muhammad in Mecca to provide an answer to their problems. Muhammad was eminently suitable for such a role for several reasons. He was an outsider who could be neutral and resolve issues impartially. Muhammad was not allied by marriage to any clan, and while he had a great-grandmother from Medina, she had come from an uninfluential clan. Moreover, as he had been rejected by Mecca, he was above suspicion as an agent supporting Meccan domination over Medina. Finally, having no major pagan shrines, Medina had no vested interest that could be threatened by a new religion. Medinans felt that they could accept and perhaps welcome the new religion if their social and political needs were met and an era of peace established.

The Prophet's migration or the *Hijra* was a major event in the history of the new religion. Later generations date 622 c.e. as the first certain date in Islamic history—as the starting point of the Muslim calendar.

The *Hijra* marks, in the words of Lewis (1958),

> [T]he turning point in the career of Muhammad and a revolution in Islam. In Mecca, Muhammad was a private citizen, in Medina the chief magistrate of a community. In Mecca he had to limit himself to more or less passive opposition to the existing order, in Medina he governed. In Mecca he had preached Islam, in Medina he was able to practice. The change necessarily affected the character, activities and doctrines of Muhammad and of Islam itself; the records pass from legend to history. (p. 41)

Muhammad's stay in Medina immediately met obstacles and was initially precarious. His devoted supporters were mainly those who had accompanied him from Mecca, the Emigrants, or the *muhajirun,* and those from Medina, known in the Tradition as *ansar,* or Helpers. The group who opposed him in Medina were known as *munafiqun,* or Hypocrites. The opposition was mainly political but nonetheless redoubtable.

Migration to Medina

In the beginning, Muhammad was only the religious leader of his own Medinan community. In political matters he was merely the head of the "clan" of Emigrants and probably less powerful than other clan chiefs. In Medina, his followers, the Emigrants who had no source of income, often worked for the Helpers or Jews as laborers. However, because of his position Muhammad was prevented from doing so. When he was not invited by his followers, he and his family often suffered. Muhammad had by then married Sawda, the widow of a follower, and Aisha, the 9-year-old daughter of his trusted follower Abu Bakr. If his small community was to survive in Medina, Muhammad had to set up a structure and organization. His own position had to be strengthened, and relations among the varied clans and groups, the initial reasons for the invitation to Medina, clarified.

It was at this time that a covenant, or the Constitution of Medina, was drawn up between the followers of Muhammad and the Jews of the oasis. The covenant defined a single community, but allowed for differences between the two religions. It is here that the talents, tact, and administrative skills of Muhammad as a group leader can be seen in the actual development of this document, which has fortunately been preserved. It is considered authentic because it contains certain conditions which were later contrary to the views of the original community of Muslims.

> The Apostle wrote a document concerning the Emigrants and the Helpers in which he made a friendly agreement with the Jews and established them in their religion and their property, and stated the reciprocal obligations as follows: In the name of God the Compassionate, the Merciful. This is a document from Muhammad the prophet [governing the relations] between the believers and Muslims of Quraysh and Yathrib and those who followed them and joined them and laboured with them. They are one community *(umma)* to the exclusion of all men. (Ibn Ishaq, 1955, p. 231)

A review of some of the details of this Constitution are interesting from the point of view of how a large group structure was defined and formed from much smaller groups. Muslims and Jews were to have equal status. "It is clearly stated that the Jews form a single community with the believers (Paragraphs 25 ff.)." Jews and Muslims "shall help one another in the event of any attack on the people covered by this document. There shall be sincere friendship, exchange of good counsel, fair conduct and no treachery between them (Paragraph 37)." In the case of war they must fight as one people and no one could make a separate peace. "If one of their number were killed, they were to make common cause against the murderer and those who helped him, and either fight them together, or accept the blood-price together (Paragraphs 19 and 21)." "They were to maintain their own internal law and order, themselves punishing any wrong doers amongst them (Paragraph 13)." Each group was to ransom any of their own members who were taken prisoner (Paragraph 2 ff.)" (Rodinson, 1980, pp. 152–159).

Muhammad had thus formed a single community or *umma* in Medina bound together by a solemn agreement. He had, in fact, converted his limited political power into a more profound religious authority. In many ways it was like the federation of clans and tribes that had existed in pre-Islamic Arabia under outstanding leaders in the past. In this case, however, it was a community that was bound together by a remarkable leader and his prophethood in what was now a religious tribe. The community has, in fact, been described as a "super-tribe" (Watt, 1961, p. 95). This conception of the *umma* as a larger clan or tribe or kinship group was also easy to conceive by Arabs who saw the world in those terms.[3] The community was not made up of individuals, but of a number of individual groups. Muhammad was not the ruler of this community. He was only the chief of his clan of Emigrants and there were eight other clans with their own chiefs. Muhammad was simply Allah's intermediary in settling differences. The constitution states:

> [W]henever any incident or dispute arises among the people of this document which it may be feared will bring harm to them, they shall refer to Allah and to Muhammad, for Allah is the most strict and faithful guarantor of the contents of this document (Paragraph 42). (Rodinson, 1980, p. 154)

A verse from the Quran (10:48), in fact, describes the function of a Prophet:

---
[3] There are traditions about the life of Muhammad in which the Byzantine emperor is spoken of as if he were a nomadic sheih dealing with tribesmen. This is an example of seeing the world in projected shapes and forms, in this instance of projected familiar group forms as well as group interactions (Watt, 1961, p. 95).

> Each community has a messenger, and when their messenger comes, judgment is given between them with justice, and they are not wronged.

This was the framework of the *umma* in Medina. Muhammad offered an ideal shape of the group that now extended the religious to the secular. It was not a document that defined a state with a supreme authority, because in the Arabia of the time that was inconceivable. It was a union of nine clans that were now one in most areas. Order within was maintained by the threats of revenge that ensured that wrongdoers would pay a price and dealings with the world outside Medina were now clearly defined.

Internal peace was restored with the end of a long-standing civil war among the two leading clans of Medina and the endless chain of blood feuds or vendettas was brought to a close.

Two of the basic needs of a group—mutual trust (and justice), safety (and security)—were thus provided for by Muhammad in the Constitution of Medina. There were to be no more blood feuds; when there was conflict, they had to seek resolution through Muhammad. Justice was clear, as the Quran explicitly laid down. No one could initiate a vendetta or perpetuate a blood feud by exacting further vengeance. Conflicts with the outside world were to be fought together, with the Jewish clans, as one unit. Muhammad had quickly and successfully brought a level of peace, a measure of trust and justice to Medina, and offered safety and security from outside threats.

In order to bind the community of believers even further, Muhammad instituted a pact of brotherhood between the Helpers and the Emigrants.

> The Apostle instituted brotherhood between his fellow Emigrants and the Helpers, and he said according to what I have heard—and I appeal to God lest I should attribute to him words that he did not say—"Let each of you take a brother in God." He himself took Ali by the hand and said, "This is my brother." So God's Apostle, the Lord of the sent ones and leader of the God-fearing, Apostle of the Lord of the worlds, the peerless and unequalled, and Ali ibn Abu Talib became brothers. Hamza, the lion of God and the lion of his Apostle and his uncle, became the brother of Zayd ibn Haritha the Apostle's freedman. (Ibn Ishaq, 1955, p. 234)

Each Helper would have an Emigrant who would be closer to him than any of the Helpers. Muhammad made an exception of himself and his family and did not choose to have a Helper as his brother because this could have destructive implications of favoritism among his followers. Muhammad had thus intuitively recognized the central principles of powerful group formation that Freud was to decipher centuries later. The horizontal identifications of brotherhood would form a powerful bond when the members of the *umma* were equally loved within a vertical tie shared with one leader.

With relative peace in the oasis at Medina, most of the clans now accepted Muhammad as a Prophet even though they had nominally accepted him as such before the *Hijra*. Opposition was not too significant except for two poets whose rantings, while they were initially considered harmless, were later considered dangerous because of their gifts.

Relationship with Jews and Judaism

Muhammad's relationship with the Jews of Medina had been positive initially. He was after all a Prophet in the Judaic tradition of Moses and had offered himself as a prophetic reformer to the Jews in Medina. Muhammad may have expected the Jews to recognize his prophetic and religious mission because of the biblical and Abrahamic aspects of his Meccan teachings. It is clear that in the early years of his stay in Medina he was attracted to and incorporated many Jewish traditions into his religion.

The Jews used to fast on the tenth of Tishri, that is, Yom Kippur, and Muhammad also made the fast of "The Tenth" *(Ashura)* an obligatory fast for Muslims.

> Aisha, may God be pleased with her, reported that the Quraysh used to fast on the day of *Ashura* in the pre-Islamic days and the Messenger of God, may peace be upon him, also observed it. When he migrated to Medina he himself observed the fast and commanded (others) to observe it. But when fasting during the month of Ramadan was made obligatory, he said: "He who wishes to observe the fast (of *Ashura*) may do so and he who wishes to abandon it may do so." (Muslim Sahih 6.423. 2499, quoted in Peters, 1994, p. 204)

Tabari describes this tradition too.

> When the Prophet came to Medina he saw the Jews fasting on the day of *Ashura*. He questioned them, and they told him that it was the day upon which God drowned the people of Pharaoh and so saved Moses and those with him from them. He said, "We have a better right to Moses than they have," and he fasted and ordered people to fast with him. (Tabari, 1987, p. 26)

Although Tabari's version has some later anti-Jewish polemic, the first version has an overt and thus possibly authentic admission that Muhammad observed this fast even before Islam (Peters, 1994, p. 204).

Muhammad's personal observation and the mandate for all Muslims to fast on the most solemn Day of Atonement or Yom Kippur, known to Arabs as the fast of "The Tenth," is evidently linked to Muhammad's claims of ties to Moses. This identity of the mission with Moses is explicit in the Meccan *suras*.

> Why are there not come (signs) like those sent to Moses? Do they not disbelieve (also) in what was earlier sent to Moses? They say: "Two sorceries that support each other" and they say "As for us we reject all (such)" Say: "Then make come a Book from God which is a better guide than these two." (Quran 28:48–49)

and

> Before it (the Quran) there was a Book of Moses, given as a guide and an act of mercy. (Quran 11:17)

Muhammad also learned while at Medina that the Jews had one solemn occasion, "The Tenth" day, when they celebrated the "sending down" of the Torah on Sinai. Another idea now emerged in the Quran. The Quran had not been revealed piecemeal but was "sent down" on a single night, the "Night of Destiny." At this time too, Muhammad began to define the belief that the Quran was not just a "recitation" but was a Book like the Torah where all of God's decrees were written down.

Prayer had been one of the earlier demands of Muhammad at Mecca. The word for it was *salat*, derived from the Aramaic of Jewish and Christian usage. It meant liturgical prayer, audibly uttered words in public worship. In Medina the custom of prayer moved closer to the Jewish custom of morning, midday, and evening prayer. *Salat* was the recitation of God's own words that were now in a book, the Quran, a word clearly related to the Syriac *Qeryana,* used to denote the "reading" or scripture lesson. Christian religious vocabulary was thus evident in its presence in Arabia.

When the first Muslims reached Medina they received permission to make a Friday public prayer at sunset, once again in the Jewish manner.

> And Mus'ab had them recite the Quran and taught them. He then wrote to the Messenger of God asking permission to perform with them the Friday service. The Prophet gave his consent and wrote to them: "On the day when the Jews make public (preparations) for their Sabbath and when the sun is setting, draw near God with two bows and deliver a sermon." Then Mus'ab ibn Umayr held the Friday prayer with them in the abode of Sa'd ibn Khaythama.... (Ibn Sa'd, Tabaqat III/I, p. 83, quoted in Peters, 1994, p. 181)

The Jewish tribes, however, posed a dilemma. Muhammad had counted on the support of these monotheists as he felt his message was very similar to what they had received in Sinai. Undoubtedly he had hoped to have a united front with their support against the pagan Meccans and other Arabs. He had therefore even adopted many Jewish practices.

The Jewish communities in Medina, however, did not identify with Muhammad nor respond to his wish for friendship and his advances to get their support and recognition. As intermediaries, the Jewish groups had some influence among the battling clans of Arabs in Medina and now they were slowly losing their influence to Muhammad. Muhammad had linked his revelations and prophecy to a long line of Jewish prophets, notably with the messages of Moses, the founder of Judaism, and Jesus, the founder of Christianity. As guardians of the ancient scriptures Medinans turned to the Jews to validate the new religion and confirm the divine inspiration. As Ibn Ishaq observed:

> About this time the Jewish rabbis showed hostility to the Apostle in envy, hatred, and malice, because God had chosen His Apostle from the Arabs. They were joined by men from al-Aus and al-Khazraj who had obstinately clung to their heathen religion. They were hypocrites, clinging to the polytheism of their fathers denying the resurrection; yet when Islam appeared and their people flocked to it they were compelled to pretend to accept it to save their lives. But in secret they were hypocrites whose

inclination was towards the Jews because they considered the Apostle a liar and strove against Islam.

It was the Jewish rabbis who used to annoy the Apostle with questions and introduce confusion, so as to confound the truth with falsity. The Quran used to come down in reference to these questions of theirs, though some of the questions about what was allowed and forbidden came from the Muslims themselves. (Ibn Ishaq, 1955, p. 239)

The Jews, however, were unwilling to validate or endorse the new religion. They declared that the Quran contradicted aspects of their ancient Old Testament scriptures, and was, therefore, false. If this was the case, their verdict was that the Quran could not be a revelation nor Muhammad a Prophet. They contemptuously rejected the claims of the gentile Prophet and opposed him precisely in the sensitive area of the veracity of his religion; the claims of Muhammad were incompatible with Judaism. This was a serious challenge to Muhammad, for if any of his followers believed the Jews, his whole *umma* could crumble. The religion of Abraham and the link to the Old Testament Prophets was already in many of the Meccan revelations and could not be excised.

The only response could be that the deviations were on the part of the Jews. It was now claimed that the Jews and Christians had "concealed" the coming of Muhammad as foretold, and had "altered" the scriptures to give false interpretations of some passages. Realizing that no support could be gained from the Jews, Muhammad dropped several Jewish practices he had adopted. The religion from then on assumed a more Arab character.

As the power and prestige of Muhammad slowly grew, there must have been some nervousness among Medinans. The repeated exhortations in the Quran to take disputes to Muhammad for settlement suggest that the practice was not always followed.

8

The Prophet at War

THE life of Prophet Muhammad, the origins of Islam in pre-Islamic Arabia, its initial beginnings in Mecca, its growth in Medina, and the ultimate empire building success of Islam—all demonstrate the formation of group identity within a representational world. Muhammad had to meet the basic needs of his group and provide the leadership necessary for it to develop into one of the most successful groups in history.

How did Muhammad meet the basic needs of this new group? We have considered economic well-being, mutual trust, and a sense of justice, as well as security to be the basic needs of the family and any group.

After the establishment of the *umma,* the next important issue was how the new Emigrants would maintain a livelihood in Medina. They could not depend on the permanent hospitality of the Medinan Muslims, nor could they farm. They must have expected to trade or prey on the trade of Mecca. Thus, the new religious Emigrants turned to arms. They developed the practice of organizing expeditions or *razzias* against Meccan caravans. The first *razzia* was a raiding party of 30 men sent by Muhammad to ambush a Meccan caravan returning from Syria along the Red Sea coast. A month later a group of 60 men tried to intercept another well-defended Meccan caravan. A Muslim, on that occasion, shot some arrows—the first warlike act of Islam. This effort and a few subsequent ones were disheartening failures. Muhammad himself led some of the later expeditions that were unsuccessful. They served, however, to increase anxiety among the

Meccans and to demonstrate to nearby nomads the strength of the new religion.

According to Lewis, European writers have expressed "much righteous indignation . . . at the spectacle of an Apostle of God leading the faithful in predatory raids on merchant caravans" (Lewis, 1958, p.44). *Razzias*, however, were a normal feature of Arab life in the desert. The usual *razzia* was directed at the animals and camels of unfriendly tribes and sometimes against their women. Well-planned surprise or overwhelming superiority were the keys to the success of these quick raids on relatively isolated segments of other tribes. Loss of life was small; however, in the rare instance when someone was killed, it was customary to appease the injured tribe with a blood gift of camels. This was sometimes disdainfully referred to as "accepting milk instead of blood."

The Emigrants went on these raids also because they considered they had been ill-treated by their fellow Meccans.[1] A revelation in the Quran (22:39–40) states "Permission is given (by God) to those who are fighting because they have been wronged . . . those who were driven from their homes for no reason but that they say 'God is our Lord.' " Another verse (16:110) describes the Emigrants as "those who after persecution emigrated, then strove and patiently endured." "Strove" in this context implied "went on *razzias*."

Another verse added somewhat later "Fight in the cause of God, and know that God hears and knows all things" (Quran 2:244).

The raids would directly bring considerable booty and provide for the economic needs and well-being of the *umma*. Indirectly the raids would allow Muslims to assess the strengths and weaknesses of the Meccans, weaken and disrupt Meccan trade, and Mecca in the process.

When the Arab practice of *razzia* was taken over by the *umma* or Islamic community, it was transformed. There were deeper

---

[1] We should consider this justification a form of rationalization for group action. Rationalization is an attempt to present an explanation that is either logically consistent or ethically acceptable for ideas, feelings, or actions whose true motives are not perceived. Rationalization, though a patent defensive function, is not usually considered a defense mechanism (Laplanche & Pontalis, 1973, pp. 375–376).

implications to aligning oneself with one side or the other. Believers were united against unbelievers and their activity was now on behalf of a religious mission. If members of a raided pagan tribe accepted Islam, they were exempted from further raiding. The Emigrants were described in another Quranic verse (8:72-75) as "those who believed and emigrated and strove with goods and persons in the way of God."

The transformation is further reflected in the use of the word *strive*. This word is translated as *jahada* and the noun *striving* is *jihad*. *Jihad*, in the course of time, technically came to mean Holy War. Thus, the mere change of name from *razzia* to *jihad* reflected and lent a compelling significance to what had become a religious activity. *Jihad* was a religious action of the expanding *umma*, against the unbelievers.

Expedition to Nakhlah—The First Bloodshed

The first Meccan blood was shed in a *razzia* in December 623 c.e. Muhammad sent out eight Emigrants carrying a sealed letter. Furthermore, instructions gave permission to those who did not want to proceed with the ambush to withdraw. This was an indicator of Muhammad's fairness. Their agreements with him did not necessitate their going to war for him.

> According to Ibn Ishaq: The Messenger of God wrote him [i.e., the leader of the group] a letter, but ordered him not to look at it until he had traveled for two days. Then he was to look at it and to carry out what he was commanded in it but not to compel any of his companions to do anything against their will. When ... [he] ... had traveled two days, he opened the letter and looked at it, and it said, "When you look at my letter, march until you halt at Nakhlah, between Mecca and al-Ta'if. Observe Quraysh there, and find out for us what they are doing." ... A caravan of Quraysh went past him carrying raisins, leather, and other goods in which Quraysh traded.... When they saw (the Muslims) they were afraid of them, since they had halted very close to them. Then Ukkashah [one of the Emigrants] came into view and he had shaved his head, and when they saw him they felt safe and said, "They are on their way to the 'umrah' (or lesser pilgrimage); there is nothing to fear from them." The (Muslims) consulted one another concerning them, this being the last day of Rajab, and said, "By God, if you leave these people alone today, they will get into the Haram (the sacred territory of Mecca)

and be out of your reach there; and if you kill them (today) you will have killed them in the sacred month." They hesitated and were afraid to advance upon them, but then they plucked up courage and agreed to kill as many of them as they could and to seize what they had with them. (Tabari, 1987, pp. 18–19)

Despite the fear that this was the sacred month of Rajab when bloodshed was forbidden, the caravan was attacked and the unsuspecting guards taken by surprise. Some Quraysh were killed, and the caravan taken to Medina with two captives. It was customary for a tribal chief to receive a fourth of the booty. The Muslims set aside a fifth for the Prophet and divided the rest among themselves before they reached Medina. They received a shocking welcome:

When they reached the Messenger of God he said, "I did not order you to fight in the sacred month," and he impounded the caravan and the two captives and refused to take anything of it. When the Messenger of God said this they were aghast and thought that they were ruined, and the Muslims rebuked them severely for what they had done, saying to them, "You have done what you were not commanded to do, and have fought in the sacred month when you were not commanded to fight." Quraysh said, "Muhammad and his companions have violated the sacred month and shed blood in it, have seized property in it and taken men captive in it. . . . However God turned this to their disadvantage, not their advantage, and when people began to say this frequently God revealed to His Messenger: "They question thee with regard to warfare in the sacred month . . . Say: 'Fighting therein is a grave offense; but graver it is in the sight of God to prevent access to the path of God, to deny Him, to prevent access to the sacred shrine and drive out its members. Tumult and oppression are worse than slaughter. . . . ' " (Quran 2:217)
When the Qur'anic passage concerning this matter was revealed, and God relieved the Muslims from the fear in which they found themselves, the Messenger of God took possession of the caravan and the two prisoners. (Tabari, 1987, p. 20)

Medinans had been concerned that the first killing of a Meccan was a serious provocation and would invite retaliation. The violation of the sacred month created further and serious misgivings. Muhammad, however, had to denounce a tie of sacredness to the month of Rajab and a pagan religion. Muhammad, moreover, had taken extreme precautions to ensure secrecy. He had given sealed instructions to the leader of the expedition: its contents were known only to him and his trusted advisors. To prevent

Meccan espionage from discovering his plans, he had even sent the party on the easterly Najd road when the goal was almost due south (Watt, 1956, p. 6). It was these elements of secret plans and surprise that led to the success at Naklah. The gauntlet was laid down. Mecca's prestige as perhaps the strongest and wealthiest people in Arabia was now dealt a bitter blow.

The Battle of Badr

Two months later, in March 624 c.e., Muhammad received word that another far larger caravan with 1,000 camels was setting out from the north down to Mecca. It was well worth plundering as only 70 men accompanied it. Muhammad raised a force of about 300 men—according to one list, 238 Helpers and 86 Emigrants. A hundred more men joined this raid than any previous expedition. When word reached Mecca about this, they sent a force of about 950 to 1,000 men led by Abu Jahl to protect their caravan at the point of greatest danger.

The caravan managed to elude the Muslims, and they instead suddenly faced an overwhelming Meccan force. The Muslims had not expected a major conflict when they had set out. Muhammad gave the Helpers a choice to return if they wished, since their oath of allegiance had not included fighting outside of Medina. They were hurt, however, by the suggestion that they could forsake him and chose to stay. To the Muslims, retreat from the superior force would have seemed an act of cowardice and involved a loss of face, so they stayed and camped out at the wells near Badr. Muhammad then gave orders to block up all the wells except the largest one nearest Mecca and the enemy, and stationed his men there. The enemy now had to fight with their water supplies blocked and on ground of Muhammad's choosing.

Ibn Ishaq describes this strategy in detail.

> I was told that men of Bana Salama said that al-Hubab ibn al-Mundhir . . . said to the Apostle: "Is this a place which God has ordered you to occupy, so that we can neither advance nor withdraw from it, or is it a matter of opinion and military tactics?" When he replied that it was the latter he pointed out that it was not the place to stop but that they should go on

to the water nearest to the enemy and halt there, stop up the wells beyond it, and construct a cistern so that they would have plenty of water; then they could fight their enemy who would have nothing to drink. The Apostle agreed that this was an excellent plan and it was immediately carried out; the wells were stopped; a cistern was built and filled with water from which his men replenished their drinking-vessels. (pp. 296–297)

The Battle of Badr began on March 15, 624 c.e. As was the custom among the Arabs, it began with individual combat among the bravest warriors. In this first exchange the Muslims won. Then arrows were fired by both sides, and Muhammad exhorted his men by offering heavenly paradise to those who were slain. In the final stages of the battle, the heavily armed and better equipped Meccans were surprisingly routed and many of their leaders, including Abu Jahl, killed.

Tabari recounts the final event when the tide of the battle turned in favor of the Muslims.

> Then the Messenger of God picked up a handful of gravel and faced the Quraysh with the words, "May their faces be deformed!" Then he threw it at them, and ordered his companions to attack. A rout followed, in which God killed many chiefs of the Quraysh and caused many of their nobles to be taken captive. While the Muslims were taking captives, the Messenger of God was in his shelter. (1987, p. 56)

Whereas the number of Meccans who died ranged from 45 to 70, and about 70 were taken prisoner, the Muslims lost only 14 in the battle. Vindication of the killings in the battle came in a Quran passage:

> You did not kill them, but God killed them; you did not shoot when you shot, but God shot, to let the believer experience good for himself. (Quran 8:17)

There was immediate conflict among those who had stayed to guard the Prophet and those who had captured men and armor and were unwilling to give them up. Ibn Ishaq describes how Muhammad faced a potential rebellion among his men.

> Then the Apostle ordered that everything that had been collected in the camp should be brought together, and the Muslims quarreled about it. Those who had collected it claimed it, and those who had fought and pursued the enemy claimed that had it not been for them there would

have been no booty and that had they not engaged the enemy they would not have been able to get anything; while those who were guarding the Apostle lest the enemy should attack him claimed that they had an equal right, for they had wanted to fight the enemy, and they had wanted to seize the booty when there were none to defend it, but they were afraid that the enemy might return to the charge and so they kept their position round the Apostle. (1955, p. 307)

Before the Prophet could order a fair and equitable distribution, a revelation resolved this conflict:

They will question thee concerning the spoils of war. Say: The spoils of war are for God and the Messenger. (Quran 8:1)

The Prophet then ordered that the booty and the captives should be brought together and no longer considered the private property of any individual. The spoils of war were later equally divided among all those who had taken part in the expedition. Property in war belonged to the new theocratic "state" and was to be used for the common weal.

This action was justified by a divine revelation in the opening of the celebrated *sura* Al-Anfal ("The Spoils" which takes its name from the above first verse of *sura* 8) which had important meaning. It brought the disunited factions and Arab tribes together under a determined leader. Instead of the squabbles between individuals fighting over the spoils of war, the *sura* allowed Muhammad to define equality in a common religious unity that could only further strengthen a sense of fairness and justice in a new and powerful group. There was "the fear of God, and obedience to Him and to His Apostle, and peace among us" (Ibn Ishaq, 1955, p. 321).

Muhammad's army had used superior tactics. They were drawn up into neat ranks and had a unified command. The Meccans, however, fought as individual clans, and disputes that had occurred before the battle suggested that there was little agreement among them. Muhammad, who had been praying, offered religious exhortation.

Then the Apostle went forth to the people and incited them saying, "By God in whose hand is the soul of Muhammad, no man will be slain this day fighting against them with steadfast courage advancing not retreating but God will cause him to enter Paradise." (Ibn Ishaq, 1955, p. 300)

Several factors thus contributed to the Meccan defeat. Besides their disunity, they had defections that reduced their numbers by a third to 600 or 700. Many Meccans did not support their leader Abu Jahl's policies. The spirit of the Muslims and their superior leadership ultimately gave them the decisive advantage in a battle they won.

The Quran, in a rare historical attestation, celebrates the victory at Badr twice.

> There has already been a sign for you in the clash of the two forces, one fighting in the way of God and the other disbelieving. And they [that is, the latter] saw twice the force before their eyes. . . . (Quran 3:13)

and in the same *sura*, some verses later.

> God had helped you at Badr, when you were a contemptible little band. So fear God and thus show your gratitude. (Quran 3:123)

The Muslims returned to Medina with a huge booty and prisoners to ransom. There were strong opinions with regard to putting all the captives to the sword. On the advice of Abu Bakr, Muhammad spared the captives until a revelation brought both of them to tears. The revelation stated:

> It is not for a prophet to hold captives until he hath made great slaughter in the land. (Quran 8:67)

However, a revelation soon after made it clear that their decision to spare the captives did not have to be revoked, as it had been accepted by God:

> O Prophet, say unto those captives who are in your hands: If God knoweth any good is in your hearts, He will give you better than that which hath been taken from you, and he will forgive you. Verily God is forgiving, merciful. (Quran 8:70)

Two prisoners were given particularly harsh treatment. They were executed at the orders of Muhammad. One of them had been hostile in Mecca towards Muhammad. Uqba of Abd Shams had thrown a sheep's uterus, filthy with blood and excrement, into the courtyard while the Prophet was praying. The other,

Nadr of Abd al-Dar, had claimed that he was as good a speaker as Muhammad and his own tales of Persia were as good as the tales of the Quran. These offenses were considered unforgivable, and both had shown no change of heart, even while captive.

The Battle of Badr was a stunning success for the Muslims after years of hardship and conflict in Mecca and Medina. Moreover, the achievement was seen as an expression of Divine goodwill. It led to a deeper faith for Muhammad and his close Companions in his prophetic mission. It vindicated his faith, after years of persecution, and convincingly demonstrated the truth of his prophecy about the punishment that the Meccan pagans would face. The victory considerably strengthened Muhammad's position in Medina. After the return to Medina, there was a period of a further consolidation of Muhammad's position. A larger number of Medinans were ready to help Muslims, and the prospect of booty attracted neighboring tribes. Muhammad was magnanimous with those who had helped him at Badr, but harsh towards the others. Two Medinans, a man and a woman who had written poems against Muhammad, were killed by some of their relations. Their verses had been critical of Medinans for allowing an outsider (Muhammad) to control their affairs and helping one who aimed to be their king. Muhammed may not have known about these poems but he did not express disapproval over the killings; nor did blood feuds follow.

Another poet met a similar fate and more details are known about his death. Ka'b ibn al Ashraf, who had an Arab father and a Jewish mother, had written a number of poems satirizing Muhammad and his Companions. Among Arabs a good poet's verses could receive wide circulation. Muhammad let it be known that he would be glad to be rid of Ka'b. Five Muslims, one of whom was a foster brother of Ka'b, volunteered to hatch a plot. They realized they could not attain their ends without deception, so they went to the Prophet to get his permission. According to Lings, they were told "they were free to say whatever would serve their purpose, for deception was legitimate in warfare, being a part of its strategy, and Ka'b had declared war on them" (Lings, 1983, p. 171). Ka'b was then lured under false pretense out of the Jewish fortress where he had sought refuge and was killed. The five Muslims then described themselves as "five honorable men, steady and true, and God was the sixth with us" (Watt, 1961, p. 129).

The Jews of Banu Nadir went to the Prophet in a panic and complained to him that one of their leading men had been treacherously killed for no apparent reason. According to Lings "it was vital to show them that if hostile thoughts were tolerable, hostile action was not" (Lings, 1983, p. 171). The Prophet according to a tradition from Waqidi said, "If he had remained as others of like opinion remain . . . he would not have been killed by guile. But he did us injury and wrote poetry against us; and none of you shall do this but he shall be put to the sword" (quoted by Lings, 1983, p. 171).

As Watt noted "such measures made it clear that Muhammad was not a man to be trifled with. For those who accepted him as a leader there were material advantages; for those who apposed him there were serious disadvantages" (Watt, 1956, p. 19).

It would seem that Muhammad was too sensitive, but there was more to it. Poetry as the only other medium of mass communication, besides religion, could pose a serious challenge. Communication media not only play a significant role, they can bind or disrupt a group. Muhammad, by taking measures against poets, managed to stifle them. At the same time he sent a clear message to others that would ultimately silence any threat from this direction.

The Jews posed the next and even greater challenge. They continued to be vocal in their criticism of Muhammad's ideas and the Quran. This undermined the very basis of his religion and the *umma*. Within a few weeks of the Battle of Badr, Muhammad moved to further consolidate his power in Medina by expelling the Qaynuqa clan of Jews.

Ibn Ishaq describes in detail the growing distance between the Jews and Muslims and the sentiment that the Jews could not be trusted.

> Some Muslims remained friends with the Jews because of the tie of mutual protection and alliance which had subsisted between them, so God sent down concerning them and forbidding them to take them as intimate friends: "O you who believe, do not chose those outside your community as intimate friends. They will spare no pains to corrupt you longing for your ruin. From their mouths hatred has already shown itself and what

their breasts conceal is greater. We have made the signs plain to you if you will understand. Behold you love them but they love not you and you believe in the book—all of it," i.e. you believe in their book and in the books that were before that while they deny your book, so that you have more right to hate them than they to hate you. "And when they meet you they say, We believe and when they go apart they bite their fingers against you in rage. Say, Die in your rage," ... (Ibn Ishaq, 1955, pp. 262–263; Quran 3:118–119)

As the anger towards the Jews in Medina intensified, Ibn Ishaq recounts several further instances and links them to revelations in the Quran that give more warning. Two examples describe the growing bitterness.

Rifa'a was a notable Jew. When he spoke to the Apostle he twisted his tongue and said: "Give us your attention, Muhammad, so that we can make you understand." Then he attacked Islam and reviled it. So God sent down concerning him: "Hast thou considered those to whom a part of the book has been given how they buy error and wish that you should err as to the way. But God knows best about your enemies. God is sufficient as a friend and helper. Some of the Jews change words from their contexts and say: We hear and disobey; hear thou as one that heareth not and listen to us, twisting their tongues and attacking religion. . . . "

The Apostle spoke to two of the chiefs of the Jewish rabbis . . . calling on them to accept Islam, for they knew that he had brought them the truth; but they denied that they knew it and were obstinate in their unbelief. So God sent down concerning them: "O you to whom the book was sent, Believe in what We have sent down in confirmation of what you have before We efface (your) features and turn them back to front or curse you as We cursed the sabbath-breakers when God's command was carried out." (Ibn Ishaq, 1955, pp. 264–265; Quran 4:44–46, 4:47)

Another revelation said,

If good befall you it is evil in their eyes, and if evil befall you they rejoice thereof. (Quran 3:120)

The reason for the expulsion of the Qaynuqa clan is not fully clarified in the sources. The Qaynuqa's connection with artisanry and trade may have linked them to Meccans, whose trade Muhammad was aggressively challenging (Donner, 1979). The ostensible basis for this expulsion of the Qaynuqa clan was a minor incident between some Jews and Muslims. It began with a trick played on an Arab woman who was sitting at a goldsmith.[1] A Jew had fastened the woman's skirt with a thorn so that when she stood up a large part of her body was exposed. A Muslim who thought this was an insulting act killed the Jew and in turn was also killed. Muhammad and a party of Muslims besieged the stronghold of the Qaynuqa Jews for a period of 15 days.

When the Jews did not get any help from their Arab allies, the Khazraj, they surrendered, agreeing to depart Medina with their families and to relinquish all their weapons. After their departure, most of their property and the internal trade of Medina moved into the hands of the Emigrants. Abdullah ibn Ubayy, of the Khazraj and the chief rival of Muhammad, lost as many as 700 of his confederates, weakening him considerably.

Two verses in a revelation justified the entire action. One stated, "If thou overcometh them in war, then make of them an example, to strike fear into those that are behind them, that they may take heed" (Quran 8:57). The other said, "If thou fearest treachery from any folk, then throw back unto them their covenant. Verily God loveth not the treacherous" (Quran 8:58). Muhammad had by this action successfully carried the momentum of his victory at Badr, to expel a threat from Medina, weaken a rival, send a clear warning to others and in the process further provide for the economic well-being of his *umma*.

This major consolidation of power in Medina resulted in some poorer tribes around Medina offering support to Muhammad. Muhammad then led at least three expeditions with about 200 to 450 men to neighboring territories to warn and to deter tribes in those areas from supporting Mecca. Mecca meanwhile was preparing a riposte. It had lost considerable prestige after the Battle of Badr, and its caravan trade was in jeopardy.

The Battle of Uhud

Almost exactly a year after Badr, 3,000 well-armed men set out from Mecca. They had 200 cavalry and 700 men with coats of

---

[1] The story of the trick also appears in legends of pre-Islamic Arabia so little credence can be given to it (Watt, 1961, p. 130).

mail. When they reached Medina, they faced a small army of 700 Medinans led by Muhammad. He chose his ground, with skill, on the hill of Uhud. The slope gave him a defensive advantage against vastly superior numbers and particularly against the cavalry.

Tabari's lengthy account of the battle of Uhud details the course of events.

> The Messenger of God had sent certain people to take up position behind his army, and said to them, "Stay here and turn back any of us who flees, and act as a guard for our rear...." However, when the archers saw the Messenger of God and his Companions in the heart of the polytheists' camp and plundering them, they hurried down to the booty. Some of them said, "Do not go against the command of the Messenger of God," but most of them went to the camp. When Khalid [a Meccan leader] saw how few archers there were left, he shouted to his cavalry, charged, and killed the archers, and then charged the Prophet's Companions. When the polytheists on foot saw that their cavalry was in action, they called to one another and renewed their attack on the Muslims, defeating them and killing some.... When the Muslims were attacked from behind and put to flight, the polytheists killed many of them. When this catastrophe befell the Muslims, they were afflicted in three ways; some killed, some wounded, and some put to flight. The latter were so exhausted by battle that they did not know what they were doing. The Messenger of God's lower lateral incisor was broken, his lip was split, and he was wounded on the cheeks and on the forehead at the roots of his hair....
>
> Hind daughter of Utbah and the women who were with her stopped to mutilate the Messenger of God's dead Companions, cutting off their ears and noses until Hind was able to make anklets and necklaces of them.... Then she ripped open Hamzah's body for his liver and chewed it, but she was not able to swallow it and spat it out. Then she climbed a high rock and screamed at the top of her voice.... (1987, pp. 114–129)

A cry arose that the Prophet was slain. Despair rapidly spread throughout the Muslim ranks until it was confirmed that he was still alive. With some degree of order, the Muslims retreated up the hill.

The battle ended, somewhat surprisingly, when the Meccans retired after inflicting even more heavy casualties. Seventy-five Muslims were killed but only 27 Meccans in this fierce engagement. The members of the Muslim infantry, however, had shown themselves to be more than a match for their opponents, and the Muslim archers had wounded most of the Meccan horses. It was at this time that the Meccans decided to withdraw rather than risk further losses in an uphill battle and the possibility of reinforcements arriving from Medina.

This battle was considered by early writers to have been a serious defeat for the Muslims. However, the main goal of the Meccans to destroy Muhammad and the Muslim community had failed. Muhammad had not only held his own against overwhelming odds, but his position in Medina, though weakened, was intact. A previous verse in the Quran (8:65) had promised an invincible military superiority:

> O Prophet, urge the believers to fight; if among you are twenty steadfast men, they will vanquish two hundred; if among you a hundred, they will vanquish a thousand....

The following verse, however, stated that God, knowing their weakness, had reduced His demands and expected one steadfast Muslim to overcome only two unbelievers! How could God have allowed this near defeat to happen to the Muslims? This question was addressed by verses in the Quran that blamed the Muslims for their disobedience at the battle of Uhud, which was also a test of their steadfastness:

> God was indeed faithful in his promise to you letting you kill them; but you slacked off, and were at variance, and disobeyed after He showed you your desire; some of you wanted this world, some the next; then He distracted you from them (and let you fare badly) to test you; but He had pardoned you, for He is gracious to the believers; you were making for the hill, turning aside for none, while the Messenger was calling you from behind; so He recompensed you sorrow upon sorrow, that you might regret neither what missed you nor what befell you. (Quran 3:152–153)

In the next few months two small parties of Muslims, sent to convert neighboring tribes, were set upon and their men killed or captured. The loss of these two parties after the losses at Uhud must have cast a pall of gloom over Muslims. After the battle of Badr, Muhammad had turned on the Jewish tribe of Qaynuqa: now after Uhud he expelled the second Jewish tribe from Medina, the Banu al-Nadir.

Muhammad had gone to collect blood money from the Jewish clan of al-Nadir. After receiving a warning from God, through Gabriel, that the al-Nadir were planning to treacherously attack and kill him, Muhammad slipped away while they were preparing a meal for him. An ultimatum was sent to the al-Nadir that they had to leave Medina in 10 days or choose death. The Jews, hoping and receiving promises of assistance from their Arab allies, chose to resist.[2]

Tabari describes how the events unfolded.

> When his companions came to him, the Messenger of God told them the story of the treachery intended by the Jews and ordered them to get ready to fight them and march against them. He then led his men against Banu al-Nadir and halted in their quarter. They fortified themselves against him in their strongholds, but he ordered the date-palms to be cut down and set fire to. They shouted, "Muhammad, you have forbidden damage to property and have blamed those who perpetrated it: what is the idea of cutting down date-palms and setting fire to them?"
>
> A group of the (Arab tribe of) Banu 'Awf Ibn al-Khazraj, . . . had sent a message to the Banu al-Nadir saying, "Stand firm and hold out, for we will not desert you. If they fight you, we will fight along with you, and if you are driven out, we will leave with you." So they waited patiently, but the group . . . (of Banu Awf) . . . did nothing, and God cast fear into the hearts of Banu al-Nadir so that they asked the Messenger of God to spare their lives and allow them to leave Medina. (Tabari, 1987, pp. 157–160)

The siege lasted 15 days. The al-Nadir capitulated when their Arab sympathizers and allies (known also as the Hypocrites to the Muslims) did not come to their aid and some of their palm trees were cut down. They now realized that even if their stronghold survived, their livelihood would be destroyed without the palm trees. Muhammad made them leave without their land and weapons, which were distributed among the Emigrants from Mecca. The Jews are described as having proudly departed from Medina with all their remaining wealth in a magnificent train of 600 camels to the oasis of Khaybar, 70 miles to the north.

According to revelations in the Quran, the People of the Scriptures, in this case the Jews, had opposed God and his Messenger and deserved a stern reprisal.

---

[2] This action against the al-Nadir after the severe losses at Uhud and the uneasy, conflictual explanations for the action against Jews (see Peters, 1994, p. 305) suggest the defense mechanisms of displacement played a part. Displacement is a mechanism in which a person redirects, often unconsciously, an emotional conflict about an object onto another less threatening object. In this instance it can be posited the group, at the behest of its leader, displaces feelings towards Mecca onto a less threatening group, the Jews (Vaillant, 1992, pp. 237–257). A leader can also consciously plan and snatch victory in the face of an earlier defeat to maintain morale.

Ibn Ishaq adds his own gloss to a *sura* from the Quran.

> Concerning Banu al-Nadir the *sura* of Exile came down in which is recorded how God wreaked His vengeance on them and gave His Apostle power over them and how He dealt with them. God said: "He it is who turned out those who disbelieved of the scripture people[3] from their homes to the first exile. You did not think that they would go out and they thought that their forts would protect them from God. But God came upon them from a direction they had not reckoned and He cast terror into their hearts so that they destroyed their houses with their own hands and the hands of the believers." (Ibn Ishaq, 1955, p. 438; Quran 59:2)

The Quran had more to say:

> And if Allah had not decreed migration for them, He verily would have punished them in this world and theirs in the Hereafter is the punishment of the Fire. (Quran 59:3)

All that they had left behind was now in the possession of the Prophet to be given to the poor and needy and particularly "the poor fugitives who had been driven out from their homes and their belongings" (Quran 59:8). The helmets, cuirasses, and swords all went to Muhammad to prepare for his next encounter with the Meccans.

After the battle of Badr the Emigrants who had come with the Prophet had secured most of the internal trade of Medina from the Jewish clan of Qaynuqa. Furthermore, with the ouster of the al-Nadir, they had the richest land in the oasis of Medina. They were no longer dependent on the hospitality of the Helpers, and their position in Medina was much stronger as their economic resources multiplied.

The years of civil discord among all the clans at Medina were almost over. Instead of strife in Medina, the *umma* could now strike far and wide with amazing strength. Unified, the *umma* was even more feared because it was known that attack was its surest means of defense. In the next few months, Muhammad led several small expeditions to thwart any attempt by Mecca to enlist the help of neighboring tribes. One notable expedition was to Dumat al-Jandal, an oasis 500 miles to the north. He took 1,000 men

---

[3] Scripture people meant "people of the scriptures," the terms for both Jews and Christians. In this instance it refers to Jews.

with him on a rapid march of almost 25 days and returned with considerable booty. Supplies to Mecca were blocked and communications with Syria interrupted by this expedition. Word soon spread about the size of this large force and its rapid march, which further deterred northern tribes from joining Mecca.

Mecca had meanwhile formed a grand alliance and made one last major attempt to crush Medina. This occurred in March 627 c.e., almost 2 years after the ill-fated attempt at Uhud. Muhammad's previous attempts at persuasion and prevention had succeeded, for only a small number of tribes joined the Meccan confederacy. The Meccans were supported by the al-Nadir, who hoped to recover the lands they had lost.

> A number of Jews who had formed a party against the Apostle . . . went to the Quraysh at Mecca and invited them to join them in an attack on the Apostle so that they might get rid of him altogether. . . . These words [of the Jews] rejoiced the Quraysh and they responded gladly to their invitation to fight the Apostle, and they assembled and made their preparations. Then that company of Jews went off to Ghatafan of Qays Aylan and invited them to fight the Apostle and told them that they would act with them and that the Quraysh had followed their lead in the matter; so they too joined in with them. . . . (Ibn Ishaq, 1955, p. 450)

The desire for revenge among the leading tribe, the Ghatafan, was also whetted by the offer of a bribe of half the crop of dates in the oasis of Khaybar.

Muhammad, however, had already received word of the impending attack and thus had a week to prepare. Most of Medina was on Muhammad's side, except the Hypocrites who were skeptical of his success. The only surviving Jewish clan, the Qurayza, tried to remain neutral. In all, Muhammad could rely on 3,000 men whom he summoned to a consultation. Salman, a Persian follower, offered a notable suggestion to deal with Meccan cavalry—a trench, or *khandaq*, a novel approach to warfare in Arabia at that time. Medina was surrounded by lava flows in all directions except the north. With the enemy almost three times the size of his own army, Muhammad could not risk meeting them in the open. Work began immediately on the northern exposed side and the trench was completed in 6 days. Muhammad then awaited the arrival of the Meccans.

The Meccan army was a huge confederation said to be 10,000 men strong, including some dependent nomadic tribes, with a 600-horse cavalry—a formidable array against the Muslims, who had few cavalry. When the Meccans reached Medina, however, they were surprised by the archers lined along the broad trench. The horsemen repeatedly attempted to force a passage across the trench but were repulsed by showers of arrows. A few Meccan soldiers did cross the trench but accomplished little, and after the loss of two men they hastily retreated.

Ibn Ishaq describes the conflict as it intensified.

> The situation became serious and fear was everywhere. The enemy came at them from above and below until the believers imagined vain things, and disaffection was rife among the disaffected to the point that Mu'attib Ibn Qushayr . . . said, "Muhammad used to promise us that we should eat the treasures of Chosroes (Emperor of Persia) and Caesar (Emperor of Byzantium) and today not one of us can feel safe going to the privy!" (1955, pp. 453–454)

The Meccan's other hope was that the Jewish clan of Qurayza would attack the Muslims from within Medina from the south. Although the Qurayza had made a treaty with Muhammad, their eventual role in an attack on Medina was unclear. The Qurayza were fearful that if Medina lost against the overwhelming odds, they would suffer at the hands of the Meccans. A Jew from Khaybar, however, persuaded the Qurayza to assist Mecca by convincing them that the Muslims would certainly lose.

This alliance was brief. A secret agent was sent by Muhammad to set the Qurayza and the Meccans into conflict. Before the agent left on his mission, he asked the Prophet for permission to tell a lie. So, playing on the fears of the Jewish clan, the agent advised them to demand hostages from the Meccans in case the Meccans abandoned their efforts too early. Then he went to the Meccans and told them these hostages would be surrendered to the Muslims and killed. This strategy succeeded in aborting any potential collaboration.

Muhammad also undermined the cooperation between the main groups of nomads in the confederacy, the Ghatafan and the Meccans, by offering them a larger bribe, a third of Medina's date harvest. Some Medinans protested that as Muslims they should not resort to such ignominy and insisted that the negotiations be terminated. Since these negotiations were not supported by any revelations, Muhammad did stop the discussions. In this battle of wits, however, the Muslims had already won, because the nomads had compromised themselves without any gain, while weakening the Meccan confederation.

The siege continued for almost a month. Provisions began to run out; the fields outside Medina had already been harvested, possibly due to Muhammad's foresight, and fodder for the Meccan horses was low. The morale of the Meccans sank and the confederacy splintered into separate ranks, with some ranks retreating. Severe cold, wind, and rain further pressured the Meccans, who had not advanced their assault against the Muslims; and thus, the last serious Meccan attempt to destroy Muhammad ended. Superior military strategy, better information, skillful use of secret agents, and the trench: all helped Muhammad avert disaster.

Meccan hopes for victory rested on their cavalry, but the trench foiled their 600-horse advantage. The greater Muslim discipline contrasted with the absence of trust or cohesion among the groups in the Meccan confederacy. Muhammad fully exploited this disunity in his diplomatic use of secret agents, and the breakup of the confederacy marked the utter Meccan failure. Mecca had tried to annihilate Islam, but now Muhammad and the Muslims were even more influential and powerful. It was Mecca's turn to fear annihilation.

The Execution of the Jews at Qurayza

Just as the battles of Badr and Uhud had been followed by the expulsion of two Jewish clans, the Qaynuqa and the al-Nadir, the Banu Qurayza, the last Jewish tribe in Medina, faced calamity after the battle of the Trench. This clan had proclaimed neutrality to maintain their pact with Muhammad, but they were involved in intrigues with the Meccan enemy. If they had trusted the Meccan confederation they would have likely opposed the Muslims and presented a considerable threat from the rear. Muhammad considered these actions treasonable and decided to destroy the last remaining Jews in Medina. After the Meccans left, Muhammad ordered his men to surround the Qurayza strongholds.

> The Apostle besieged them for twenty-five nights until they were sore pressed and God cast terror into their hearts. . . .
> Then they [Banu Qurayza] sent to the Apostle saying, "Send us Abu Lubaba (for they were allies of al-Aws), that we may consult him." So the Apostle sent him to them, and when they saw him they got up to meet him. The women and children went up to him weeping in his face, and he felt sorry for them. They said, "Oh Abu Lubaba, do you think that we should submit to Muhammad's judgment?" He said, "Yes" and pointed with his hand to his throat, signifying slaughter. Abu Lubaba said, "My feet had not moved from the spot before I knew that I had been false to God and His Apostle." Then he left them and did not go to the Apostle but bound himself to one of the pillars in the mosque saying, "I will not leave this place until God forgives me for what I have done. (Ibn Ishaq, 1955, pp. 461–462)

The Qurayza surrendered unconditionally despite the ominous signs of their future. At this time the clan of the Aws pleaded with Muhammad to forgive them as the Qaynuqa, the allies of the Khajraj, had been forgiven by him in the past. Muhammad instead agreed to allow a leader of the Aws clan to decide the Jews' fate if the Aws swore to abide by his decision. Sa'd ibn Mu'adh was chosen to deliver the verdict.

> Sa'd asked, "Do you covenant by Allah that you accept the judgment I pronounce on them?" They said Yes . . . Sa'd said, "then I give judgment that the men should be killed, the property divided, and the women and children taken as captives. . . . " Then they surrendered, and the Apostle confined them in Medina in the quarter of Bint al-Harith, a woman of Banu al-Najjar. Then the Apostle went out to the market of Medina (which is still its market today) and dug trenches in it. Then he sent for them and struck off their heads in those trenches as they were brought out to him in batches. Among them was the enemy of Allah Huyayy ibn Akhtab and Ka'b ibn Asad their chief. There were 600 or 700 in all, though some put the figure as high as 800 or 900. As they were being taken out in batches to the Apostle they asked Ka'b what he thought would be done with them. He replied, "Will you never understand? Don't you see that the summoner never stops and those who are taken away do not return? By Allah it is death!" This went on until the Apostle made an end of them. (Ibn Ishaq, 1955, p. 464)

The sentence has been criticized by European writers for its "savage and inhuman character" (Watt, 1956, p. 215). It is puzzling that those who participated in the events and the transmitters of the tradition show little concern for the harsh nature of the sentence. Watt suggests that Sa'd must have realized that to allow tribal allegiance to the Jews (for they had been unfaithful to Muhammad and not to the Aws) would have renewed the fratricidal conflicts in Medina. Ties to the Islamic community had preceded all other ties. As Sa'd was led towards Muhammad, he is rumored to have said, "the time has come for Sa'd that no one's blame should touch him in respect of God." This presumably meant that he would do his duty and serve Islam over old confederate ties. To prove that all the Aws concurred in the decision, two of the condemned were given to each member of the clan of the Aws to execute. The participation of the Aws as a group in the execution of their former allies served a purpose. The shared action could have reduced individual guilt and conflict among the members at that time and even later. Muhammad by having Sa'd, a leader from the Aws, make the decision had already given the Aws responsibility for their former clients' execution. Muhammad had weighed group and clan affiliations in this decision too. Muhammad was careful in distancing himself from the plan. Had he ordered the shedding of blood he would have risked alienating some of the Aws, who as confederates of the Qurayza, would have felt compelled to avenge their deaths.

Muslim jurists have argued also that the Banu Qurayza had broken a treaty with the Prophet by negotiating with his enemies. Muhammad therefore had a right to break their pact and declare a state of war. *Sura* 8 of the Quran seems to refer to this incident:

> The worst of beasts in the sight of God are those who reject Him: they will not believe. They are those with whom you made a treaty, then they break their compact every time and they fear not God. So if you come up against them in war, drive off through them their followers, that they may remember. And if you fear treachery from any group, dissolve it [that is, the pact] with them equally, for God does not love the treacherous. (Quran 8:55–58)

9

The Conquest of Mecca

MUHAMMAD now turned his attention to Mecca. Instead of capturing Mecca and slaughtering his most bitter enemies, Muhammad's vision was now statesmanlike. This new vision, carried out in a deliberate manner, began with numerous expeditions to subdue the neighboring tribes that had assisted Mecca. Some tribes approached Muhammad directly and asked for peace, and he accepted them henceforth as allies or confederates. One document that has been preserved is noteworthy, because Muhammad accepts the tribe as allies without insisting they become Muslims or pay legal alms (*zakat*).

However, the old methods were resumed when a warning was sent to the al-Nadir Jews who had gone to Khaybar. Secret assassins killed two of its old leaders at Khaybar, the oasis to the north. The al-Nadir had been involved in plots with the Meccans that threatened Medina, and the al-Khazraj, who competed with the al-Aws, decided to take action.

> Thus, when the al-Aws killed Ka'b ibn al-Ashraf on account of his hostility to the Messenger of God, al-Khazraj said, "They will never take superiority from us by doing that." They conferred together to find a man comparable to Ibn al-Ashraf in hostility to the Messenger of God and called to mind Ibn Abi al-Huqayq, who was in Khaybar. They then asked the Messenger of God for permission to kill him, and this he gave. Five men of al-Khazraj, set out.... The Messenger of God put 'Abd Allah ibn 'Atik in command of them and forbade them to kill women or children. Setting out, they reached Khaybar and entered Ibn Abi al-Huqayq's house by night. As they went, they shut the door of every room.... (Tabari, 1987, pp. 101–102)

They had little difficulty in mortally wounding the old man. They escaped pursuit and reached Medina safely a few days later.

With the remaining threats to Medina removed, expeditions were sent to Dumat al-Jandal on the road to Syria, in August and September 626 C.E. The expeditions weakened trade ties with Mecca and blockaded the trade routes critical to its survival: a vulnerable Mecca was now ripe for takeover. Future Muslim strategic expansion meanwhile also lay on the road to the north. The first trading caravan was sent north at this time. These actions anticipated expanding Islam's influence in that direction as well as strengthening and increasing its prosperity.

In March 628 C.E., following the fast of *Ramadan,* Muhammad dreamed that he had entered Ka'ba in Mecca with his head shaven and its key in his hand. He told his Companions the dream and invited them to make the lesser pilgrimage or *Umra* (the *Hajj* was the greater pilgrimage). Fourteen to sixteen hundred pilgrims set out with camels to be sacrificed.

> He called together the Arabs and neighboring Bedouin to march with him, fearing that the Quraysh [in Mecca] would oppose him with arms or prevent him from visiting the temple, as they actually did. Many of the Arabs held back from him, and he went out with the Emigrants and the Helpers and such of the Arabs as stuck to him. He took the sacrificial victims with him and donned the pilgrim garb so that all would know that he did not intend war and that his purpose was to visit the temple and to venerate it. . . . (Ibn Ishaq, 1955, p. 499)

When the Meccans heard about this they sent 200 cavalry to bar the Muslims. By taking a devious and difficult route, however, the Muslims eluded them and reached Hudaybiyya at the edge of the sacred territory of Mecca, when Muhammad's camel refused to budge.

The Meccans, as guardians of the sanctuary, faced a dilemma; if they prevented their enemies, the Arab pilgrims, from entering the Holy House, they would gravely transgress their sacred trust; but if they allowed them to enter Mecca, they would present Muhammad with a tremendous moral victory. The performance of the Muslims' sacred and ancient rituals would make Islam even more attractive, and by its inclusiveness, allow it to supersede their disparate beliefs. They chose, therefore, to fight to the east.

Messengers sped in and out of Mecca, but finally a treaty was signed between Mecca and Muhammad.

> Then they [the Quraysh of Mecca] sent Urwa ibn Mas'ud to the Apostle. . . . He came to the Messenger and sat before him and said: "By God, I think I see you deserted by these people (here) tomorrow." Now Abu Bakr was sitting behind the Messenger and he said, "suck al-Lat's nipples. Should we desert him?" . . . Then he [Urwa] began to take hold of the Apostle's beard as he talked to him. Al-Mughira ibn Shu'ba was standing by the Apostle's head clad in mail and he began to hit his [Urwa's] hand as he held the Apostle's beard saying, "Take your hand away from the Apostle's face before you lose it!" Urwa said, "Confound you, how rough and rude you are!" The Messenger smiled and when Urwa asked who the man was he told him that it was his brother's son, al-Mughira ibn Shu'ba, and he [Urwa] said, "O wretch, it was only yesterday that I was wiping your behind!" (Ibn Ishaq, 1955, p. 502)
>
> Then Quraysh sent Suhayl ibn Amr to the Messenger with instructions to make peace with him on condition that he went back [to Medina] this year, so that none of the Arabs could say that he made a forcible entry. . . . After a long discussion peace was made and nothing remained but to write an agreement.
> Then the Messenger summoned Ali and told him to write "In the name of God, the Compassionate, the Merciful." Suhayl said, "I do not recognize this; but write, 'In thy name, O God.'" The Messenger told him [Ali] to write the latter and he did so. Then he said, "Write, This is what Muhammad, Messenger of God, has agreed with Suhayl ibn Amr." Suhayl said, "If I witnessed that you were God's Messenger I would not have fought you. Write your own name and the name of your father." The Messenger said, "Write, This is what Muhammad ibn Abdullah has agreed with Suhayl ibn Amr: they have agreed to lay aside war for ten years during which men can be safe and refrain from hostilities on condition that if anyone comes to Muhammad without the permission of his guardian he will return him to them; and if anyone of those with Muhammad comes to the Quraysh they will not return to him. We will not show enmity one to another and there shall be no secret reservation or bad faith. He who wishes to enter into a bond and agreement with Muhammad may do so and he who wishes to enter into a bond and agreement with Quraysh may do so". . . . (p. 504)

This agreement further stated that Muslims would not reenter Mecca until the next year. The Meccans would at this time vacate their city for 3 days to enable the lesser pilgrimage to be carried out. Initially, this treaty would seem to signify a loss for Muhammad. The Muslims, however, could not have conquered Mecca with their small force, so the treaty was a compromise that preserved the prestige of Mecca and indirectly turned more power over to Muhammad.

There was a great deal of dissatisfaction among Muhammad's men during the treaty negotiations.

> The Apostle's Companions had gone out without any doubt of occupying Mecca because of the vision which the Apostle had seen, and when they saw the negotiations for peace and a withdrawal going on and what the Apostle had taken on himself they felt depressed almost to the point of death. (Ibn Ishaq, 1955, p. 505)

Some nomadic tribes had not joined the pilgrimage because they sensed there would be no booty. Muhammad, in the middle of a crisis, had chosen to consolidate and make more absolute his hold over his followers. At a critical stage in the negotiations, Muhammad called on all the Muslims to pledge acceptance of all his decisions and to hold together and fight to death. This pledge is called the Pledge of Good Pleasure (*Ridwan*). A revelation (Quran 48:18) notes that, "God was well pleased with the believers when they pledged allegiance unto thee beneath the tree."

The terms of the treaty with Mecca produced resentment, however; protests mounted and became intense. For a time the Muslims would not sacrifice their animals or shave off their hair to complete their pilgrimage. When Muhammad set off on the return journey, he led a sullen group disturbed by the apparent failure of the expedition. A revelation (Quran 48:1) left no doubt, however, that the expedition was to be considered a victorious one, for it opened "Verily we have given thee a clear victory." Referring to the dream that had prompted the pilgrimage, the revelation (48:27) reassuringly proclaimed:

> God hath truly fulfilled for His Messenger the vision: God willing, ye shall enter the inviolable mosque in safety, not fearing, with the hair of your heads shaven and cut. But He knoweth what ye know not and before that hath He given you a near victory.

From a long-term perspective, the expedition was clearly favorable to Muhammad. He negotiated a treaty with the Meccans as their equal and the cessation of war would allow Muhammad time to further expand Islamic influence.

Ibn Ishaq declared this event a victory.

No previous victory in Islam was greater than this. There was nothing but battle when men met; but when there was an armistice and war was abolished and men met in safety and consulted together, none talked about Islam intelligently without entering it. In those two years double as many or more than double as many entered Islam as ever before. (Ibn Ishaq, 1955, p. 507)

The Pledge of Good Pleasure had brought the Muslims closer to their leader, who could now lay claim to their allegiance in whatever manner he chose, including dying, if he so demanded. It was no longer necessary to defeat Mecca. On the return from the expedition, a verse (Quran 60:7) was revealed that caused rejoicing: "It may be that God will establish love between you and those with whom you are at enmity."

The Conquest at Khaybar

The Muslim enmity for the Jews was far from over. The "near victory" promised in the recent revelation—a victory which would also be rich in spoils (Quran 48:19)—could be none other than the conquest of Khaybar, one of the richest communities of Arabia. The exiled al-Nadir and the Khaybarite kinsmen continued to be hostile to Medina. Neither group had participated directly in the Trench campaign, but their allies, the Ghatafan, had sided with the Quraysh.

Muhammad knew that the Muslims' disappointment continued to simmer because of the fruitless Meccan expedition and that he could not let their virtue and sacrifice go unrewarded. Six weeks after his return from Mecca, Muhammad set out to capture one of the richest communities in Arabia, the prize oasis of Khaybar. Another revelation clearly stated that only those who had gone on the pilgrimage were to be rewarded by joining this expedition.

The march to Khaybar was secret and swift, although Khaybar did receive word of the plans. People refused to believe the rumors because Khaybar's many fortresses were considered impregnable. Moreover, Khaybar had 10,000 armed men and expected 4,000 more men from their allies, the Ghatafan, to join them, while the invading forces numbered 1,600. Understanding that lack of unity was their great weakness, the Jews fought in separate groups from their mountain citadels. A revelation about the Medinan Jews applied to the Khaybarites too.

> They will not fight against you in a body save in fortified villages or from behind walls. Ill feeling is rife amongst them. Thou countest them as one whole, but their hearts are divided. That is because they are a folk who have no sense. (Quran 59:14).

The Muslims attacked each fortress in turn, a tactical response that made the disparity in numbers meaningless. Although the Khaybarites were expert marksmen and periodically advanced beyond their fortresses, they were repulsed. One by one the fortresses fell, secretly aided in part by some Jews who wanted to save their own families. After the first two strongholds fell, the others quickly agreed to similar terms of surrender.

Ibn Ishaq discusses the capture of Khaybar in quick brief strokes as follows:

> The Apostle besieged the people of Khaybar in their two forts al-Watih and al-Sulalim until when they could hold out no longer they asked him to let them go, and spare their lives, and he did so. Now the Apostle had taken possession of all their property—al-Shaqq, Nata, and al-Katiba and all their forts—except what appertained to these two. When the people of Khaybar surrendered on these conditions they asked the Apostle to employ them on the property with half share in the produce, saying, "We know more about it than you and we are better farmers." The Apostle agreed to this arrangement on the condition that "if we wish to expel you we will expel you." (p. 515)

The division of Khaybar by Muhammad among his followers clearly links the rationale for this assault to the recent disappointments at al-Hudaybiyya. "Khaybar was apportioned among the men of al-Hudaybiyya without regard to whether they were present at Khaybar or not" (p. 521).

When Khaybar capitulated, the nearby oasis of Fadak avoided catastrophe by quickly seeking similar terms.

> When the Apostle had finished with Khaybar, God struck terror to the hearts of the men of Fadak when they heard what the Apostle had done to the men of Khaybar. They sent to him an offer of peace on condition that they should keep half of their produce. Their messengers came to Medina, and he accepted their terms. Thus Fadak became his private

property, because it had not been attacked by horse or camel. (Ibn Ishaq, 1955, p. 523)

A new condition was thus introduced to the terms of the truce between the Khaybar people and Muhammad. The Jews could continue to cultivate their land but owed half the produce to the new Muslim owners. There was no need to destroy them; they could labor for Islam. This new requirement would become a central feature of the later Islamic Empire in its relationships to conquered groups. The land was no longer divided among individuals but among clans, with one-fifth going to Muhammad.

The victory over Khaybar marked the end of any major Jewish influence in Arabia. Three other Jewish oases including Fadak quickly gave in to Muhammad on similar terms. Muhammad had conquered a far richer and stronger force because he built a strategy on the Jews' disunity. The Khaybarites too had been overconfident and even failed to prepare water supplies for a prolonged siege; when their weaknesses became apparent they were quickly defeated. Once again their Arab allies, fearing Muslim reprisals, did not assist them.

Between the fall of Khaybar in May 628 c.e., and the final surrender of Mecca in January 630 c.e., Muhammad sent numerous expeditions to subdue neighboring tribes including three expeditions to Syria, journeys which enormously advanced his prestige and power and allowed him to return to his ultimate goal: the conquest of Mecca. While holding to the dictates of the Meccan treaty, Muhammad nevertheless allowed new Meccan converts to harass or attack Meccan caravans from a base outside Medina. Because of the drastic deterioration of their trading, these men sought formal acceptance into Muhammad's community, while Muhammad was not technically held responsible for their actions.

In March 629 c.e., Muhammad and 2,000 men made the lesser pilgrimage to Mecca in accordance with the treaty of al-Hudabiyya. The Meccans withdrew for three days, but were impressed by the Arabian character and strength of Muhammad's religion. Meanwhile, Muhammad sought reconciliation with his own clan of Hashim and their new leader, another uncle, Abbas, who was a banker. To strengthen his matrilineal kinship ties and his ties to Abbas, Muhammad married Abbas's sister-in-law. This convinced two Meccans, Khalid and Amr, to convert to Islam, as they, like other Meccans, were now convinced the Hudabiyya treaty was a great moral victory for Muhammad, and that his entry into Mecca would eliminate further Meccan resistance.

Muhammad's truce with Mecca ended in 629 c.e. The Khuza'a, who had formed an alliance with Muhammad under the terms of the Hudabiyya treaty, killed a man from the Bakr tribe who had written verses hostile to Muhammad. The Bakr were old Meccan allies; and with Meccan-supplied weapons, surprised the Khuza'a in a night raid and inflicted some losses. This was promptly reported to Muhammad.

Ibn Ishaq outlines the beginning of the conflict:

> When the peace of Hudabiyya was concluded between the Apostle and Quraysh one of the conditions . . . was that anyone who wanted to enter into a treaty relationship with either party could do so; the Banu Bakr joined Quraysh and Khuza'a joined the Apostle. . . .
> The Banu Bakr . . . attacked Khuza'a by night while they were at al-Watir their well, killing one of their men. Both parties fell back and continued the fight. The Quraysh helped Banu Bakr with weapons and some of them fought with them secretly under cover of the night until they drove Khuza'a into the sacred area. (Ibn Ishaq, 1955, pp. 540–541)

Fearful of their role in the conflict and its impact on their trading in Medina, the Meccans sent their leader, Abu-Sufyan, to seek a compromise with Muhammad. Muhammad was adamant, however, and refused to negotiate with Abu-Sufyan, because the Meccans had broken their treaty with him.

> The Apostle ordered preparations to be made for a foray. . . . Later the Apostle informed the men that he was going to Mecca and ordered them to make careful preparations. He said, "O God, take eyes and ears from Quraysh so that we may take them by surprise in their land," and the men got themselves ready. (Ibn Ishaq, 1955, p. 544)

The war preparations were kept secret while a small party was sent north to disguise the goals of the real expedition. Ten thousand men eventually set out in January 630 c.e. Even as they approached Mecca, the Meccans were unaware of Muhammad's plans. Muhammad ordered the lighting of 10,000 fires that night as they camped outside the city to emphasize the size of the force they would soon face. Abu-Sufyan was sent out with other leading Meccans to negotiate, but Muhammad rejected their overture. Abu-Sufyan, overwhelmed by the size of the forces, agreed to formally submit to Islam with the promise that a general amnesty would be granted for himself and those who claimed his protection: those who locked their houses and stayed indoors and those who entered the great mosque.

On January 11th, 630 c.e., Muhammad's forces, divided into four columns, advanced on Mecca from four different directions. There was little resistance, and only the column under Khalid actually fought. Thirty Meccans and two Muslims were killed. Mecca, the last major prize, had now fallen to Muhammad. The general amnesty had been effective, and bloodshed was minimal.

> The Apostle has instructed his commanders when they entered Mecca only to fight those who resisted them, except a small number who were to be killed even if they were found beneath the curtains of the Ka'ba.
> Among them was 'Abdullah ibn Sa'd, ... The reason he ordered him to be killed was that he had been a Muslim and used to write down revelations; then he apostatized and returned to the Quraysh and fled to 'Uthman ibn 'Affan whose foster-brother he was. The latter hid him until he brought him to the Apostle after the situation in Mecca was tranquil, and asked that he might be granted immunity. They allege that the Apostle remained silent for a long time till finally he said yes. When 'Uthman had left he said to his Companions who were sitting around him, "I kept silent so that one of you might get up and strike off his head!" One of the Helpers said, "Then why didn't you give me a sign, O Apostle of God?" He answered that a prophet does not kill by pointing. (Ibn Ishaq, 1955, p. 550)

Of the four who were proscribed, three were killed: al-Huwayrith, who had insulted the Prophet when he was in Mecca; the apostate who had composed verses against Muhammad; and one of his two singing girls who sang satirical songs about the Messenger.

Ibn Ishaq continues his account of the most celebrated moments in Islamic history.

> [T]he Apostle after arriving in Mecca when the populace had settled down went to the temple and encompassed it seven times on his camel touching the black stone with a stick which he had in his hand. This done he summoned 'Uthman ibn Talha and took the key of the Ka'ba from him, and when the door was opened for him he went in.

> [According to another tradition] The Apostle entered Mecca on the day of the conquest and it contained 360 idols which Iblis (Satan) had strengthened with lead. The Apostle was standing by them with a stick in his hand, saying, "The truth has come and falsehood has passed away; verily falsehood is sure to pass away" (*Sura* 17:82). Then he pointed at them with his stick and they collapsed on their backs one after the other....
>
> A traditionist told me that the Apostle stood at the door of the Ka'ba and said: "There is no God but Allah alone; He has no associate. He has made good His promise and helped His servant. He has put to flight the confederates alone ... O Quraysh, God has taken from you the haughtiness of paganism and its veneration of ancestors.... Then he added, "O Quraysh, what do you think that I am about to do with you?" They replied, "Good. You are a noble brother, son of a noble brother." He said, "Go your way for you are the freed ones." (Ibn Ishaq, 1955, pp. 552–553)

Arabian paganism had been finally destroyed in the Meccan Haram. The shrines of the powerful Goddesses al-Uzza and Manat, and with some difficulty, the goddess al-Lat at Taif, were the next to fall.

Muhammad stayed for 2 to 3 weeks in Mecca. Some of the old familiar privileges were taken away from the Meccans, but the custody of the Ka'ba stayed in the same family, and the right of giving water to the pilgrims stayed with the family of al-Abbas. Most of the Meccan citizens embraced Islam, as Muhammad accepted them with forgiveness. A revelation reflected the spirit.

> This day there shall be no upbraiding of you nor reproach. God forgiveth you and He is the most Merciful of the merciful. (Quran 12:92)

The despised Meccan Prophet had returned from exile in triumph as a conqueror: he had harassed and provoked, then threatened and fought, but now, in reconciliation finally won the acceptance of Mecca.

Barely 3 weeks after the fall of Mecca a new military threat loomed to the east, which was the last major challenge to Muhammad's political might. A group of tribes, the Hawazin, had an army three times the size of the Muslim army and were longtime enemies of the Meccans. Muhammad was aligned with Mecca now and set off with an army of 12,000. Muhammad struck a swift and fatal blow at Hunayn, crushing the challenge. About 6,000 women and children, all the animals, and 4,000 ounces of silver, became the Muslims' booty.

A verse in the Quran refers to this encounter at Hunayn.

> God hath given you victory on many fields, and on the day of Hunayn, when ye exulted in your numbers, though they availed you naught, and the earth, vast as it was, was straitened for you. Then ye turned back in flight. Then God sent down His Spirit of Peace on His Messenger and upon the believers, and sent down hosts you could not see, and punished those who did not believe. Such is the reward of disbelievers, and afterwards, God relenteth unto whom he will, for God is forgiving, Merciful. (Quran 9:25–27)

The victory of Hunayn was consolidated by the siege of Ta'if, where the shrine of the goddess al-Lat was located.

Tabari describes what happened next.

> When fifteen days of siege had passed at al-Ta'if the Messenger of God consulted Nawfal ibn Mu'awiyah and asked his opinion about continuing the siege. He replied, "O Messenger of God, they are like a fox hiding in its den. If you persist in your siege, you will capture it, and if you leave it, it will not harm you...."
>
> It has been reported that the Messenger of God said to Abu Bakr while he was besieging Thaqif in al-Ta'if, "O Abu Bakr, I saw [in a dream] that I was presented with a large bowl filled with butter and that a cock pecked at it and spilt it." Abu Bakr replied, "O Messenger of God, I don't think that you will attain what you desire from them today." The Messenger of God responded that he did not think so either. (Tabari, 1990, p. 24)

This interesting dream and the consultation may have played a part in the decision made by the Prophet. The siege was abandoned in 2 weeks. The Thaqif fought bravely, and the Muslims had casualties. A walled town could not be easily taken, even with the newly acquired siege engines. A long battle would make Muhammad's men restive, shed more blood, and ultimately make a reconciliation with the Thaqif more difficult (Watt, 1956, pp. 70–73, 99–101).

The prestige gained at Mecca and Hunayn would diminish and the booty gained at Hunayn was still waiting; Ta'if could be acquired by other means. Muhammad's disappointment in the stalemate, rather than a victory, is a possible reason for his sharp treatment of a man who accidentally kicked him on the return journey.

A fifth-share of the considerable Hunayn booty went to Muhammad; the rest was distributed to Muhammad's impatient men.

> The Messenger of God gave [gifts] to those "whose hearts were to be reconciled (*al-mu'allafa qulubuhum*)," who were certain men of eminence, in order to conciliate them and to win over their hearts. He gave a hundred camels each to the following.... (Tabari, 1990, pp. 31–32)

They were the Quraysh, who had recently seen their pagan world shattered by Islam in Mecca. Abu-Sufyan and his family received 300 camels, and other leading Meccans each received 100 camels. The Prophet had acted magnanimously to reduce the frustration and bitterness of the newly conquered and to strengthen their nominal commitment to the new religion. It was in this manner that Muhammad attained one of his greatest achievements; effecting a genuine reconciliation with his most implacable foes, the leaders of Mecca.

The 4,000 Helpers from Medina, who like the other impoverished Emigrants only received four camels each, voiced resentment at these lavish gifts given to Muhammad's own people and family.

> When the Messenger of God had distributed those gifts among the Quraysh and the Bedouin tribes, and the Helpers got nothing from it, this group of Helpers took [the matter] to their hearts and talked volubly about it until one of them said, "By God, The Messenger of God has joined his kinsfolk!" Sa'd ibn Ubadah went to the Messenger of God and said, "O Messenger of God, this group of Helpers have a grudge against you for what you did with the booty and how you divided it among your own people, and by giving great gifts to the Bedouin tribes while this group of Helpers got nothing...."
>
> When all of them had assembled, he went and informed the Prophet, who came to them. After due praise and exaltation of God, he addressed them saying: "O community of Helpers, what is this talk I hear about you? [What is] the grudge you have harbored in your hearts [against me]? Did I not come to you when you were erring and God guided you; [were you not] needy and then made rich by God; [were you not] enemies and [did not] God reconcile your hearts? ..."
>
> O Helpers, you harbor a grudge [against me] because of the worldly things by which I conciliate a people so that they may embrace Islam, while I entrust you to your Islam. Are you not pleased, O Helpers, that the people should take away sheep and camels while you go back to your homes with the Messenger of God? (Tabari, 1990, pp. 36–37)

Muhammad thus reassured them that they were important to him and that he would be living with them in Medina and not at Mecca.

Muhammad's actions toward the defeated Meccans were not the lavish generosity of a middle-aged victor, but a deeply felt personal act. In transcending the enmities, of years of humiliation, conflict, and war, he gave large gifts to those "whose hearts were to be reconciled." Muhammad was reconciling too with his own past and his own family, clan, and tribe. It was an act of generosity rarely rivaled in history, for fratricidal war has often descended to its own logical conclusion—total and absolute destruction. Muhammad in this supreme act of reconciliation, painfully resented by his own followers, converted a proud people, his defeated rivals, to his cause by offering respect, trust, and honor. The results were gratifying, for the Quraysh went on to provide future Islam with its leading warriors and statesmen.

Erik Erikson (1969) in his own middle age was to observe that the creative human need in the middle span of life was *generativity*. In his seminal study of the middle-aged Mahatma, he was to note striking parallels between Gandhi's militant nonviolence and the practice of psychoanalysis. Just as Freud had heard in "free association" the revelations of troubled individuals that psychoanalysis endeavored to help and change, Gandhi had listened to his own "inner voices" to challenge and face the truth through Satyagraha. Psychoanalysis and Satyagraha shared an affinity—transformation was only possible when both partners, unequal to begin with, changed in a process that had renounced violence. Just as therapeutic listening and persuasion sought to cure the aberrations of individuals in a psychoanalytic encounter, a puny, loin-clad Gandhi was to challenge, using only moral force and nonviolent resistance, the might of the British Empire—a fateful encounter that was to be the beginning of its end.

The reconciliation with the hated other that Muhammad achieved in Mecca offers a model of hope. The prophecy in the Quran (60:7) "It may be that God will establish love between you and those with whom you are at enmity" had come to pass. The harsh experiences of the days of conflict and war with Mecca had ended as Muhammad offered a flexible and adaptive response to bring his people together. The revelation that the revered founder of Islam fulfilled is the most powerful message that Islam has for a changed world of today where our capacity for mutual and assured destruction poses immeasurable risk.

10

The Last Years of the Prophet

MUHAMMAD set out on his last major expedition a few months after his return to Medina. The year 630 c.e. had marked the final victory of the Byzantines over the Persians. In a major campaign, Emperor Heraclius had reversed the losses suffered at the hands of the Persians, who had previously overrun Egypt, Syria, and Asia Minor. In March 630 c.e., Heraclius had restored the Holy Rood to Jerusalem.

Muhammad must have heard of these events to the north and realized that a show of power was necessary. His followers and allied tribes received orders to send all their armed and mounted men to this Syrian campaign. Thirty-thousand men, 10,000 of whom were mounted, set for Tabuk near the Gulf of Akaba. The purpose of this mission is unclear, although one tradition suggests that the Muslim community's livelihood depended upon the booty from the Prophet's raids. Muhammad insisted that it was the religious duty of all able-bodied Muslims to participate, which strengthened the campaign and reduced the possibility of dissident opinion in Medina.

This was not a popular expedition with some of the Muslims. The Byzantines had a formidable reputation; the heat was oppressive, and there was drought. Ibn Ishaq and Tabari in their accounts, as well as a *sura* in the Quran, are vehement in their criticisms of these malingerers.

> Those who were left behind rejoiced in their inaction behind the back of the Apostle of God; they hated to strive and fight with their goods and

persons in the cause of God. They said, "Do not go forth in the heat." Say: "The fire of hell is fiercer in heat." If only they could understand!

Let them laugh a little; much will they weep in recompense for what they do.

If, then, God bring you back to any of them, and they ask your permission to go out with you (on a raid), say: "Never shall you go out with me or fight an enemy with me. For you preferred to sit inactive on the first occasion. So sit now with those who lag behind." (Quran 9:81–83)

There were no battles or engagements described in the accounts of this expedition.

> When the Messenger of God reached Tabuk, Yuhanna ibn Ru'ba, governer of Ayla, came to him, made a treaty with him, and offered him the poll tax (*jizya*). The people of Jarba and Adhruh also offered him the poll tax, and the Messenger of God wrote a document for each one of them which is still in their possession. (Tabari, 1990, p. 58)

Treaties were concluded with small Jewish and Christian communities near the Gulf of Aqaba offering them guaranteed protection upon an annual payment. They were allowed to manage their own affairs and were not asked to become Muslims, but relations with outsiders were now under the protection of "God and His Messenger," the Islamic state. The treaty ended a remarkable expedition by the Islamic troops deep into the Byzantine empire to the town of Tabuk.

On his return the Prophet stopped at the Mosque of Dissent in Dhu Awan. Muhammad suspected the builders had ulterior motives in constructing this mosque and ordered its destruction by fire. Tabari (1990) observes,

> [C]oncerning them [the builders of the Mosque] it was revealed in the Quran: "And those who have taken a mosque for [working] mischief and disbelief, as well as disunion among the faithful and as an outpost for those who already fought God and His Messenger, will swear, 'We desired nothing but good.' God witnesses what sort of liars they are." (p. 61; Quran 9:10)

The "Hypocrites" who did not join in the campaign were cast out for a period of 50 days, a severe punishment that weakened any internal opposition to Muhammad, and probably also prevented internal dissension from destroying this small state after his death.

The next year beginning April 630 was the "Year of Deputations," as the ninth year of the *Hijra* is called, in which numerous tribes and subtribes sent delegations to form an alliance with Muhammad.

The news of Mecca's fall and the collapse of the tribal confederation at Hunayn quickly spread over western Arabia. Arab tribes now understood the extent of Muhammads's growing power and the need to join his *umma*. Muhammad's *umma* was originally more of a political entity than a purely religious one, established to govern Medina, with Muhammad as "the Prophet" of this community. With the increasing power of Muhammad, and particularly after the fall of Mecca, acceptance of Islam was now a condition for joining the *umma*.

> When the Apostle had gained possession of Mecca, and had finished with Tabuk, and Thaqif had surrendered and paid homage, deputations from the Arabs came to him from all directions.
> In deciding their attitude to Islam the Arabs were only waiting to see what happened to this clan of the Quraysh and the Apostle. . . . When Mecca was occupied and the Quraysh became subject to him and he subdued it to Islam, and the Arabs knew that they could not fight the Apostle or display enmity towards him they entered into God's religion "in batches" as God said, coming to him from all directions. . . . (Ibn Ishaq, 1955, pp. 627–628)

Accepting God's religion and Muslim *umma* membership required payment of the *zakat* or *sadaqa*, an alms tax, that supported the community treasury. The *zakat* was a religious obligation, one of five basic elements later called the "Pillars of Islam" (Peters, 1994, p. 243). A revelation presciently anticipated the risk of new members reneging on their commitments at a later date. This in fact did happen after Muhammad's death.

> But if they violate their oaths after they have pledged, and taunt you for your religion, fight the leaders of unbelief, for their oaths are nothing to them. (Quran 9:11–12)

Sometimes rival factions within tribes sought their own relationships with Muhammad. Abu-Bakr, his chief associate and an expert in genealogy, understood the complex relationships between different subdivisions of a tribe. Guided by Abu-Bakr, Muhammad smoothly and tactfully negotiated the alliances without alienating other sections of these tribes. For the envoys who came from all over Arabia, obligations to Islam were stressed; they were also enjoined to welcome the messengers sent to collect the religious taxes.

Many of the new converts had weak spiritual motivation and a revelation reflected this awareness:

> The Arabs of the desert say: We have faith. Say thou: Faith Ye have not, but say "we submit," for faith hath not yet entered your hearts. And if ye obey God and His Messenger, He will not withhold from you ought of (the reward of) your deeds. (Quran 49:14)

Islam thus accepted a hierarchy of submission, with submission without faith being of the lower degree. Muhammad was practical in accepting degrees of membership in his *umma*. It is evident he did not see the world in absolute or categorical terms: he accepted "gray areas" as long as they posed no threat to him or his religion.

This growing strength of Islam brought hardened attitudes towards idolaters. They were given 4 months of respite to move about safely; after that period, God and His Messenger were freed of any obligation to them. The only *sura* (the *Sura* of Repentance, 9:1–129) to open without the Names of Mercy, because of stern commandments against idolaters, now clearly states:

> Then, when the sacred months have passed, slay the idolaters wherever you find them, and take them (captive) and besiege them and prepare for them each ambush. But if they repent and establish worship and pay the poor-due, then leave them their way free. (Quran 9:5)

Two exceptions to this commandment were made: individuals under a special treaty with the Prophet, and those who sought protection were instructed in Islam.

There were other threats. A man from a Christian tribe named Musaylimah claimed that he was a prophet, and sent a letter to Muhammad beginning "From Musaylimah the Messenger of God to Muhammad the Messenger of God," and suggested they divide the earth into equal spheres of influence. Muhammad replied with contempt, addressing the letter "From Muhammad the Messenger of God to Musaylimah the liar. . . ." There were also two men who, as impostors, claimed prophethood, and a woman who claimed to be a prophet.

The Hajj pilgrimage of 632 c.e., "the pilgrimage of farewell," established the ceremonial form for Mecca and its environs as a purely Muslim ritual, and unbelievers were forbidden to attend. The pagan meaning of some ceremonies has been lost, but other ceremonies were incorporated into the new ritual bringing new meanings; for instance, the lapidation of stone pillars, reinterpreted as the stoning of devils, was now part of the new ritual.

The news of the false prophets and some minor insurrections may have added to Muhammad's stress. His health gradually deteriorated after he returned from the great Hajj pilgrimage. By June 632 c.e., Muhammad's health worsened, but he continued to attend to his duties and lead the prayers in the mosque. As his suffering from fever and severe headaches increased, his wives let him stay principally in his beloved Aisha's apartment, and Abu-Bakr led the daily prayers in the mosque. On June 8, 632 c.e., Muhammad lost consciousness and died with his head on his dear Aisha's lap.

When Abu-Bakr heard of the Prophet's death, he went to Aisha's house and then to the Mosque.

> He paid no attention to anything and went [straight] to the Messenger of God in Aisha's house where he was lying in a corner covered by a striped garment of the Yemeni fabric. Abu-Bakr went close [to the Prophet], uncovered his face, kissed him, then said, "With my father may you be ransomed, and with my mother! Indeed, you have tasted the death which God had decreed for you. No [other] death will ever overtake you. . . ."
>
> After praising God and extolling Him, he said, "O people, those who worshipped Muhammad, [must know that] Muhammad is dead; those who worshipped God, [must know that] God is alive [and] immortal." He then recited the verse: "Muhammad is only a messenger, and many a messenger has gone before him. So if he dies or is killed, will you turn back on your heels? He who turns back on his heels will do no harm to God; and God will reward the grateful." By God, it was as if the people did not know that this verse was revealed to the Messenger of God until Abu Bakr recited it that day. The people took it from him, and it was [constantly] in their mouths. 'Umar said, "By God, as soon as I heard Abu Bakr recite it, my legs betrayed me so that I fell to the ground, and my legs would not bear me. I knew that the Messenger of God had indeed died." (Tabari, 1990, pp. 184–185)

For a time, Medina was in confusion. Muhammad had not named a successor or designated anyone to continue the administration of the Islamic state; Abu-Bakr had been appointed only to lead the prayers. The Medinans wanted someone from their own clan to be the leader rather than a Qurayshite Emigrant; they wanted someone who would not put the interests of his own clan or tribe first. The ideal candidate was a man close to Muhammad and a Qurayshite who had emigrated earlier, but also a man who was detached from his own tribe and who could pull together the loyalties of all the varied tribes. Abu-Bakr was ultimately chosen "successor" (*Khalifa*) or Caliph of the Messenger of God.

11

The Growth of a Charismatic Leader

THE building of Muhammad's *umma* or community of believers was vital to the success of Islam. In his role as a prophet and leader, Muhammad's revelations provided guidance and structure to the ideal shapes of this nascent group. The scattered, fragmented clans and tribes were molded into a new political and religious community. Polytheism gave way to a universal monotheism that was initially identified with the Judaic tradition. Some clans' matriarchal patterns were changed to a clearer patriarchal structure, allowing a form of polygamy. The sporadic tribal raids or *razzias* to support the community over time became the Holy War, or *jihad,* against the unbelievers.

How did these transformations come about? Muhammad's early experiences as an orphan in the pre-Islamic world of Mecca are crucial to understanding his vision of the world. These early experiences are reflected in his representational world: first as a child, and later as a young adult. The adult Muhammad, the Apostle of God, received revelations that in their slow evolution defined and created the representational world for his *umma*.

Hope is the first basic strength that is nurtured in infancy, according to Erikson. Little information, however, is available describing the early years of Muhammad's life. His father, Abdullah, died before he was born, during a caravan journey to trade in Syria. The infant Muhammad was sent to a clan that lived in the desert for the first few years of his life, as it was the custom that the child be suckled and weaned by a foster mother. A few years after his return to his home, at the age of 6, his mother, Amina, died leaving him in the care of his grandfather Abd al-Muttalib.

It is acknowledged that Muhammad always had an acute sense of smell and vision (Lings, 1983, p. 167). We can assume then that in his early childhood all his senses—smell, taste, touch, sight, hearing—were uniquely sensitive to his surroundings. Throughout his life we note both a need for warm, sensitive mothering and a need to mother others. He demonstrated an intense wish to take care of abandoned creatures and an identification with the oppressed; a need to master and change life for all those who were weak and needy was clearly evident.

A quotation from one of Freud's earliest writings is apposite:

> At early stages, the human organism is incapable of achieving this specific action (i.e. toward a riddance of a given excitation). It is brought about by extraneous help, when the attention of an experienced person has been drawn to the child's condition by a discharge taking place along the path of internal change (e.g., by the child's crying). This path of discharge thus acquires an extremely important secondary function—viz., of bringing about an understanding (*Verständigung*) with other people; and the original helplessness of human beings is thus the primal source of all moral motives. (Freud, 1954, p. 379, quoted in Erikson, 1975, pp. 63–64)

Erikson makes an interesting note that Freud does not speak of "mother" or the "environment" but of an "experienced person" (*"ein erfahrenes Individuum"*) who is described as helpful vis-à-vis the "helpless" one. Erikson (1975) observes that Freud, in his shift from a neurological to a psychological point of view, anticipated a new morality based on the "mutuality of function" which must "evolve from psychoanalytic and ecological considerations" (p. 64).

The identification with loved ones and the internalization of their mandates and patterns of behavior:

> [I]s the means by which character is initially organized . . . identification is also the means of securing the love of important persons and of making oneself safe from attack (either from the actual persons or from the internalized representations of persons), but identification also serves the function of mastery. (Weinstein & Platt, 1973, p. 99)

The ideal shape of the self is defined in part by the internalization of the ideal shape of the other. Thus, children possess parents who appear omnipotent and whom they admire and idealize. Parents, in turn, hold familial, cultural, and social ideals for the children to attain. Real situations and experiences allow for transformation and actualization of these ideal shapes. An abstract ideal may, for instance, take the place of an infantile ideal. In the attainment of these ideals, as defined by social standards and expectations, love, once sought from the other, is now derived from pride in accomplishment. This process further builds self-love and esteem. As the child matures, with the increasing capacity of the ego functions of discrimination and judgment, ideals are modified by changing assessments of reality (Weinstein & Platt, p. 100).

What identity did Muhammad have as a child? His mother was alive until he was 6 years old. We can assume a satisfactory mutuality was attained between mothered child and mothering adult. This afforded a safe pole and identity from which Muhammad could reach out for the other pole, the first love objects. Identity is built upon this satisfactory mutuality between the mothering adults and the mothered child. "The fate of childhood identifications, in turn, depends on the child's satisfactory interaction with a trustworthy and meaningful hierarchy of roles as provided by the generations living together in some form of family" (Erikson, 1959, pp. 121–122).

The early years of Muhammad's representational world would have been characteristic of the representational world of the average child in Mecca, except for his orphan status. We do not know nor can we attempt to fully reconstruct his inner world. We can be certain that the "symbolic universes," "social products with a history" of the Quraysh clan and the world of the Bedouin would be reflected in Muhammad's representational world (Berger & Luckmann, 1966, p. 97).[1]

Muhammad grew up in the world of Mecca among the sedentary Bedouin. Clan life had its own well-defined "symbolic universe" that regulated all the peoples' roles in Mecca and in the surrounding Bedouin. Poets and soothsayers, or *kahins*, passed on traditions and history in the rich Arabic language. Muhammad's

---

[1] Their concept of a symbolic universe (close to Durkheim's religion) is where history's socially objectivated and subjectively real meaning takes place.

mother's and foster mother's roles were defined by this tradition, and when his mother died, clan tradition dictated that his grandfather and then his uncle become his caretakers. The orphan Muhammad undoubtedly had his share of hardships and experienced feelings of loss and abandonment. We can only assume this, however, as there is no evidence to suggest the extent of Muhammad's sense of this loss.

Most traditional cultures view the replacement of one person by another person in the same role as adequate; individuals are nothing but their roles. The acknowledgment of individual uniqueness is a very late development in history.[2] In the harsh desert climate of Muhammad's home, life could be brutal and short; orphanhood was not uncommon. It is partly for this reason that we have very little biographical detail about Muhammad's childhood. Abd al-Muttalib, Muhammad's grandfather, was about 80 years old when he assumed Muhammad's care. The grandfather died two years later, and Abu Talib, his uncle, took over this responsibility. The clan would presume Muhammad had adequate parenting as some member of the family was expected to look after the orphan.

Muhammad's needs for nurturance and shelter were thus met by the family and clan. In Eriksonian terms, it was these "generations living together in some form of family" that provided Muhammad with that "trustworthy and meaningful hierarchy of roles" and a substitute for his parents. It was his mother, grandfather, uncle, and other elders of the clan of the Hashim who as a group provided Muhammad with the familial, cultural, and social ideals. His extended clan family provided him not only with the elements that build basic trust but also gave him important elements of the ideal shape of his self.

In Muhammad's representational world the ideal shapes would be based partly on identification with the ideal shapes of his extended family and its history. What was the ideal shape of his family in Mecca? Muhammad's family belonged to the clan of the Hashim of the Quraysh tribe. There is a considerable body of lore related to the Quraysh, some of which may have been

---

[2] Dereification, the "seeing through" of roles as roles, is a late development in human history and individual biography.

embellished over time. From his family, the clan, and local poets, Muhammad heard the stories about the attainments of his ancestors Qusayy, Hashim, and Abd al-Mutalib. In this oral culture, bards and poets would celebrate the achievements of his ancestors and other Arabs as they told stories in Arabic of the rulers and kings of Pre-Islamic Arabia. In fact, after Muhammad, the next 500 years "may be seen in the light of the expansion of this one tribe to the dimensions of a world power" (Rodinson, 1980, p. 39).

The ideal shape of Muhammad's family and clan was that of a family that had contributed significantly to Mecca and its history. However, the actual shape of the family and clan was far from this ideal. The clan of Hashim was poor and held little power in Mecca. Muhammad's uncle, Abu Talib, as the leader of the clan of the Hashim, could offer no more than protection to Muhammad, though the clan stood by him throughout his life in Mecca. No one dared to touch him as this would have certainly led to feuds and vendettas with the entire Banu Hashim clan.

We know nothing of Muhammad's first loves and little of his adolescence. We assume that the presence of his family, particularly his grandfather and later his uncle, gave him recognition, an indispensable support for the difficult tasks of this age. Muhammad had to resynthesize identifications from childhood in a unique way and consolidate his identity formation by accepting the roles offered to him in the social setting of that historical period.

During adolescence and young adulthood Muhammad must have been challenged, in Eriksonian terms, by his social world and its ideals. It would be important for him to identify with goals that would merit commitment and to develop an awareness of his skills and strengths; he would need hope, purpose, and competence to deal with the tasks of this stage of his life. Muhammad would also be challenged by family and clan ties of loyalty. Trusting himself, with an appropriate mistrust of simple approaches and easy resolutions and possessing a commitment to his values and ideals, to his friends, family, clan and "nation": all would be important.[3] A mature and flexible commitment would not foreclose promising choices, while a total dedication could lead to a

---

[3] Arabia in the sixth and seventh century was not a nation, in the modern sense. It had clans, tribes, and some city states, but Arabs did have some sort of distinctive identity partly based on language and history that we could call "national."

rigid fanaticism. With the capital accrued from experiences at previous stages, he would build an identity described in psychoanalysis as ego-synthesis of basic drives, endowment, and opportunities.

Adulthood and Marriage to Khadija

At the age of 25 Muhammad married Khadija, a wealthy widow who was 40 years old and one of the more successful entrepreneurs in Mecca. A verse in the Quran (93:1–8) acknowledges that he had not been forsaken for God found him an orphan yet gave him refuge, found him poor yet made him rich, found him wandering yet guided him. It was this providential marriage and not God's miracle that altered Muhammad's representational world, a world now expanded to include a marriage partner and a share in a successful business ownership. Muhammad's actual shapes now changed from being a poor orphan and a young adult with limited success to being a successful Meccan.

With his marriage Muhammad faced an experience that involved a commitment and a relationship of mature love. This presupposed a sharing of life and work and of productivity nurtured by the bond of adult sensuality and common goals. Two already defined identities, one not to be submerged by the other, could now have the opportunity to grow and expand (Erikson, Erikson, & Kivnick, 1986, p. 279). The commitment and a relationship of mature love, described as intimacy by Erikson, has been called an object relationship by other psychoanalysts.[4] The circle of potential intimacies, however, can be broadened to involve many others, including extended family, companions, and idealized identity models of legend and history.

Muhammad's marriage reflected his ability to make such a commitment to sharing and intimacy. In turn, support from Khadija had a renewed impact on his commitment to others. Respect for Khadija was marked by his unwavering affection and gratitude. Perhaps because of Muhammad's early loss of his mother he had

---

[4] There is no consistent theory of object relationship in psychoanalysis nor is the term the happiest of phrases (e.g., Weinstein & Platt, 1973, pp. 43, 103).

a special attachment to this older woman.[5] Muhammad described Khadija as the best of all women of her time, and said that he would live in peace and tranquility with her in a house built of reeds in paradise. He spoke so often of Khadija that after her death his young, new wife, Aisha, said she was seized with more feelings of jealousy and rage when Khadija was mentioned than she had ever felt for anyone else. In the polygamous world of Mecca, merchants and travelers were allowed to take other wives for a limited period, but Muhammad was bound to Khadija alone until her death. Indeed, he condemned the practice of temporary marriages.

Khadija and Muhammad had four daughters and one son; their son died at an early age. The death must have contributed to a great deal of unhappiness and dissatisfaction.

Erikson defined adulthood as a time when

> We have reached the stage of generativity which encompasses a long period of responsibilities that demand stamina and dedication. The challenge is to be productive in all manner of ways and the strength to be developed is that of care. Caring embraces taking care of whatever one produces, children, of course, but also all that one does or makes or is part of. It involves playing an active role in the social institutions that create the coherence of a given social structure at a given historical time. Not to be in any way productive and participant in the social network in which one lives, and works, and loves must result in stagnation—a sense of the end of growth, both personally and as a member of the community.... (Erikson et al., 1986, p. 285)

If we accept this view, it is of interest to note that the most creative and dynamic period of Muhammad's life was indeed his adulthood. We can clearly see him remarkably taking on the challenges and tasks of this stage with energy and perseverance. Caring for his wife and family was obvious, but when this caring was extended to the weak and the poor, and the entire Meccan society, it became his life task. He took an active role in not only modifying and changing the social structure of that historical period, but in creating an entirely new socioreligious structure—a structure that would alter history. Muhammad's adulthood was

---

[5] Surrogate love permits even children who have suffered neglect to survive and flourish. Anna Freud sought "psychological" mothers all her life (Vaillant, 1993, p. 255).

thus a period of major growth and creativity for himself and on behalf of the carefully nurtured community he created.

Muhammad's first public preaching occurred almost 3 years after what he identified as his first revelation when he was 40 years old. This interval of doubt and silence could be considered a period of Muhammad's ongoing crisis of adulthood until there was a public resolution. Besides his own personal dissatisfaction, the Prophet had been unhappy with the social malaise in Mecca. The state of poverty of his clan and his own experiences as an orphan must have starkly highlighted the distance between the ideal shapes and actual shapes of Muhammad, his family, and clan. This added to his conflicts. Few Meccans had such an interest in the moral, religious, and intellectual issues that preoccupied Muhammad. His earliest concerns involved morality and the helpless. The ethical concerns for the poor and weak, including orphans, that were the domain of all clan leaders in a pastoral nomadic economy, were of no interest to the newly rich mercantile leaders. The rise of a mercantile class led to individual interests overwhelming those of the group (the clan or tribe) and to a neglect by Meccans of the chiefs' traditional duty to protect the poorer clan members. Muhammad too had experienced this as a child and later as a young adult. Tribal opinion and mores that maintained the clan code through poets' stories and traditions and supported it in the public forum, had little or no impact in Mecca. The ethical codes and values of the desert could be neglected easily in the city. This led to a breakdown of tribal and clan solidarity and a deterioration in the religious life of Meccans (Watt, 1961, p. 51). The merchants, because of their wealth, were unconcerned with the higher powers or their duties toward the weak and helpless, such as widows and orphans.

An early passage in the Quran states:

Woe to every slanderer, scoffer,
who gathers wealth and counts it,
thinking wealth will make him immortal. (Quran 104:1–3)

The Quran (89:18–21) not only criticized the Meccans, but asserted that these faults would lead to eternal punishment. The man who is condemned on the Last Day is described as:

> He was not believing in God Almighty,
> not urging to feed the destitute;
> today he has no friend here. (Quran 69:33–35)

The Meccan chapters of the Quran are mainly religious. They deal predominantly with God's goodness and power, the wickedness of idolatry, the inevitability of divine judgment, and man's responses: worship, gratitude, and generosity. Man was not to amass wealth, oppress, or neglect.

> As for the orphan, oppress not,
> As for the beggars, refuse not,
> As for thy Lord's mercy, expatiate. (Quran 93:9–11)

There was also direct criticism of the Meccans:

> You respect not the orphan,
> urge not to feed the destitute,
> savour the heritage greedily,
> Love wealth ardently. (Quran 89:18–21)

Interestingly, these passages are nearly all that is expressed about human relations in the early part of the Quran. There is no mention of relations with family, marriage, life, attitudes towards parents or children, or property. These fundamentals of social life were taken for granted.

At this stage, Muhammad probably had not intended to establish a separate and distinct religious community, but it is clear that he was troubled by the contemporary social malaise and the decline of values in Mecca. However, as the first revelations reveal, Muhammad did not wish to make major changes in the religious practices of Mecca. He was concerned about the loss of clan and tribal practices of the old ethical culture in the city's mercantile climate. The poor, the destitute, and the orphans were being neglected. The Quran emphasized the religious consequences of the troubles and offered a more satisfactory and corrective alternative to the dispossessed. The supportive climate, ideals, and virtues of solidarity were to be brought from the desert to the urban setting.

Initially there were no novel ideas or innovations in the new preaching. He threatened and warned of hellfire except for the righteous for whom there were promises of the pleasures of Paradise. The other Meccan divinities were neither denied nor affirmed; they were ignored. There were no denunciations, of "those who assign companions to Allah," as there are in the later revelations that insist on a unique supreme deity. The new approach was also not revolutionary. What was unique was that the individual would be judged by God without consideration of kinship, family, or tribe. Men functioned as individuals within a group very similar to a clan or tribe. Although Islam was still like other clans or tribes, it had its own Prophet. The seeds of development in the future were laid down in this simple concept: religion linked the individual to the group which was the new social unit. The ideals of group support that Muhammad never had in his clan and tribe were to be replaced by a new religious tribe that would support everyone.

The revelations reminded Muhammad not only of his own beginnings but of the nature of his tasks. There was an interval when he received no revelations and was mocked for being forsaken. However, at this gloomy moment, Muhammad is reminded of God's special goodness to him:

> Thy Lord hath not forsaken thee nor doth he hate thee;
> And verily the latter portion will be better for thee than the former.
> And verily thy lord will give unto thee so that thou wilt be content.
> Did he not find thee an orphan and protect (thee)?
> Did he not find thee wandering and direct (thee)?
> Did he not find thee destitute and enrich (thee)? (Quran 93:3–8)

As Muhammad was nearly 50 years old, the prophecy in this *sura*, "the latter portion will be better for thee than the former," must have seemed absurd to those who heard it. Yet these last 10 years of Muhammad's life are in fact one of the more remarkable records of success in history.

It is here that what could be called a "crisis" at the deepest personal level for Muhammad occurs. He was by now well settled, married with four daughters, and prosperous in trade. But he had no son. His eldest child, a son named Qasim, had died before his second birthday. This loss was significant: Muhammad was even known as Abu al-Qasim, the father of Qasim. Muhammad adopted his young cousin, Ali, the son of his uncle Abu-Talib, and a young slave, Zayd, who was a gift from Khadija at the time of their marriage.

These adoptions, however, could not make up for the deep sense of loss that Muhammad must have felt at the death of his son. At a social level, most traditional patriarchal cultures emphasize the need for a male heir to carry the family name. Not having a son was a deep source of shame in Arabia, and an adoptive son could not substitute for a male biological heir, nor reduce the sense of shame. Muhammad was cruelly taunted for not having a male heir, and because of this mockery, Mecca was becoming unbearable to him.

A passage in the Quran gave a retort to the disbelievers who had taunted the Prophet and called him *abtar* (or mutilated) as he had no son and therefore, none to uphold his family or religion after him (Rodinson, 1980, p. 54).[6]

> Yes, we have given you abundance
> So pray your lord and sacrifice;
> it is your enemy who is the *abtar*. (Quran 108)

We can see in this revelation, together with previous revelations, an integration of several levels that included a resolution of Muhammad's personal crisis as well as a resolution of critical local and "national" issues. Muhammad was the leader of a nascent group. At a personal level he had identified with the orphan, the wanderer, and the destitute, and in meeting their needs he was in part giving to others what had not been given to him. His great-great-great-grandfather, *Qusayy,* had been the first person to establish a permanent settlement at the sanctuary in Mecca and is considered the ancestor of all the leading Meccan clans. Hashim, the great-grandfather of Muhammad, also had been a leading figure in Mecca. Would Muhammad leave a similar legacy? Instead, without a male heir, Muhammad was being called *abtar,* an added insult and humiliation in seventh-century Arabia.

---

[6] In fact his own uncle Abu Lahab had rejoiced when the Prophet's son died. He had gone to the pagans and given them the good news that Muhammad was now childless, cut off from his roots and his own people. There would be no one to remember the Prophet when he died. Without a male heir his links to the past, the future, and even his memory would vanish at his death.

It implied that he was not creative or procreative, in a biological sense.

Was Muhammad tormented and angered by the mockery? The intensity of the response suggests this. The brief revelation initially reassured him that God had given him abundance, that his task was to pray and sacrifice. The last verse shows anger, and the resolution offered is that the enemy was *abtar!* The personal crisis and an attempt at resolution are revealed in this short, intense, and ultimately poignant revelation.

The retort described in the revelation above has been considered vengeful. Mockery, however, could be considered a powerful trigger for the creative response of a leader who, instead of a male heir, would leave behind an immense new group linked to a new religion that would become "immortal." Also was it not a dark and ominous hint that these Meccan enemies would leave behind no such heritage, and that their very lives could be in peril? Painful conflicts rooted in humiliation can create their own powerful response. The vehemence of Muhammad's revelatory response indicates the depth of the pain.

Islam and the Impact of Judaism

Meccans could not live in isolation, nor was Mecca isolated. Intelligent Meccans, particularly those who traded with the north, were aware of the world outside the desert vastness of Arabia. The Jewish and Christian worlds had an impact on Arabia at the "national" level. Their religions rested on sacred books received from heaven, revered for their antiquity, with miraculous acts to support their worth. They had organized houses of worship, a well-defined clergy of priests and rabbis, formal liturgical prayers, sacrifices, and rituals. Compared to monotheistic Christianity and Judaism, the other religions that were practiced in the Arabian Peninsula reflected simpler beliefs and idol worship.

Could it have been disturbing and threatening for Arabs to have nothing comparable to the complex religious edifices of their neighbors? Arab traders, including Muhammad, had seen direct evidence of these powerful group-binding universalist religions. They had heard of and seen the enormous influence of the two most powerful empires in the world, the Byzantine and Persian (Sasanian) Empires, at the edges of the Arabian desert. The most celebrated Arab states, the Lakhmids and the Ghassanids, were mere clients and vassals of Persia and Byzantium. Wickedness at home and humiliations abroad reflected the challenges that sensitive Meccans could have experienced. Muhammad was to provide not only a personal answer but an answer for all Arabs in the rich Arabic language of its poets.

The earliest passages of the Quran seem to be similar to Judeo-Christian monotheistic beliefs. In these passages there are references to concepts of God the Creator, of revelation and resurrection, and of a day of judgment. This vision was distinctly more complex than the beliefs of pre-Islamic Arabs who had many capricious minor gods and no final universal justice which demanded accountability for periods of injustice and anarchy on earth.

Muhammad has been accused of learning from and listening to men who spoke a foreign language (Quran 16:103) and who told legends about the ancients (Quran 25:5). In order to uphold the belief that the Quran was a miraculous act, orthodox Islam holds that Muhammad was illiterate and could not read or write. It is clear from the biblical material in the Quran that Muhammad had, in fact, never read the Bible. However, many Judeo-Christian concepts were widely known to intelligent Meccans and thus available in oral form. The fact that the revelations were also in very good Arabic suggested authenticity and refuted slanderous imputations that they were borrowings from Jews and Christians.

In its outward form, the community had acquired only a few rites. The members were initially called "the Faithful" (*Mu'min* in the singular). Much later those who had surrendered to Allah were called Muslims. Initially, Muhammad's faithful were few in number. They performed *salat*, a pious act that involved prostrating themselves deeply from the waist, and recitations of the sacred revelations (Quran), the word of Allah to Muhammad. This form of prayer was similar to the readings (*qeryana* in Syriac) in the Syrian church. *Salat* was clearly derived from the Aramaic to refer to liturgical prayer of the Jews and Christians. Prayers were performed at sunrise, sunset, and during the night, similar to Christian practice. Furthermore, during prayer, as observed by the Jews, everyone turned towards Jerusalem.

The first convert to Islam was Muhammad's wife Khadija, who comforted and supported him from the time of his first revelations. Soon he gathered a small group of converts. A few were from influential clans, but others were from outside the clan system and needed clans to protect them. Early sources described these converts as "young men and weak persons."[7] "Weak persons" referred to those who did not have good clan protection.

By incorporating the biblical prophets into the Quran, the revelations allowed Muhammad to draw closer links to Judaism and Christianity. Later, at Medina an even more elaborate connection was established as Muhammad positioned Abraham at the center of his new religion. The Jews and Christians believed that Abraham (Ibrahim in Arabic) was the father of both Arabs (through Ishmael) and the Jews (through Isaac). Abraham was the first to believe in one Almighty God, and the promises made to him had preceded Judaism and Christianity. Essentially, Muhammad proclaimed that since Abraham was the first to surrender to the will of God, or Allah, he was therefore the first Muslim. Muhammad thus had a ready answer to those who called him to follow Judaism or Christianity:

> And they say: Be Jews or Christians
> then ye will be rightly guided.
> Say (unto them O Muhammad):
> Nay but we follow the religion of Abraham,
> The upright, and he was not of the idolaters. (Quran 2:135)

In several quick strokes, the Quran, through these revelations, had transcended Judaism and Christianity, the major religious challenges to Arabia. In one conceptual leap, Islam was not only older but now more universal, with an ancient heritage that could rival its predecessors. Islam had restored the pure religion of Abraham, and Muhammad had defined a new and special historical religious relationship between Abraham, the first ancestor, his own Arab people, and direct spiritual descendants. The historical past and present were now linked by a glorious religious claim to the future.

---

[7] A list that provides the names and some biographical details of approximately 50 of the earliest converts has been preserved (Watt, 1961, pp. 36–37).

We can see how personal conflicts experienced by Muhammad in Mecca, during his own adult crisis, and conflicts that other sensitive, thoughtful Meccans could also have experienced at the local and "national" level were dealt with, integrated, and now at least, cognitively transcended by the revelatory responses. An Arab messenger had provided, in Arabic, an ideal shape for his group and for all Arabs: a set of beliefs that challenged the Judeo-Christian world. The more developed forms of religion, powerful civilizations, and associated empires nearby would no longer be attractive for some Arabs, or be experienced as threats by other Arabs.

Islam did not develop in one full form. It was evolutionary, slow, careful, deliberate, and almost logical in its response to these challenges. The rate of change occurred at a pace that allowed easy assimilation; and, interestingly, similar qualities have been ascribed to Muhammad. Islam now provided Arabs with a satisfying Arabic religion and identity.

Though he seemed to dissociate Abraham from Judaism and linked him with Islam, Muhammad had adopted many Jewish practices. Jewish symbols and rituals were incorporated into the ideal shapes of the *umma*. For instance, Jerusalem was accepted, from the beginning, as the *qibla*, or the direction to be faced in prayer. Muhammad may have stressed the importance of Friday, because it was the day of preparation for the Jewish Sabbath.

On an individual level, the process of associating oneself with a significant other has been called identification.[8] The adoption of, or identification with, many Jewish practices and customs by the leader Muhammad, and considered acceptable and necessary for the group, can be called group identification, a process whereby a leader and an entire group of followers adopt some of the practices of another group.

Another group identification with Jewish customs was prayer in the middle of the day. A revelation allowed the faithful to eat the food of the people of the Book and to marry their women. While all the strict dietary laws of the Jewish faith were not followed, eating "pork or blood, or any animals that had either died

---

[8] Internalization and identification are important concepts that allow linkages between the intrapsychic world of the individual to society and its history (Berger & Luckmann, 1967, p. 131; Weinstein & Platt, 1973, pp. 25–26).

a natural death, had their necks wrung or been sacrificed to idols" was not allowed (Rodinson, 1980, p. 159). The Muslims even adopted certain Jewish modes of dress.⁹

At the cognitive level Islam had already offered a transcendent monotheistic religion. Simple earlier tribal practices—the worship of multiple idols, a form of pagan polydaimonism—yielded at the affective and behavioral level to identification with complex Judaic religious practices. Total transcendence and mastery over any religious and ideological threat from the nearby Judeo-Christian or the Persian worlds was almost complete.

The ideal shapes of the *umma* at this time in Medina included several additional aspects in the representational world of their group: the initial religious revelations from Mecca and Medina; the constitution of Medina (not based on revelation but demanding adherence defined by solemn agreement and clan commitment); several Jewish customs; and the actual presence of the leader, the Prophet. How the ideal shapes of the *umma* were internalized varied depending upon the individual's perspective of the total representational world of the *umma*. Individuals could choose and internalize those aspects of the offered shapes that would reflect a unique and personal commitment to the *umma*. (Both conscious and unconscious elements would play a role in this "choice.")

The strength of the emotional ties to the leader and the religion helped the individual internalize aspects of this representational world and further supported identification among the members of the group or *umma*. The sharing of symbolic objects (such as the Ka'ba and the Book, the Quran, that the recitations have turned into), symbolic actions (such as the religious rituals of prayer), a common language (Arabic), eating practices (the avoidance of "bad" foods), and a common manner of dress: all further strengthened this individual and group identification.¹⁰

---

[9] Christianity too had incorporated doctrines and practices from the existing religious world of the ancient Middle East and synthesized them into a new perspective (Albright, 1957).

[10] Berger and Luckmann (1967) concede that internalization occurs after identification. Though they indicate the possibility of a genuine dialectic between social and psychological phenomena, they see the self only as a reflected social entity and unfortunately stop at the possibility of what they consider is an "untenable alliance with either Freudian or behavioristic psychology" (Notes 6–7). Their rich concept of symbolic universe thus loses validity as a broad construct by excluding the possibilities of an individual, in this instance Muhammad, creating an entire symbolic universe.

A Charismatic Leader

A hortatory effort to guide and support the process of identification and internalization is clear from the first passages of the Quran (after the seven verses of the *al-Fatihah* or opening). The effort included support for belief, prayer, and action; acceptance of ongoing guidance; and the promise of future prosperity to the God-fearing followers. There was also a temporal link to the revelatory past and the certainty of the future. Past, present, and future became linked in one vast divine sweep.

> This beyond doubt is the Book, a guidance unto the God-fearing, who believe in the unseen and perform the prayer and give of that which we have bestowed upon them;
> and who believe in that which is revealed unto thee
> and in that which was revealed before thee,
> and who are certain of the hereafter;
> these are they who follow guidance from their Lord
> and these are they who shall prosper. (Quran 2:2–5)

Joining cognition, affect, behavior and reward here and in the hereafter, within an anxiety-relieving perfection of the past and future rolled into a timeless present, creates a sense of wholeness and magical oneness for the individual and provides a powerful support for submerging individual identity into a merging group.

A group's unity cannot tolerate any discord. A revelation gave this miraculous support to the Prophet:

> If thou hadst spent all that is in the earth,
> thou would not have united their hearts
> but God hath united their hearts. (Quran 8:63)

Muslim identification and togetherness were not complete, however, among a group who were nominally Muslims but who opposed Muhammad politically, a group usually known as *munafiqun,* an Arabic word initially translated as *Doubters,* from Ethiopic, the language of the Christian church in Abyssinia. It meant doubters or skeptics, those who were of two minds. A revelation stated that:

> They utter with their mouths a thing which is not in their hearts. Allah is best aware of what they hide. (Quran 3:167)

A prominent member of a clan who had political ambitions to become leader of Medina, prior to Muhammad's arrival, led the "doubters." Opposition to these "doubters" hardened after they, as a group, deserted in a battle. The term *doubters* is now more frequently translated as *Hypocrites*.

Muhammad turned his attention to another group, the Jews in Medina after the Badr victory. When the Jews refused to validate or endorse Muhammad's message, and did not recognize him as a Prophet, he made changes that reduced the influence of Judaism. The direction of prayer, *qibla*, faced Mecca now, not Jerusalem; and the observation of the Jewish fast, Day of Atonement, became an observation of the fast of the month of *Ramadan*, now the holiest month for Muslims. Some interpreted this change as a gesture to win the support of some anti-Jewish clans, but these changes were significant. Muhammad moved from wishing to be a prophet in the Judaic tradition and identifying with Jewish customs and beliefs, to developing a separate and distinct identity. The Arab identity of Islam was now complete.

How are we to understand Muhammad's intense reactions towards Jews and his subsequent changes in the adopted Judaic practices? It was in Medina that Muhammad first encountered large Jewish communities, and in his isolation he identified with them. He sought acceptance by the Jewish community; he wanted to be considered a prophet in the Judaic tradition, so it is not surprising that he absorbed many Jewish practices and customs. Could there have been elements of an unconscious transference onto his hosts in this adoptive city in whose religion he sought a common identity? Erikson (1969) describes such an experience when he visited a foreign country and felt annoyance towards his host: he described it as "an unconscious transference onto any host—that is the attribution of a father or older-brother role to anyone in whose home one seeks safety or in whose influence one finds security" (p. 74). He further describes his response as anchored in his own early infantile experiences of having found a loving stepfather in an adopted country.

Muhammad as an orphan had similar experiences in Mecca: he found a loving grandfather and later a caring uncle and some members of his clan. In Medina he sought safety in a protective, and what he hoped would be a nurturing parental clan whose culture, or rich religious tradition, offered solace. His disappointment, when he was rejected as a prophet by the Jews of Medina, is apparent in the immensity of his subsequent reactions to the Jews in Medina and evidenced by the very different treatment accorded to the Jews of Khaybar. In fact the terms of his settlement with the Jews of Khaybar became the model for future Islamic conquests. In general in his later years he no longer harbored a grudge: Jews and Christians were treated the same way as *dhimmis,* a protected people.

A sociological perspective offers some insight into another approach to groups that borrow ideas.

> Every society importing the foreign idea ... inevitably focused on the source of importation—an object of imitation by definition—and reacted to it. Because the model was superior to the imitator in the latter's own perception (its being a model implied that), and the contact itself more often than not served to emphasize the latter's inferiority, the reaction commonly assumed the form of *Ressentiment.* ... *Ressentiment* refers to a psychological state resulting from suppressed feelings of envy and hatred (existential envy) and the impossibility of satisfying these feelings. (Greenfeld, 1992, p. 15; *Ressentiment* was a term coined by Nietzsche and later developed by Max Scheler).

Ressentiment also results in the transformation of values. The new values are "transparent," a form of denial, in the links to earlier forms that are now disclaimed.

Muhammad—His Personality and Role as a Leader

The creation of the *umma,* now a powerful religious community, and the formation of its representational world was influenced by the revelations Muhammad received and by his personality as a leader and as an Apostle of God. The marriages of Muhammad after Khadija's death, and his expressed views about sexuality defined the forms of marriage and family for the *umma.* (The sexual and aggressive drives are the two major instinctual drives in the Freudian psychoanalytic tradition.) The radical and aggressive transformation, however, of petty tribal raids to *jihad,* or Holy War, under Muhammad's leadership profoundly determined the shapes of the *umma* and ultimately its formidable successes.

How do we understand Muhammad as a man, with a distinctive personality, and as a leader? We cannot trace a single crucial event or factor that is central to understanding Muhammad or his life as it unfolded (Rieff, 1963).[11] Nor can we link "psychopathology" (Lifton, 1974) as a basis to explain Muhammad's evolvement into the historical figure he became.[12] What we can clearly identify in the description and activities of Muhammad's life are "ego" strengths.

The *ego* as a metaphorical term has many elusive aspects. Freud used it "to convey the self-preservative executive ego, the agile rider of Plato's two horses: Selfless conscience and selfish instincts" (Vaillant, 1993, p. 7). Later the term evolved to include conscience, instincts, people, and reality as well. In Vaillant's words, the ego "encompasses the adaptive and executive aspects of the human brain: the ability of the mind to integrate, master and make sense of inner and outer reality" (p. 3). He went on to add that "The ultimate developmental ego tasks are wisdom, the fusion of care and justice, and the capacity to consider the needs, rights and past histories of others even as we pay heed to those same facets in ourselves" (p. 8).

It is in relation to the perceptions of and responses to inner and outer realities that mechanisms of defense[13] play a critical role in coping with, and ultimately adapting to, both inner and outer worlds. Critical to the understanding of an individual is the role of defense mechanisms that can be inferred from thoughts, feelings, and actions (Vaillant, 1993, p. 3). The actions of Muhammad, in his adaptation to events in his inner and outer worlds, allow us to draw conclusions about the role of the most common of these mechanisms. These defense mechanisms were transformed to group defense mechanisms when the *umma* shared, supported, and followed in their behavior the action sanctioned by the Apostle of God.

---

[11] Freud was influenced by German historicism and Judeo-Christian millennial thought, so that one crucial event explained all history. If history is predestined, however, there can be no history.

[12] The linking of major historical events only to psychopathology is too reductionistic and deterministic.

[13] While academic psychology has had a mistrust of defense mechanisms, psychoanalysis has ignored rigorous empiricism. Defenses were seen by Freud as pathological, rooted in childhood, linked exclusively to sexual conflict, and ignored in their role in modulating relationships (Vaillant, 1993, p. 13).

There are apparently some authentic descriptions of Muhammad in his youth (Watt, 1961, p. 229). He was of average height, with a large head and prominent forehead. His face was neither round nor plump; he had a hooked nose, large black eyes, a fair complexion, and a pleasant smile. The hair on his head was long, thick, black, and slightly curly. He was a big-boned man; his chest and shoulders were broad and sturdy, and his body was perfectly proportioned. He walked as if pacing downhill—others had difficulty meeting his stride—and when he turned, his whole trunk as well as his head moved. Erikson too had remarked on the perambulatory velocity and vigor of other great men such as Gandhi, Freud, the meditative St. Francis, and Kierkegaard (Erikson, 1969, p. 108).

At the age of 63, Muhammad is said to have "the stature and grace of a much younger man, his eyes were still bright, and there were only a few white hairs in his black hair" (Lings, 1983, p. 337). Watt describes Muhammad as "given to sadness" (Watt, 1961, p. 229),[14] and there were long periods of silence when he was deep in thought; yet he never rested but was always busy. His time was carefully apportioned and he never spoke unnecessarily. He spoke rapidly; his words were always precise and sufficient to clarify the meaning; there were no embellishments. His feelings were firmly under control. When he was annoyed he turned aside; when pleased, lowered his eyes. In dealing with people he was tactful, though occasionally he could be severe; he was generally gentle. His laugh was mostly a smile. His youthful nickname of al-Amin the reliable, captured his serious cast of character.

Muhammad's personal charisma had the greatest impact on his followers. Charisma is often synonymous with the prophetic role in Weber's analysis (Weber, 1963). A charismatic leader has exceptional personality qualities. He is a person endowed with superhuman power or supernatural capabilities whose followers, by their devotion and trust, freely accept his authority, validate his charisma, and legitimate his influence. The intrapsychic processes that linked the prophet and his followers involves a process of mutual idealization. "The prophet assumes . . . a position of

---

[14] For a note on sadness among religious leaders and "a traditional temptation of the homo religiosus," see Erikson, 1958, p. 34.

power and influence that sets him aside . . . and endows him with special capacities and prerogatives" (Meissner, 1988, p. 32). The needs of the followers are met and fulfilled by identification with the prophet, his mission, and his teaching. The reciprocal ties between the leader and followers further enhances idealization of each other as well as the group, allowing some gratification of narcissistic needs.

Even though the Quran is remarkably free of humor and is filled with high seriousness, and at times irascibility, there are many stories and vignettes in his legends that describe a lighter side to Muhammad's personality and his charisma. He laughed easily and joked and shared happy and sad moments with children and his wives. He was reasonable, rational, and tactful; and as evinced in Medina, successfully mediated problems between the clans. He demonstrated loyalty to others, and inspired loyalty from others in turn. He conceptualized complex events, but consulted with trusted aides before major events, and then planned necessary actions accordingly; he was calculating and shrewd. All of these qualities made him a natural group leader who, even if he had not been a Prophet and a Messenger of God, would have inspired his followers.

Other stories tell of Muhammad's gentleness and tender feelings (Lings, 1983, pp. 134, 211, 288; Watt, 1961, p. 102). These intimate images of Muhammad offer an interesting human counterpoint to the picture of his larger role in the conduct of social and public affairs. The smaller, vivid details, which have an inner consistency, bring to life broader historical and biographical events.

The wife of a Companion, Jafar, who was killed in a battle, described how Muhammad broke the news to them. When she was busy with her household chores, Muhammad came to her house and asked for the three sons of Jafar. When she brought them to him, he placed his arms around them, and smelling them as a mother would a baby, burst into tears. He then told her that Jafar had been killed. He left her home only after leaving instructions that food should be prepared for the household as they were in mourning. He met the daughter of another Companion, Zayd, who had died in the same battle: he clasped the child into his arms and wept without restraint.

Muhammad also had a special fondness for playing with children. His wife, Aisha, at the age of 10 was still playing with toys, and he would join in her games with a youthful spirit and laughed when she called some of her dolls "Solomon's horses." He loved his granddaughter, Umanah, and took her once or twice to the mosque, perched on his shoulder, while he recited the Quran. Many children were his friends. One child, with whom he joked and entered into childish games, appeared very sad one day and told Muhammad that a pet nightingale had died; he did whatever he could to reduce his grief. Muhammad's thoughtfulness also extended to animals. Just before the conquest of Mecca, his men passed by a bitch with a litter of newborn pups. He gave orders not to disturb the pups and posted a man to stand guard until all the contingents had passed.

Muhammad was charismatic, so jealousy was inevitable and frequent among his several wives. Although he was aware of their feelings, he would tease them about their jealous natures. Once he brought an onyx necklace into the room where his family was assembled and announced he would give the necklace to the one dearest to him. After keeping them in suspense and guessing, he clasped it around the neck of his granddaughter, Umanah. The Prophet also had an exceedingly sensitive side. Muhammad had become very attached to a Coptic Christian slave girl, Mariyah, sent by the ruler of Egypt. His wives, concerned that he spent too much time with her, became jealous and hounded him until he swore he would not see Mariyah again. A revelation, now known as the *Sura* of Banning, brought resolution to this crisis. It opened with a rebuke to the Prophet for yielding to his wives:

> O Prophet, why bannest thou, to please thy wives,
> that which God hath made lawful unto thee?

After absolving him of the oath, the next verse addressed the wives:

> It may be, if he divorced you, that his lord will
> give him wives in your stead who are better than
> you, submissive unto God, believing, devout,
> penitent, inclined unto worship and fasting,
> widows and virgin maids (Quran 66:1–5)

The wives now chastened by the threat were not allowed to see him for a month, after which time calm was restored.

A Controversial Marriage

The most controversial of Muhammad's marriages was his marriage to Zaynab in March, 627 c.e. It has been "criticized by his contemporaries, and has been the object of virulent attacks by European scholars" (Watt, 1961, p. 156). Zaynab had been married to Zayd, formerly a Christian slave given to Muhammad by Khadija, and now his adopted son. Muhammad had gone to Zayd's house, but Zayd was out, and he saw Zaynab, scantily clad, and supposedly was smitten by her. He declined to enter her house and went away saying to himself: "Praise be to God, praise to the Manager of Hearts." On Zayd's return, Zaynab told him of Muhammad's visit, his refusal to enter the house, and his cryptic utterance as he left. Zayd immediately went to Muhammad and offered to divorce Zaynab. Muhammad said no, and to keep Zaynab; but Zayd could no longer tolerate his marriage and divorced Zaynab. After an appropriate waiting period, Muhammad arranged his own marriage to Zaynab. This action has been justified in the Quran which states:

> When you told the man (Zayd) whom God had favoured and whom you have favoured yourself, "Keep your wife and worship God," you were concealing within yourself what God was to reveal. You feared (the judgement of) men, but you should rather fear God. When Zayd divorced her, we gave her to you in marriage, so that for the believers there may be no guilt in (marrying) the wives of their adopted sons when they divorce them.... Muhammad is the father of no men among you. He is the Messenger of God and the seal of the prophets. (Quran 33:37–40)

The criticism of this marriage was based on several grounds, but the principal complaint was that Zaynab was the wife of an adopted son; therefore, their relationship was incestuous. The Quranic verse challenged this, implying that treatment of an adopted son as a real son was objectionable. Medina had a strong matrilineal tradition and marital relations in pre-Islamic Arabia were considerably looser. The relationships toward adoptive sons,

A Charismatic Leader

therefore, had a different meaning in this newer approach and brought a complete break with the past.

Later Muslim writers stress the asexual nature of the marriage to Zaynab. Muhammad, they state, was only changing the social rules related to adoption and contracting a marriage for political reasons (Rodinson, 1980, p. 207). Zaynab, according to these writers, at 35, was past her prime, and therefore could not have been desirable. It was unlikely, Watt (1961) states, that a man at the age of 56 could be "carried away by a passion for a woman of thirty-five or more" (p. 158). Other Christian writers, however, stress the "highly inflammable passions" of the Prophet (Rodinson, 1980, p. 207). Rodinson points out that it is the Islamic traditions and histories that suggest it was not a Western fiction. It is these sources that describe Muhammad's disturbed state of mind after glimpsing Zaynab. Furthermore, she was described as being remarkably beautiful. Public opinion, quoted in the Quran itself, would not have questioned the marriage if it were a mere legal or social issue. A *hadith* (or tradition) in fact has jealous Aisha caustically alluding to some Doubters who claimed that Muhammad had withheld some revelations: "If the Prophet had concealed anything of the revelation, it would have been those verses he ought to have kept hidden" (Tirmidhi, Sahih, Kitab 44, quoted in Rodinson, 1980, p. 207). It was not the amorous nature of the Prophet, according to Rodinson, that invited comment but "what struck them as odd was that the rule should have been so exactly calculated to satisfy desires which were for once in conflict with social taboos" (Rodinson, 1980, p. 207).

Attitudes towards Sexuality

It is the amorous nature of this incident, however, that has invited the most derisive comment. While the effect of Zaynab's physical attractiveness on the Prophet is not mentioned in earlier sources, it is clear that later Muslims maintained there was "no monkery in Islam" (Watt, 1961, p. 158). Their ascetic tradition, like the Jewish one, did not include celibacy. A *sura* from the Quran supports this. "But monasticism they (the Christians) invented—we ordained it not for them only seeking Allah's pleasure..." (Quran 57:27). Muhammad's chivalrous character and virility were magnified and imaginatively embellished over time (the ability of leaders is often magnified by their followers). Pickthall, in a comment on the Quran, clearly accepts that "The Prophet has never been regarded by Muslims as other than a human Messenger of God; sanctity has never been identified with celibacy. For Christendom, the strictest religious ideal has been celibacy; monogamy is already a concession to human nature. For Muslims, monogamy is the ideal, polygamy the concession to human nature" (Pickthall, 1930, p. 405). This somewhat defensive tone could be understood as a response to the harsh views and polemical, sanctimonious writings of some Western orientalists regarding Muhammad's marriages and sexuality.

The acceptance of sexuality and sexual drives is clear in the strictures against the extremes of asceticism. It is alleged that Uthman, one of the most ascetic of Muhammad's Companions, who had been an ascetic before joining Islam, was so intent on controlling his desires that he requested permission from the Prophet to be made a eunuch and to spend the rest of his life as a wandering beggar. "Hast thou not in me a fair example?" reportedly said the Prophet. "And I go into women, and I eat meat, and I fast, and I break my fast. He is not of my people who maketh men eunuchs or maketh himself a eunuch" (Muhammad ibn Sa'd-Kitab at-Tabaqat al-Kabir, as quoted in Lings [1983, p. 165]).

The revelations, moreover, continually stressed the importance of thanking God for the blessings of life.

> Beautified for mankind is love of the joys (that come) from women and offspring, and stored up heaps of gold and silver and horses branded (with their mark) and cattle and land. (Quran 3:14)

> And of His signs is His creation for you of consorts from amongst yourselves, that ye may find rest in them, and His ordaining of love between you and mercy.
> Verily therein are signs for people who reflect. (Quran 30:21)

Natural pleasures consecrated by thanks to God were forms of worship. The Prophet even spoke of the pleasures of the senses and of prayer in the same context:

> It hath been given me to love perfume and women and coolness hath been brought to mine eyes in the prayer. (Muhammad ibn Sa'd. I/2, 112, quoted by Lings [1983, p. 166]; "Coolness of the eyes" is a favorite Arabic expression for joy and delight)

The Question of Matrilinearity

Muhammad made several other contributions toward the establishment of a more patrilineal system. The change was from a tribal matriarchal system where the family structure was weak, as the tribe provided several supports, to a more patriarchal family based system. This would enhance the role of both parents in child rearing. For instance, one marriage reform in the Quran prescribes that when a woman is divorced, which was common in Arabia, she should have a "waiting period" of three months before remarriage. In a matrilineal system, where property passed through the maternal line, proof of paternity was relatively unimportant. A total change in this system to a patrilineal system would not have been easily accomplished. The Quranic injunction of a waiting period of three months prior to remarriage would now leave little doubt about a child's paternity and was a major step in the transformation towards a patrilineal society.

Other aspects of this move towards a patrilineal structure were reflected in Quran verses revealed after the Battle of Uhud. These verses focus on the plight of orphans and widows, and define some of the rights of women considered deprived among the pagan Arabs. One verse is the basis of the Islamic system of polygamy:

> If you are afraid that you will treat the orphans unjustly, then marry what women seem good to you, twos and threes and fours; if you are afraid you will not deal equitably, then one; or (the captives) that your right hands possess; then you are more likely not to be unfair. (Quran 4:3)

The marriage reforms of the Quran should be considered with regard to the social context of the time. Islam may have regularized and imposed a patriarchal structure. Watt suggests that unscrupulous guardians might have prevented their female wards from marrying so they would have unrestricted access to their wards' property. The Quran, by encouraging a man to have several wives, would allow girls who were old enough to be properly married (Watt, 1961, p. 154). The family would also be based more on the individual than on the group and clan, as the older custom had defined. The Quranic rules of inheritance further attempted to ensure a fairer distribution of property among individuals, including women.

Some of Muhammad's marriages were to widows of Emigrants who had died in the battles at Badr and Uhud, while others were attempts to form alliances for political reasons. These alliances can be seen in the marriages he arranged for his daughters and those of his associates.

Muhammad, in his marriage to Zaynab, received revelations that stressed the difference between the Prophet and his followers. The permission he received from God to have more than four wives was for him alone, not for the rest of the believers. His wives were given the title of "mothers of the faithful" and were forbidden to marry anyone else after his death.

Sexuality has to be understood within the cultural, social, and historical context. In pre-Islamic Arabia a considerable amount of evidence suggests the social system was a matrilineal one, except in some areas such as Mecca, where it was patrilineal (Watt, 1961, p. 153). In the matrilineal system, marriage did not mean a woman left her family: the husband came to visit her for periodic visits, and a woman could have polyandrous relationships with two or more husbands from different clans. According to Watt (1961), one report, which may exaggerate pre-Islamic marital customs, suggested that some women had up to 10 husbands (p. 153). Another report states that some women were sexually involved with any man who came to them (p. 154).

Muhammad's marriages need to be examined within the social context of his culture. He grew up in a culture with few or no ascetic traditions and no tradition of strict monogamy. A culture that permits polygamous relationships allows a freer attitude towards sexuality; celibacy would be almost incomprehensible. Separation or divorce would be considerably easier. The Quran now laid down a structure that defined marriage along more patrilineal lines but also retained some features of the matrilineal tradition by allowing a limited form of polygamy. The individual family instead of the clan and tribe would become more important.

Muhammad: A Warrior Prophet

Psychoanalytic theory states that the second major instinctual drive is the aggressive drive. The expressions of the aggressive drive are modified by the ego and its defenses under the pressures of inner urges and outer reality. It is this area—the expression of aggression—that Muhammad as religious leader received even more criticism. The Christian world, whose kind and gentle leader was crucified, has been dominated by images of a religion of peace and found it "scandalous and even wicked that Muhammad had to fight his way to peace, power and victory. Islam had been dubbed the religion of the sword, a faith which has abandoned true spirituality by sanctifying violence and intolerance" (Armstrong, 1992, p. 164). Earthly success for Christians was not a spiritual triumph. Rejection of this world, suffering and dying for Christ, and a long history of persecution and martyrdom in the early Christian church had defined a view of religion and religious leaders based on love, charity, and humility.

Muhammad was a very different religious leader, one who turned to arms to support a community that at that time had no other means of support. It was this use of force, however, that radically altered the actual shapes of the group and offered a new ideal shape. Initially, raids or *razzias* were a tribal practice, directed mainly to the capture of camels or other animals of a neighboring clan or tribe. Surprise and superiority in quick raids were successful, with a very small loss of life. The first raiding party in 623 c.e. was a small group of 30 men who ambushed a Meccan caravan. A month later 60 men intercepted another, better defended caravan, and some arrows were fired by a Muslim. This small beginning was the first warlike act of Islam. Other expeditions, some led by Muhammad, were unsuccessful and disheartening failures.

The later raids or *razzias*, however, became more aggressive as the *umma* transformed them into religious missions directed by revelations against the unjust Meccans and unbelievers. In one ambush at Naklah, a Meccan was killed; and the transformation was soon complete. A rationalization of this transformation is reflected and justified in the Quranic verses.[15]

> Warfare is ordained for you, though it is hateful unto you; but it may happen that ye hate a thing which is good for you, and it may happen that you love a thing which is bad for you. Allah knoweth, ye know not. (Quran 2:216)
>
> For persecution ... (by the Meccans) ... is worse than killing. (Quran 2:217)

The *jihad* against Mecca continued, however, until it surrendered. This was certainly facilitated further by the rapid and vast increase in the number of armed men. No longer were these small tribal *razzias* with little or no loss of life. If a pagan tribe that was raided accepted Islam, however, they were exempted from further raids. This acceptance was another transformation, because this meant permanent peace with this tribe, increased numbers for Muhammad, and a measure of stability within the *umma*.

Two months after the first killing at Naklah 300 men fought at the Battle of Badr (624 c.e.). A year later 700 defenders fought at Uhud against 3,000 Meccans. At the Battle of the Trench, 2 years later, 3,000 defenders were pitted against 10,000 Meccans. At the conquest of Mecca (630 c.e.) there were 10,000 men, and in the same year Muhammad led 30,000 men, 10,000 of them mounted, on his Syrian campaign to the north to challenge the Byzantine Empire. Thus, in the short span of 7 years the small *razzias*, beginning with 30 men, had become a force of 30,000 men, a thousand times larger.

Muhammad had become an accomplished military leader and had built a formidable force in the *umma*. He dressed for battle with a "turban about his helmet and donned his breastplate, under which he wore a coat of mail belted with a leather

---

[15] Rationalization, a very common process, offers an explanation that is either logically consistent or ethically acceptable for actions whose true motives may not be perceived. Despite its defensive function it is not a mechanism of defense (Laplanche & Pontalis, 1973, pp. 375–376).

sword-belt. He had ... girt on his sword and slung his shield across his back" (Lings, 1983, p. 175). In the Battle of Uhud a horseman, with a drawn sword, came at Muhammad. Muhammad took a spear from a Companion, shook off others who had closed in to protect him, as if they were no more than flies on a camel's back, and stepped in front of them all. It was with a grim and deadly earnestness that he faced the horseman and before he could be struck, mortally wounded the attacker in the neck with a powerful thrust. As one of his Companions described, 'When the Messenger of God made a deliberate effort toward some end, there was no earnestness that could compare with it" (Lings, 1983, p. 187).

At the Battle of Badr, Muhammad exhorted his men to advance and not retreat with the promise, from God, of Paradise to those who were slain. He devised a battle cry *"Ya mansur amit"* (O thou whom God hath made victorious, slay) which resounded on the battlefield as his men surged forward. Besides the war cry *"Allahu Akbar"* (God is great), at the siege of Khaybar, Muhammad added *"Kharibat Khaybar"* (Khaybar is crushed) in a "triumphant play upon the letters of the name" (Lings, 1983, p. 265).

Muhammad was fair to captives in war, as shown in the Battle of Badr. They were not killed as custom allowed, but were freed on ransom. The captives and the booty were not the property of the individual captor but were the property of the group. The group included everyone who had taken part in the expedition, which supported the needs of the group over the individual's, and reinforced group solidarity.

Muhammad always sought counsel before going into battle, particularly from his two trusted Companions, Abu Bakr and Amar. These consultations were supported by a revelation that stated:

> Consult them about affairs, and when thou art resolved, then trust in God. (Quran 3:159)

Significant contributions to battle planning and war strategy are part of Muhammad's legacy. After plans were decided, Muhammad insisted that the preparations be kept secret. He also employed deception and guile to maintain the element of surprise in an attack and employed elements of psychological warfare. In the final attack on Mecca he ordered his men to spread out and to each light a fire after dark. Ten thousand campfires could be seen on the outskirts of the sacred territory, suggesting a far larger force than existed and significantly increasing the Meccans' fears.

Muhammad used a secret agent at the Battle of the Trench in Medina to provoke conflict between the Jewish Qurayzah clan and the Meccans. "This agent asked permission to lie and the Prophet said, 'Say what thou wilt to draw them off from us for war is deception'" (Lings, 1983, p. 225, quoting traditions from Ibn Ishaq and Waqidi). On one occasion Muhammad sent Muslims from the tribe of Khajraj as secret assassins who went with his blessings to kill one of the Jewish leaders of Khaybar as a warning not to fraternize with the enemies of Islam, the Meccans.

The Promise of Immortality

The pagan Arabs who were experienced raiders fought by charging in a disorganized fashion, often retreating, and then returning to the battlefield. In the Battle of Badr, the Prophet arranged a line formation, the *Tabiya*, with great success. The men were ordered into straight regular ranks, and Muhammad walked alongside them, pushing back anyone out of line with an arrow. The following revelation (in *Sura* as-Saff—"The Ranks") supported such a formation:

> Lo, Allah loveth those who battle for his cause in ranks, as if they were a solid structure. (Quran 61:4)

His men were no longer individually well trained and bellicose nomads but a mass of men that could act in unison with a brute ferocity that was effectively controlled, even during battle. The organizing principle that Muhammad defined was the group equivalent of an integrative and synthetic ego function that channeled and directed the aggressive instinctual drives of a multitude of separate individuals.[16]

---

[16] On the role of drill and command structures that provided European armies in the seventeenth century with "the equivalent of a central nervous system" see the very

In a recent work, McNeill suggests that people who move together in drill tend to bond in a manner that consolidates group solidarity (McNeill, 1995). He adds that the "euphoric response to keeping together in time" increases "muscular bonding" which is the "surest, most speedy and efficacious" way to create a community "that our species has hit upon." McNeill convincingly demonstrates that moving together creates a selfless camaraderie that offers a competitive advantage and increases the effectiveness of an army in a military endeavor. Thus Muhammad, by training and moving his men into battle in ranks, may have increased their muscular bonding and group solidarity, and ultimately their effectiveness, when they fought as a solid structure.[17]

It was the promise of martyrdom and paradise that was probably the most potent factor that Muhammad brought to the annals of warfare. In the Battle of Badr, Muhammad had exhorted his men by saying:

> By Him in whose hand is the soul of Muhammad, no man will be slain this day . . . but God shall straightway enter him into paradise. (Quoted in Lings, 1983, p. 147)

At the Battle of Uhud, a Helper said:

> O Messenger of God. We have before us one of two good things: either God will grant us mastery over them . . . , or else God will grant us martyrdom. I care not which it may be, for verily there is good in both. (Quoted in Lings, 1983, p. 176)

Throughout history battles were often ritual engagements governed by rules of combat. Soldiers fought for kings or emperors, but emotional ties to distant rulers are often weak, so to fight until death would be uncommon for an entire army. Muhammad's promise that no one would be slain, and the tempting

---

enlightening discussion by McNeill (1982, pp. 123–124). What McNeill calls the "equivalent of a central nervous system" hints at what we would call the synthetic function of a group ego formed within a shared representational world that defined and directed group action in war.

[17] There are several traditions which enjoined the faithful to pray in "rows." This supported structure and organization in another area. This promoted a sense of equality and solidarity. The prayer ground was "the first drill ground of Islam" (Hitti, 1968, p. 39).

offers of a heavenly paradise, transformed the odds of war by offering a new form of symbolic immortality.

Symbolic immortality is more than a simple denial of death. According to Lifton (1974), it is part of a "compelling, life enhancing imagery binding each individual to significant groups and events removed from him in place and time" (p. 37). He suggested that a sense of immortality may be expressed in many ways. Biologically it is expressed by links to ancestors and living through children. From a theological perspective, immortality is evidenced in beliefs of life after death. Immortality is also expressed creatively through "works" that survive beyond the individual. Mystics experience immortality in a oneness with nature and by transcending, if temporarily, time and death. He added further that "much of human history consists of the struggle to achieve, maintain, and reaffirm a shared or collective sense of immortality under constantly changing psychic and material conditions" (Lifton, 1974, p. 37). Most of these forms of immortality, the biological, theological, and creative as well as mystical, are individual forms of immortality that are defined, supported and sanctioned by the family, community, or culture.

Muhammad offered a totally different form of immortality in war for an entire group of armed warriors. Death did not really exist for them; they had absolutely nothing to lose. Instead they could gain victory on earth or look forward to paradise where pleasures and happiness abounded. Life and death were both transcended. War was a celestial game in the magic realm between heaven and earth.

Lifton quotes another leader, the leader of a secular "religion," who had in another much later time defined this issue well.

> A leader who can instill these transcendent principles (of revolutionary immortality) in his followers, can turn the most extreme threat and disintegration into an ordered certainty of mission, convert the most incapacitating death anxiety into a death conquering calm of near invincibility. (Lifton, 1968, pp. 69–70)[18]

Muhammad offered theological immortality as well as group immortality to his Companions in war. The intensity and the

---

[18] Mao had attempted to replace the biological mode of immortality offered by the Chinese family system to the newer revolutionary immortality, to maintain his revolution

excitement of a battle setting is charged with emotional fervor and fear as comrades lie wounded and dying nearby. Reason and instinct do not allow us full comprehension of men who fight to the death. The warrior's denial of the elemental fear of death, reinforced by a group denial, could increase group fearlessness while reducing the possibility of stark fear and panic that is rapidly communicated and often determines defeat or disaster in battle. The offer of paradise for martyrdom and dying for one's faith made Islamic warriors even more formidable, and nearly invincible, as they faced their foes with their own death-conquering calm.

The promise of martyrdom for the group and Islam could also be considered a form of altruistic sacrifice: to kill or be killed for the sake of a group (Durkheim, 1897/1951).[19] Durkheim, in writing about altruistic suicide, common in the past from Gaul to Japan, noted that:

> [The individual] must be almost completely absorbed in the group and the latter accordingly, very highly integrated. For the parts to have so little life of their own, the whole must indeed be a compact continuous mass . . . massive cohesion is indeed that of societies where the above practices obtain" (Durkheim, 1897/1951, p. 221).

Muhammad offered a massively cohesive world where the social, political, and religious worlds were one.

Islam had no place or need for altruistic suicide, but dying for the faith offered a novel form of aggression directed outward. McNeill (1982) observed that "Moslem victories rested entirely on a new social discipline and religious faith that united all the tribes of Arabia into a single armed polity without affecting the design of weaponry in the slightest" (p. 21). He went on to note that "the rise of Islam and the establishment of the early caliphate proves that ideas, too, matter in human affairs and can enter decisively into the balance of forces as to define lost lasting and fundamental human patterns" (p. 21).

---

as it faltered and as he became older. The rapid demise of Marxist secular revolutionary "ideology" contrasts with the relative "immortality" of religious belief systems.

[19] According to Durkheim, altruistic suicide is suicide as a duty. The weight of society is brought to bear on an individual who is led to destroy himself. The sacrifice is imposed by society for social ends. War offers a form of socially accepted altruistic homicide and with the ever present risk of personal death a form of group altruistic suicide.

It was the group denial of fear and anxiety, the promise of martyrdom, and the pleasures of paradise that provided "the social discipline" for Islamic warriors to conquer Arabia and soon large parts of the known world. The religious faith in the ideal shape of the community and in dying for the group in *jihad* that Muhammad offered in his revelatory "ideas" further supported and ultimately altered the balance of forces from Gibraltar to the borders of China.

What was the nature of leadership Muhammed provided? Approaching this study from the view of the analyst as well as the historian, we rely on the Quran, the rich traditions recorded, and the available biographies. There is always caution when studying remote historical figures and distant events. We have, however, a well-differentiated theoretical structure that suggests the importance of developmental events and their impact in later life, events which offer reasonable judgments about emotional ties in relationships and attachments to symbolic social structures. We also can assess ego skills and meanings from patterned behavior. What is striking in the available historical detail is how Muhammad as a leader, in a slow, careful manner, developed his group: the community of Islam.

The pre-Islamic world consisted of small groups of clans and tribes. The harsh imperatives and dangers of life in the desert dictated the individual's dependency on his extended family and clan for survival. The basic needs—trust, economic, and safety—of an individual that are met by the group would be evident on a daily basis. As no larger social unit existed outside the tribe, an individual could not rely on laws for support or protection from the dangers presented by the desert and other tribes.

Muhammad grew up in this traditional world of clans and tribes. The history he heard from bards and storytellers was the history of groups and of their unique leaders in Arabia. The clan tradition of manliness or *muruwah* that defined the ideal man were ideals that supported the clan and allowed success in the struggle for a desert existence. Other than the ideal individual, the individual—as an individual—did not exist. It is thus understandable that there are few details of Muhammad's life before the age of 40, in his maturity in any event, when he became a leader of a group in Mecca. The Arabs' culture saw the world largely in terms of groups, clans, or tribes, in interaction. Unless an individual was a leader or chief, he was just a member of a group. Individuality had little meaning; groups depended on their chiefs, whose decisions to march to new pasture or to go to war determined the survival of a group.

Muhammad grew up in this world of groups, and he understood that his success depended on the group he built. His personal identity was initially largely a group identity. His representational world had been shaped by his extended family, the Hashim clan, and the Quraysh tribe in Mecca. The *actual* shapes of his world, however, were very different from the *ideal* shapes of his world at every level. He suffered severe conflicts: he was a man who had an illustrious ancestry but who had no son; he was a member of a clan whose fortunes had declined; and he lived in a pagan world surrounded by powerful empires and universalist religions. Resolution of the conflicts began when he received revelations from God that offered him a new role as a religious leader, and these revelations brought him into serious conflict with his own people and subsequently led to his persecution. The small group he formed was forced into exile, and they migrated to Medina. A small subgroup had previously departed for Abyssinia.

Growing up with a long tradition of clans and tribes, and personally experiencing the impact and power of groups, made Muhammad sensitive to group issues. Thus in his plans and actions it is evident that groups were critical to his decisions. When he realized he was no longer safe in Mecca without the protection of his clan, he negotiated with other clans in Medina. The Medinans saw him as someone who would stop their fratricidal clan wars and they offered him the role of an arbitrator in settling the ongoing clan feuds.

Soon after his arrival Muhammad drew up the Constitution of Medina, which was a turning point in his life. He realized that the religious doctrines he espoused had little meaning without support from a political body. The only model of authority then available was that of a tribal chief, and the chief's authority was the consensual authority, begrudgingly given by those who considered him just a first among equals. His main role was to settle disputes if called upon and, more critically, decide when the tribe had to move or respond to threats from other tribes. The size and power of a tribe, limited by range and geography, could not increase much until it divided into subtribes and clans, but there was no reason to join other tribes except to become a confederation for defense or offense. The wealth of a nomadic tribe also could increase only by enlarging its flocks or by initiating *razzias* on other tribes. It would seem the tribal model with the limited power of a chief offered Muhammad few useful ideas that would further the spread of his religion and increase its numbers or strength. Even in the towns the *Mala*, or tribal council, had only limited moral and persuasive authority among the recognized nobles.

Muhammad converted his limited political power as the head of a small body of migrants to a religious authority over several Muslim, pagan, and Jewish tribes. The original Medinan *umma* confirmed the tribal customs and organization; each tribe retained its privileges and its obligations to others within the tribe. In the *umma*, however, all the other rights were waived and all disputes were resolved by Muhammad. Muhammad thus carefully preserved the social traditions and tribal values of pre-Islamic Arabia: he did not supplant; he supplemented. Muhammad had only dealt with the civil and political relations of his members and those outside; relations between members—marital and property rights among members of the same tribe—retained their pre-Islamic heritage. For the new members of the *umma* there was minimal interference, only huge potential gain. It was these careful, limited, and judicious inclinations of the Prophet that would aid in his success. A vast and sudden change threatens stability by being a threat in itself. There was a new group solidarity bound together by his personality. A tribe could maintain its tribal identity and forge in addition a new and larger, powerful identity based in the beginning on simple practices. After the initial "submission" (*islam*) one only had the daily prayer, almsgiving, and a commitment to worship Allah.

There were important differences that the *umma* fashioned. Religion replaced blood as the defining social bond. The *umma* banned blood feuds, and settled disputes by arbitration, which increased unity. The Sheikh of the *umma*, Muhammad, had absolute religious authority given by the people to God who had conferred them onto His Messenger and chosen Apostle; his powers were not conditioned by the tribe's approval or easily revoked. Muhammad was the head of a new supertribe, a religious "tribe." From the beginning he held both civil and religious authority. Previously there had been no political authority and no real state, religion alone could provide such authority. Muhammad now became both God's representative and the head of a state, and in this role, he received a historically alien authority. Instead of becoming a religion within a state or a state religion it became the very state!

It was this authority, with the establishment of mutual trust and justice, however, that would cement and unite so many independent and autonomous tribes. The drawing up of a constitution was extraordinary and added to his authority; but it was the transforming of the *razzias* into the *jihad* that radically altered the shapes of his new *umma* and its fortunes.

As a leader, Muhammad was trusted by his followers; his Companions were ready to offer their lives for him. He consulted with them often and followed their advice, as many traditions confirm; he took his group into unventured territory. He was cautious, prudent, careful; he planned well. He took calculated risks and in spite of some reverses, he still kept his *muhajirun* (Emigrants) and *ansar* (Helpers) followers. A major wrong move might have been disastrous for his group, but he was shrewd, calculating, farsighted—even visionary.

Muhammad conceptualized and integrated complex abstract relationships, just as he was able to integrate perceptions of events among varied tribes before taking action. He applied ruse and guile when at war, and he was fair, deliberate, and tactful when he made peace with tribes.

He was thus flexible and adaptable with good "testing of reality." Those tribes he could not directly convert, he persuaded in part by punitive raids from Medina, but he primarily applied diplomacy. He played on conflicts between different factions, offering the advantage of an alliance with an increasingly strong *umma* or a share in the booty from Muslim *razzias*. Thus, the security experienced within Medina was extended to larger areas by building a web of relationships and later by treaties or direct conquests.

The linking of biography and creative product can reveal defenses used by the individual; these defenses are not the imaginings of an analyst. Defenses are not manifestations of pathology but are extraordinarily human instruments of adaptation. The life of Muhammad amply illustrates mature defenses, such as altruism, sublimation, humor, and anticipation (mature defenses have been correlated with several measures of successful adult outcomes [Vaillant, 1992]). There is evidence too of tragic displacement, as seen in his ambivalent relationships with the Jewish community in belief and practice, a community Muhammad so closely identified with when he came to Medina.

It is this maturity of defenses, and once again his integrative skills, that allowed Muhammad to become a statesman. He reconciled with the most implacable of his foes, the Quraysh of Mecca; and in future years the Quraysh were to provide some of the outstanding leaders of Islam. Muhammad embraced into his community people who were not yet ready for Islam; thus, supplying a model of trust and acceptance for his associates, and establishing a model for unity and ideal group relations. Muhammad provided an auxiliary ego and a set of functions for the group—reality testing, adaptive defense styles, and integrative capacities—that were critical for survival in the beginning and ultimately became a model for the group's headlong and impressive expansion.

It was the tradition of aggression and war and Muhammad's claims to the exclusivity of a position, however, that left problems: a persistent theme of Islamic history. A "claim to exclusive validity for one's own position . . . (is) . . . fatal to the open search for truth. Such a claim to exclusivity has been, indeed, a standing temptation of all the monotheistic communities" (Hodgson, 1974, p. 186).

In summary, the representational world of the *umma* was almost entirely defined by Muhammad. He incorporated some of the shapes from pre-Islamic Arabia. He modified and merged old tribal traditions and institutions. The revelations from Allah linked a hoary past to a glorious future, so that for believers, earth became linked to paradise; and for sinners, to hell. The challenges from a Judeo-Christian world were incorporated and transcended in Arabic to a purely Arab vision. Every community need was provided for within the new ideal shapes that led to structures which defined family, clan, legal systems, beliefs, rituals, practices, and, ultimately, the shapes of an *umma* and a religion. These shapes became the basis of a new culture with its own icons and symbols, and gave birth to a new civilization. The Quran, a record of his revelations, and the *Hadiths,* the collections of the sayings of the Prophet, were immortalized after his death, and these writings became the foundation of the entire representational world of Islam. They became the basis of a religious "constitution" that to this day provides the guiding principles of Islam. For large stretches of its history, the ideal shapes of Islam in its representational world were close to the actual shapes.

The Prophet, thus, not only provided for the basic needs but provided for almost every need of his *umma*. Mutual trust on every level was the key. In the short span of slightly more than two decades Muhammad altered life in Arabia forever. He clearly understood that to alter the simple forms of tribal life and bring them together and to challenge the great empires of his day, nothing less than a total transformation was required; anything else would have failed. He succeeded.

12

The Empire of Islam

THE death of Muhammad brought a crisis in the young Muslim *umma* and an immediate question about the survival of the state. The Prophet left no directives for choosing a successor; there was no tribal council, like the *majlis,* to exercise authority. In his unique role as God's exclusive exponent on earth, Muhammad was precluded from nominating a successor, and the only Arab precedent for succession was the tribal election of a new chief. The men closest to Muhammad felt all Muslims were bound by a contract and that they had a special duty to guide the pattern of life founded by the Prophet; and thus through the collaborative action of three men, Abu Bakr, Umar, and Abu Ubaida, Abu Bakr was chosen as the *Khalifa* or "Deputy" of the Prophet.

As Caliph, Abu Bakr exercised authority in a different manner from that of the traditional Arab tribal sheikh. He was not a prophet; he had executive powers and authority over the community and the region. It was his control of the army, however, that gave him political and military authority, which over time became essential to the office of Caliph.

In the theologically based view of later historians, the first challenge the Caliph faced became known to tradition as the Wars of the *Ridda,* or Apostasy. The refusal of tribes to recognize the authority of Abu Bakr, however, was not a relapse to paganism but a termination of a contract on the death of a party. The Prophet's death and the selection of a replacement, a selection in which they had not participated, led most tribes to suspend both their treaty relationships and the tribute (*zakat*). Abu Bakr immediately undertook military subjugation of these tribes. In the process an army was created. The Muslims found a savior in the military genius of Khalid ibn Al-Walid. In several quick and bloody campaigns he attacked and subdued the resistant tribes. Many tribes with small factions or clans who previously recognized Muhammad were now forced to accept Islam and pay the *zakat* taxes.

Several new prophets did arise in nearby areas, but they were declared false. It was subsequently declared that Muhammad was the last of the prophets; there could be no other. The essential oneness of Muslims was now asserted and this unity was soon proved, even before the "Wars of *Ridda*" were over, when the Arabs launched aggressive raids on the Byzantine and Sasanian empires.

Implicit in Muhammad's teaching was a claim to universalism and universal authority. His *haram* had no natural boundary limits: he sent military expeditions into Byzantine lands, and he supposedly sent missions to the rulers of all the great states, seeking submission to his religious message. The major expedition into Syria planned before Muhammad's death was duly sent, but it was the momentum and enthusiasm of the "Wars of *Ridda*" that pushed the Muslims into the frontier regions of the great empires.

At the beginning of the seventh century, the two rival Empires of Byzantine and Persia ruled the Near and Middle East. The Byzantine Empire—Greek and Christian in culture and religion, Roman in its administration—was ruled from Constantinople with the basis of its power the huge plateau of Anatolia and Egypt and Syria to the south. Egypt's Coptic population and the Aramaic of Syria did not share the Greek culture or race; they resented the crushing taxes imposed by the Empire and the persecution of their Monophysite churches by the imperial (Greek) church. The Jews in Palestine had suffered even more from Byzantine oppression.

The Persian Sasanid Empire resembled Byzantium in that its core was the Iranian plateau, and it ruled over a religiously disaffected people in Iraq. The majority of the people were Christian, Jewish, or Manichean who had suffered under the Mazdean

The Empire of Islam

hierarchy. The last of the wars between Persia and Byzantium were fought between 602 and 628, leaving Byzantium the weakened victor, but both sides were too weak and exhausted to face the unsuspected menace from the south. Islam was ready to burst upon them. Under the energetic generalship of Khalid ibn al-Walid, now known as the "Sword of God," the raids against these exhausted empires proved immensely successful and yielded vast amounts of booty.

In 634 c.e. 2 years after Muhammad's death, Abu Bakr died. Abu Bakr's successor, Umar, decided to systematically occupy the imperial agricultural provinces. Syria was invaded; the surprise raids led to the occupation of Damascus. In 636 c.e. the Byzantine army at Yarmuk in Syria was totally destroyed. At a critical moment the Arab auxiliaries, a major portion of the Byzantine army, defected to the Muslims. Most other Syrian cities soon fell with little struggle. The Muslims turned their highly organized effort next against the Sasanians in Iraq, and in a historic battle at Qadisiyya in 637 c.e., the main Iranian forces were crushed. The Sasanian capital, Ctesiphon, surrendered after offering brief resistance. Once again, the Arab auxiliaries of the Sasanians went over to the Muslims. Most of the Iraq cities also capitulated. Morale among the Byzantines in Syria and among the Sasanians in Iraq collapsed, and no major effort was made to challenge the Muslims. The disaffected peasant and urban populations in both these states offered little resistance and in fact welcomed the conquerors. The city population accepted individual treaties on a friendly basis with the Muslims who also lowered their onerous taxes.

With the conquest of the Fertile Crescent, Arab tribes poured in large numbers to join the victorious armies at their garrison towns. The increased military potential prompted an expedition in 639 c.e., led by another powerful general, Amr ibn al-As, to conquer the riches of Egypt. Once again dissatisfaction with Greek rule led the Copts, who had been bitterly persecuted, to aid the invaders. By 641 c.e. most of the country was occupied and in 642 c.e., the local Byzantine capital of Alexandria fell, too. The Arabs had applied desert power just as effectively as sea power was used by modern empire builders. The desert was familiar and accessible for communication, reinforcement, supplies, and retreat when necessary. The Arab military bases were therefore built strategically at the edge of the desert.

Ultimately, the entire Sasanian empire was overrun, though the Arabs failed to overcome the Byzantines' homelands. After it became evident that the Byzantines could not be conquered in Anatolia by land, the Arabs took to the sea. With the aid of Egyptian and Syrian naval skills, Cyprus was taken; by 655 c.e., the Byzantine fleet was shattered. The wars of conquest, the new motif of Arab history and symbol of its unity, temporarily came to a halt. These conquered lands were the basis of an enduring new Empire of Islam.

The Arabs resumed their last major advances under Abd al-Malik and al-Walid (705–715 c.e.). The Berbers in the Maghrib (North Africa) joined with the Arabs' superior power to form a secondary center of conquest in the west Mediterranean. A raid was launched in the year 710 into Spain, rapidly followed by the occupation of great parts of the Iberian peninsula. Further to the southeast, an Arab force conquered the Indian province of Sind, by land and by sea. In Central Asia, Arabs achieved resounding victories and established control over the lands beyond the Oxus, occupying Bokhara and Samarqand. The frontier between Muslims and the Chinese in the high mountains was halfway between the capitals of the two imperial powers.

Within a hundred years of the death of the Prophet almost all the peoples and centers of ancient civilization belonged to Islam. Muslim scholars saw themselves at the center of the world, stretching from Spain across North Africa to the Middle East and up to the borders of China and India in the east.

What were the reasons for not only the survival of Islam after the Prophet's death but its astonishing success? The principles of group formation defined by Muhammad brought about the survival of Islam after his death and its subsequent phenomenal success. These principles had proven their success in Arabia, but now they had also been successfully tested outside Arabia.

There were two concerns among the leaders in Medina: how to spread Islam and how to express its power. And the objectives of these concerns were often merged. Quran reciters were sent to teach the essentials of Islamic faith, and persuade Arabs to join in the military campaigns. The Quranic injunctions implied a moral and financial solidarity that was the foundation of the military enterprise. The raids of the Medinan Muslims for booty were not enough, and with the flexible and adaptive lessons learned from Muhammad's skills, the expeditions were to become campaigns of conquest. Muslims would now occupy cities and introduce Muslim government.

Muhammad's decisions at Khaybar were wisely extended to all the newly conquered lands. The newly defeated Arab or non-Arabs were to be ruled, not governed. Christian Arabs even participated in the conquests, but no attempts were made to convert unbelievers. The privileges and corruption of the old orders were to be replaced by the fair social order of Islam that would demonstrate the superiority of its religion. The empire in turn would validate the social, financial and religious significance of Islam.

In Medina, Muhammad had replaced the constant feuding society of Medina with a society under a single leader and arbiter. Islam faced a similar need in the newly conquered lands: to bring order and discipline among the frequently lawless desert tribesmen. The answer that Muhammad had offered in Medina—a central mechanism for arbitrating conflict—was adaptively extended to the new territories. The conquered provinces had different laws and customs; there was no unified law in the Empire. In several states the surrender terms respected the local customs and laws; in others, there was greater freedom to impose newer laws. The conquerors did not, however, interfere with civil and religious administration. Just as earlier in Arabia most of the tribes that joined Islam were allowed to retain their social customs and practices, the threat of new rule was reduced if the rhythms of daily life experienced little interference. Moreover the possibility of increased stability and even fewer taxes increased the attractiveness of Islam.

Another of Muhammad's solutions, the central provision of the needs of the disadvantaged, was modified for the vast ruling Arab community that had settled outside Arabia. An organization, the army *diwan*—a register of all Arab Muslims in the armies of conquest—was set up. The booty from the conquered territories was distributed as pensions to the individuals listed in this *diwan*.

The Caliphate's success relied upon the distribution of the heady largess or booty which attracted more Arab tribes to even more conquest. To maintain the warriors' morale required a perpetuation of the system. The captured booty was distributed, with the Caliph receiving the one-fifth appropriation of the late Prophet for distribution to the state and the poor. The immovable booty—the taxes from the land—was kept (as *fay*) to be apportioned later by the army *diwan*. Muslims paid only a small religious levy; all other taxes, the *jizya* and *kharaj*, were paid by the non-Muslim subjects. Conversion to Islam could effectively reduce the state's income!

The religious and military character of the Arab community was further defined by the *diwan*. The *diwan* demarcated the social standing of all Arab Muslims, even those who had fought and lost in the Wars of *Ridda*, and a higher social status was accorded to those who had submitted first to the faith. This reinforced the unity of the ruling Arab elite and separated them from the ruled.

The Muslims initially settled only in garrison towns in the new lands, living off the tribute allotted by the *diwan*. God's order was represented by a mosque in each garrison. The commander of the garrison led the worship in the mosque, and attended to both the military and religious affairs of the community. He settled disputes within the strictures of the Quran. The new order in the conquered lands was thus based on the moral order defined by Muhammad.

———— * ————

Attempts to conceptualize and understand mass behavior—the behavior of groups—have not been completely successful. Studying the genealogy of the group process and the formation of group identity allows an approach to the study of all groups from family, clan, tribe, ethnicity, and class to nation. This study of the life of the Prophet Muhammad and the *umma* he created adds a new dimension to this analysis. Groups must be studied as a totality of needs and functions that derive from the individual.

The basic needs are physiological needs, the need for safety and security, and "basic trust." The institutional counterparts to these individual needs are a free economy, a security structure that provides safety from internal dangers and external threats and a legal system that can fairly enforce its laws. A successful group would need a leader who has mature defense mechanisms. A leading idea or a "constitution" could substitute for a leader by providing shape and structure to a group. For a group to function in an integrated, cohesive manner it must constantly adapt to its inner and outer world. Specialized and differentiated subgroups must develop and work together to achieve common goals, and maintaining mutual trust at every level of the group is vital to this process.

As the rise of Islam tellingly reveals, the *umma* became immensely more powerful than the sum of its tribal parts by supporting all the needs of its members, as well as the new needs of the group as they become necessary at each moment in history. An understanding of the model of the group the Prophet created offers hope even to those who are not believers.

Braudel and others of the *Annales* school have emphasized the study of the *longue durée* (Braudel, 1980). They measure the forces that shape collective existence. In their view the substance of history is found in the deeper, more permanent fabric of life: the relations between biological forces, social structure, and the environmental surround. This historical long view, however, can easily add to pessimism and even despair, as an important recent study suggests. In Southern Italy as compared to Northern Italy, the Hobbesian dilemmas of collective action have hampered attempts to cooperate for mutual benefit in economics as well as in politics. This has been "the tragic fate of southern Italy for a millennium" (Putnam, 1993, p. 178). History is seen as not always efficient in weeding out social practices that impede progress; collective irrationality once attained tends to be self-reinforcing. The influence of a unique leader such as Muhammad counters such a view. In the span of just 22 years from his Call to his death, he permanently altered longstanding social structures and changed world history.

The study of the rise and fall of large groups, such as nations, has a vast and voluminous history. Historians and philosophers have pondered these issues for centuries. The rise of the West has been attributed to several factors by historians. Standard accounts do not, however, provide a compelling explanation for this rise (Olson, 1982). They have suggested several causal factors, from geographic, political, social, scientific, technological, to economic and military. Except for the scientific and technological influences that are more recent in history, most of the above factors did play a part in the rise of Islam and were influenced by the ideas of Muhammad. Two factors instrumental in Islam's rise were economic and military, and they deserve comment, even if briefly. This is not the place for a comprehensive argument; one example for each will suffice. Muhammad, born to a trading culture in the seventh century, offered a laissez-faire approach to Islam's economy; the Quran for instance is sprinkled with trade terms. This approach permitted several centuries of free trade and prosperity and is a stark contrast to another economic philosophy which until recently was almost a religion, Marxism. Marxism provided an ideological blueprint for society and has had an impact that still reverberates throughout the world. Marxism offered "a peculiar mixture of science and prophecy that is both the major intellectual flaw of Marxism and the source of its immense mythopoetic appeal" (Berger, 1986, p. 4). Philosophy and science were intertwined in Marxist work, but it was its hostility to capital and business that first invited and then propelled the downfall of communist states. The puzzling, hopeful, and at times euphoric, reception of Marxist ideas demonstrates, however, the catastrophic impact of unsound economic ideas in human history.

Economic factors, it is disturbing to note, have been closely associated with the military. It is clearly evident in the growth of Islam from a small *umma* to a great empire. The role of war in the rise of the West, not too surprisingly, has had similar features. The history of the rise and fall of some of the leading countries of Europe shows a very significant correlation over the long term between their revenue-raising capacity and their military strength. Great Britain was the forcing house for the emergence of the military–industrial complex. Its rise is interesting. Britain, the first modern nation, had its own identity forged also by two powerful forces: religion and war. The invention of Britain was closely bound with Protestantism and war with the hated other, at first Catholic Spain and later Catholic France. "War—recurrent, protracted and increasingly demanding war—had been the making of Great Britain" (Colley, 1992, p. 322).

The study of the role of war in the making and the expansion of societies has disturbing implications today. The industrialization of war and the quantum jump in our capacity to kill and destroy continues to spawn a dangerous and unstable world. We study aggression and war with profound ambivalence. There are, however, no simple solutions, nor is there yet some feel a compelling need for despair.

The study of the rise or decline of groups and nations as the most dominant of forces in this century continues to be a critical need. History in fact is a history of groups, and at times, of unique individuals who have forever altered its shapes. There are, however, no universal inductive lessons from history. Monocausal explanations of events are too simplistic. Nor does epistemology suggest that a monocausal explanation is valid. Multicausal explanations alone have the power and parsimony to explain the impact of a large number of linked phenomena. It is critical to the study of multicausal factors that all of the components be examined together for their impact on a group rather than addressing the issues separately, and in isolation. The study of the life of Muhammad and the unparalleled rise of Islam amply demonstrates that the study of a group should encompass its entirety.

Nowhere is the need for a multicausal approach more necessary and critical than for states in transition and in the formation of the largest of groups, the nation state.

The collapse of imperialism left in its wake over a hundred new nations. The pious exhortation to form democracies, left behind as the legacy of imperial retreat, foundered rapidly in the quick collapse of democracy, in many nations, into dictatorships, tyranny, and the rule of corrupt oligarchies. The forces that shaped democracy were itself ill understood. Democracy, the outcome of a slow historical process, reached its fullest expression with universal adult suffrage in Western countries only in the late 1940s; in the electoral process, the selection of a government is often seen as an end itself, rather than a mere beginning. It is less clearly understood that constitutional structures should guarantee rights that are based on the developmental needs of an individual. When these rights allow economic well-being and safety, and are supported by the rule of law, they form the basis of liberal constitutional democracies.

One brief example of the problems faced by the change to a democracy may make this clear. The transition of Russia from communist rule to democracy in 1991, after the much vaunted universal triumph of democracy, amply describes the perils, the slow agony, and the rapid descent into terror. The attempt to move to a market democracy collapsed in spectacular fashion, leaving the country in bankruptcy and without a government. The inability to develop the economic, legal, and financial structures to collect taxes, regulate banks, police the state against a robber baron oligarchy, and create a working judiciary had left a former superpower ruderless. The institutional abyss was a direct cause of the debacle.

Thus in the opening years of the twenty-first century the intellectual challenge and task remains a better understanding of all groups—from the smallest, the family, to the largest, a nation state. They share after all many features in common. Despite the dire warnings of Malthusians, with the aid of science and technology, we have had the potential to offer well-being to everyone on our planet. This promise has been honored in its breech.

Today it is only in the few liberal democracies that a child can grow and develop in a safe environment that extends from the family to every institution in his or her developmental journey. It is only in such a setting that an individual can develop potential to its fullest. For the rest of the planet where democracy is nonexistent and illiberal democracies flourish (Zakaria, 1997) the fate of a child is very different. The fate of too many is stunted by abject poverty and misery, by wars and conflict.

References

Albright, W. F. (1957). *From Stone Age to Christianity: Monotheism and the historical process*. Garden City, NY: Doubleday.
Anderson, B. (1991). *Imagined Communities Reflections on the Origin and Spread of Nationalism*, rev. ed. New York: Verso.
Andrews, G., Pollock, C., & Stewart, G. (1989). The determination of defense style by questionnaire. *Archives of General Psychiatry, 46,* 455–460.
Armstrong, K. (1992). *A biography of the Prophet*. New York: HarperCollins.
Assmann, J. (1997). *Moses the Egyptian: The memory of Egypt in western monotheism*. Cambridge, MA: Harvard Univ. Press.
Baldwin, A. (1961). The Parsonian theory of personality. In M. Black (Ed.), *The social theories of Talcott Parsons* (pp. 153–190). Englewood Cliffs, NJ: Prentice-Hall.
Balter, L. (1978). Leaderless groups. *International Review of Psycho-Analysis, 5,* 331–350.
Bell, D. (1960). *The end of ideology: On the exhaustion of political ideas in the fifties*. New York: Free Press.
Bell, J. E. (1980). Family therapy. In H. I. Kaplan, A. M. Freedman, & B. J. Sadock (Eds.), *Comprehensive textbook of psychiatry* III (2:2217–2224). Baltimore: Williams & Wilkins.
Bergen, B. J., & Rosenberg, S. D. (1971). The new neo-Freudians: Psychoanalytic dimensions of social change. *Psychiatry, 34,* 19–37.
Berger, P., & Luckmann, T. (1967). *The social construction of reality: A treatise in the sociology of knowledge*. Garden City, NY: Anchor Books. (Original work published 1966)
Berger, P. L. (1986). *The capitalist revolution: Fifty propositions about prosperity, equality and liberty*. New York: Basic.
Bertalanffy, L. Von (1969). *General systems theory: Essays in its foundation and development* (rev. ed.). New York: Braziller.
Braudel, F. (1980). *On history*. Chicago: University of Chicago Press.
Broderick, C., & Smith, J. (1979). The general systems approach to the family. In W. Burr, R. Hill, F. Nye, & I. Reiss (Eds.), *Contemporary theories about the family* (pp. 112–129). New York: Free Press.
Buhl, F. (1930). *Das Leben Muhammeds* (H. H. Schaeder Trans.). Leipzig: Quelle & Meyer.
Campbell, D. T. (1983). The two distinct routes beyond kin selection to ultrasociality: Implications for the humanities and social sciences. In D. L.

Bridgeman (Ed.), *The Nature of prosocial development: Interdisciplinary theories and strategies*. New York Academic Press.

Colley, L. (1992). *Britons: Forging the nation 1707–1837*. New Haven, CT: Yale Univ. Press.

Cooley, C. H. (1909). *Social organizations*. New York: Charles Scribner.

Cooley, C. H. (1964). *Human nature and the social order*. New York: Scribner's. (Original work published 1902)

Davis, K. (1959). The myth of functional analysis as a special method in sociology and anthropology. *American Sociological Review, 24*, 757–772.

Deutsch, M. (1954). Field theory in social psychology. In G. Lindley & E. Aronson (Eds.), *Handbook of social psychology* (Vol. 1, pp. 182–185). Cambridge, MA: Addison-Wesley.

Donner, F. M. (1979). Muhammad's political consolidation in Arabia up to the conquest of Mecca. *Muslim World, 69*, 229–247.

Durkheim, E. (1950). *The rules of sociological method*. Chicago: Free Press. (Original work published 1895)

Durkheim, E. (1951). *Suicide*. New York: Free Press. (Original work published 1897)

Durkheim, E. (1976). *The elementary forms of religious life*. London: Allen & Unwin. (Original work published 1912)

Eisenstein, E. L. (1968). Some conjectures on the impact of printing on Western society and thought: A preliminary report. *Journal of Modern History, 40*, 1–56.

Encyclopedia of Islam (1936). Muhammad s.v.

Erikson, E. H. (1958). *Young man Luther: A study in psychoanalysis and history*. New York: Norton.

Erikson, E. H. (1964). *Insight and responsibility: Lectures on the ethical implications of psychoanalytic insight*. New York: Norton.

Erikson, E. H. (1966). Gandhi's autobiography: The leader as child. *American Scholar, 35*, 632–646.

Erikson, E. H. (1969). *Gandhi's truth: On the origins of militant nonviolence*. New York: Norton.

Erikson, E. H. (1975). *Life history and the historical moment*. New York: Norton.

Erikson, E. H. (1980). Identity and the life cycle. New York: Norton. (Original work published 1959)

Erikson, E. H. (1985). *Childhood and society*. New York: Norton. (Original work published 1950)

Erikson, E. H., Erikson, J. M., & Kivnick, H. Q. (1986). *Vital involvement in old age*. New York: Norton.

Ettin, M. F. (1993). Links between group process and social, political and cultural issues. In H. I. Kaplan & B. J. Sadock (Eds.), *Comprehensive group psychotherapy* (3rd ed., pp. 699–716). Baltimore: Williams & Wilkins.

Evans, R. I. (1967). *Dialogue with Erik Erikson*. New York: Harper.

Freud, S. (1953). Three essays on the theory of sexuality. In J. Strachey (Ed. & Trans.), *The standard edition of the complete psychological works of Sigmund*

Freud (Vol. 7, pp. 123–243). London: Hogarth Press. (Original work published 1905)

Freud, S. (1954). *The origins of psycho-analysis: Letters to Wilhelm Fleiss, drafts and notes: 1887–1902.* New York: Basic.

Freud, S. (1955a). Totem and taboo. In J. Strachey (Ed. & Trans.), *The standard edition of the complete psychological works of Sigmund Freud* (Vol. 13, pp. 1–161). London: Hogarth Press. (Original work published 1913)

Freud, S. (1955b). Group psychology and the analysis of the ego. In J. Strachey (Ed. & Trans.), *The standard edition of the complete psychological works of Sigmund Freud* (Vol. 18, pp. 65–143). London: Hogarth Press. (Original work published 1921)

Freud, S. (1961). The ego and the id. In J. Strachey (Ed. & Trans.), *The standard edition of the complete psychological works of Sigmund Freud* (Vol. 19, pp. 1–66). London: Hogarth Press. (Original work published 1923)

Freud, S. (1964). An outline of psycho-analysis. In J. Strachey (Ed. & Trans.), *The standard edition of the complete psychological works of Sigmund Freud* (Vol. 23, pp. 139–207). (Original work published 1940)

Galanter, M. (1989). *Cults: Faith, healing, and coercion.* New York: Oxford Univ. Press.

Geertz, C. (1973). Ideology as a cultural system. In *The interpretation of cultures: Selected essays.* New York: Basic.

Gellner, E. (1964). *Thought and change.* London: Weidenfeld & Nicholson.

Greenberg, J. R., & Mitchell, S. A. (1983). *Object relations in psychoanalytic theory.* Cambridge, MA: Harvard Univ. Press.

Greenfeld, L. (1992). *Nationalism: Five roads to modernity.* Cambridge, MA: Harvard Univ. Press.

Hartmann, H. (1965). Psychoanalysis as a scientific theory. In *Essays on ego psychology: Selected problems in psychoanalytic theory* (pp. 318–350). New York: International Univ. Press.

Hitti, P. K. (1968). *The Arabs: A short history.* New York: St. Martin's Press. (Original work published 1948)

Hobsbaum, E. J. (1990). *Nations and nationalism since 1780: Programme, myth, and reality.* Cambridge, U.K.: Cambridge Univ. Press.

Hodgson, M. G. S. (1974). *The venture of Islam: Conscience and history in a world civilization* (Vol. 1). Chicago: Univ. of Chicago Press.

Hofstadter, R. (1966). *The paranoid style in American politics and other essays.* London: Cape.

Holt, P. M., Lambton, A. K. S., & Lewis, B. (1970). *The Cambridge history of Islam.* New York: Cambridge Univ. Press.

Horowitz, D. (1985). *Ethnic groups in conflict.* Los Angeles: Univ. California Press.

Hughes, J. A., Martin, P. J., & Sharrock, W. W. (1995). *Understanding classical sociology. Marx, Weber, Durkheim.* London: Sage.

Huntington, S. P. (1993). The clash of civilizations. *Foreign Affairs,* 72, 22–49.

Huntington, S. P. (1996). *The clash of civilizations and the remaking of world order.* New York: Simon & Schuster.

Hutchinson, J., & Smith, A. D. (Eds.). (1994). *Nationalism.* Oxford, U.K.: Oxford Univ. Press.
Ibn Ishaq (1955). *The life of Muhammad: A translation of Ishaq's Sirat Rasul Allah.* (A. Guillaume, Trans., Introduction & notes). London: Oxford Univ. Press.
Ibn al-Kalbi (1952). *Book of idols.* Princeton, NJ: Princeton Univ. Press.
Isaacs, H. R. (1975). *Idols of the tribe: Group identity and political change.* Cambridge, MA: Harvard Univ. Press.
Joffe, W. G., & Sandler, J. (1968). Comments on the psychoanalytic psychology of adaptation with special reference to role of affects and the representational world. *International Journal of Psycho-Analysis, 49,* 445–454.
Kaplan, R. D. (1996). *The ends of the earth: A journey at the dawn of the 21st century.* New York: Random House.
Klein, R. H., Bernard, H. S., & Singer, D. L. (1992). *Handbook of contemporary group psychotherapy: Contributions from object relations, self psychology and social systems theory.* Madison, CT: International Univ. Press.
Laplanche, J., & Pontalis, J.-B. (1973). *The language of psychoanalysis.* New York: Norton.
Lazell, E. W. (1921). The group treatment of dementia praecox. *Psychoanalytic Review, 8,* 168.
Le Bon, G. (1920). *The crowd: A study of the popular mind.* London: Fisher Unwin.
Lewin, K. (1947). Frontiers in group dynamics. *Human Relations, 1,* 5–41.
Lewis, B. (1958). *The Arabs in history.* New York: Harper & Row.
Lewis, B. (1982). *The Muslim discovery of Europe.* New York: Norton.
Lifton, R. J. (1968). *Revolutionary immortality: Mao Tse-tung and the Chinese cultural revolution.* New York: Random House.
Lifton, R. J. (1974). On psychohistory. In R. J. Lifton & E. Olson (Eds.), *Explorations in psychohistory* (pp. 21–41). New York: Simon & Schuster.
Lings, M. (1983). *Muhammad: His life based on the earliest sources.* Rochester, VT: Inner Traditions.
Mackay, C. (1980). *Extraordinary popular delusions and the madness of crowds.* New York: Harmony.
Mannheim, K. (1985). *Ideology and utopia: An introduction to the sociology of knowledge.* New York: Harcourt Brace. (Original work published 1936)
Marx, K. (1977). *Selected writings.* D. McLellan (Ed.). Oxford: Oxford Univ. Press.
Marx, K., & Engels, F. (1970). *The German ideology.* New York: International. (Original work published 1847)
Maslow, A. H. (1954). *Motivation and personality.* New York: Harper & Row.
Mayall, J. (1982). *The community of states: A study in international political theory.* London: Allen & Unwin.
McDougall, W. (1920). *The group mind.* Cambridge, U.K.: Cambridge Univ. Press.
McLuhan, M., & Fiore, Q. (1967). *The medium is the message.* New York: Bantam.
McNeill, W. H. (1982). *The pursuit of power, technology, armed force and society since A.D. 1000.* Chicago: University of Chicago Press.

McNeill, W. H. (1995). *Keeping together in time: Dance and drill in human history.* Cambridge, MA: Harvard Univ. Press.
Mead, G. H. (1962). *Mind, self and society.* Chicago: Univ. of Chicago Press. (Original work published 1934)
Meissner, W. W. (1988). The origins of Christianity. *The Psychoanalytic Study of Society* (Vol. 13, pp. 29–62). Hillsdale, NJ: Analytic Press.
Merton, R. (1949). *Social theory and social structure.* New York: Free Press.
Milburn, M. A., & Conrad, S. D. (1996). *The politics of denial.* Cambridge, MA: MIT Press.
Mills, C. Wright (1959). *The sociological imagination.* New York: Oxford Univ. Press.
Munich, R. L. (1993). Group dynamics. In H. I. Kaplan & B. J. Sadock (Eds.), *Comprehensive group psychotherapy* (3rd ed., pp. 21–32). Baltimore: Williams & Wilkins.
Nairn, T. (1977). *The break-up of Britain.* London: New Left Books.
Olmstead, M. S., & Hare, A. Paul (1978). *The small group* (2nd ed.). New York: Random House.
Olson, M. (1982). *The rise and decline of nations: Economic growth, stagflation and social rigidities.* New Haven, CT: Yale Univ. Press.
Pagels, E. (1995). *The origin of Satan.* New York: Random House.
Parens, H., & Saul, L. J. (1971). *Dependence in man.* New York: International Univ. Press.
Parkin, F. (1992). *Durkheim.* Oxford: Oxford Univ. Press.
Parsons, T. (1949). *The structure of social action.* Chicago: Free Press.
Parsons, T. (1964). *Social structure and personality.* New York: Free Press.
Peters, F. E. (1994). *Muhammad and the origins of Islam.* Albany, NY: State Univ. New York Press.
Pfaff, W. (1993). *The wrath of nations: Civilization and the furies of nationalism.* New York: Simon & Schuster.
Pickthall, M. (1930). *The meaning of the glorious Koran: An explanatory translation.* New York: Dorset Press.
Pine, F. (1988). The four psychologies of psychoanalysis and their place in clinical work. *Journal of the American Psychoanalytic Association, 36,* 571–596.
Post, J. (1991). Saddam Hussein of Iraq: A political psychology profile. *Political Psychology, 12,* 279–289.
Pratt, J. H. (1922). The principles of class treatment and their application to various chronic diseases. *Hospital Social Service, 6,* 401.
Putnam, R. D. (1993). *Making democracy work: Civic traditions in modern Italy.* Princeton, NJ: Princeton Univ. Press.
Reiss, I. (1965). The universality of the family: A conceptual analysis. *Journal of Marriage and the Family, 27,* 443–453.
Rieff, P. (1963). The meaning of history and religion in Freud's thought. In B. Mazlish (Ed.), *Psychoanalysis and history* (pp. 23–44). Englewood Cliffs, NJ: Prentice-Hall.
Ritzer, G. (1996). *Sociological theory* (4th ed.). New York: McGraw-Hill.

Rodinson, M. (1980). *Muhammad.* New York: Random House.
Ross, D. (1991). *The origins of American social science.* Cambridge, U.K.: Cambridge Univ. Press.
Roth, B. E. (1993). Freud: The group psychologist and group leader. In H. I. Kaplan & B. J. Sadock (Eds.), *Comprehensive group psychotherapy* (3rd ed., pp. 10–21). Baltimore: Williams & Wilkins.
Rothstein, A. (1985). Models of the mind: Their relationships to clinical work, *Workshop Series of the American Psychoanalytic Association,* Monogr. 1. New York: International Univ. Press.
Runyan, W. McK. (1982). *Life histories and psychobiography: Explorations in theory and method.* New York: Oxford Univ. Press.
Sagan, E. (1991). *The honey and the hemlock: Democracy and paranoia in ancient Athens and modern America.* New York: Basic.
Sandler, J., & Rosenblatt, B. (1962). The concept of the representational world. *The Psychoanalytic Study of the Child* (Vol. 17, pp. 128–145). New York: International Univ. Press.
Schafer, R. (1967). Ideals, ego ideal, and ideal self. In R. R. Holt (Ed.), Motives and thought: Psychoanalytic essays in honor of David Rapaport (pp. 131–176). *Psychological Issues,* Monogr. 18/19. New York: International Univ. Press.
Scheidlinger, S. (1993). History of group psychotherapy. In H. I. Kaplan & B. J. Sadock. (Eds.), *Comprehensive group psychotherapy* (3rd ed., pp. 2–10). Baltimore: Williams & Wilkins.
Schmidt, C. (1982). The use of the Gallop Poll as a psychohistorical tool. *The Journal of Psychohistory, 10,* 141–162.
Schwartz, R. M. (1997). *The curse of Cain: The violent legacy of monotheism.* Chicago: Univ. Chicago Press.
Shapiro, T., & Perry, R. (1976). Latency revisted: The age 7 plus or minus 1. *The Psychoanalytic Study of the Child* (Vol. 31, pp. 79–105). New Haven, CT: Yale Univ. Press.
Al-Tabari (1988). *The history of al-Tabari: Vol. 4.* Albany, NY: State Univ. New York Press.
Al-Tabari (1988). *The history of al-Tabari: Vol. 6. Muhammad at Mecca.* Albany, NY: State Univ. New York Press.
Al-Tabari (1987). *The history of al-Tabari: Vol. 7. The foundation of the community.* Albany, NY: State Univ. New York Press.
Al-Tabari (1990). *The history of Al-Tabari: Vol. 9. The last years of the Prophet.* Albany, NY: State Univ. New York Press.
Trotter, W. (1916). *Instincts of the herd in peace and war.* London: Fisher Unwin.
Turner, B. S. (1974). *Weber and Islam: A critical study.* London: Routledge & Kegan Paul.
Turner, J., & Maryanski, A. Z. (1979). *Functionalism.* Menlo Park, CA: Benjamin/Cummings.
Vaillant, G. E. (1977). *Adaptation to life.* Boston: Little, Brown.
Vaillant, G. E. (1992). *Ego mechanisms of defense: A guide for clinicians and researchers.* Washington, DC: American Psychiatric Press.

Vaillant, G. E. (1993). *The wisdom of the ego.* Cambridge, MA: Harvard Univ. Press.
Volkan, V. D. (1988). *The need to have enemies and allies.* Northvale, NJ: Aronson.
Watt, W. M. (1953). *Muhammad at Mecca.* London: Oxford Univ. Press.
Watt, W. M. (1956). *Muhammad at Medina.* London: Oxford Univ. Press.
Watt, W. M. (1961). *Muhammad: Prophet and statesman.* New York: Oxford Univ. Press.
Weber, M. (1930). *The Protestant ethic and the spirit of capitalism* (T. Parsons, Trans.). London: Allen & Unwin.
Weber, M. (1958). *The religion of India: The sociology of Hinduism and Buddhism.* Chicago: Free Press. (Original work published 1916–1917)
Weber, M. (1963). *The sociology of religion.* Boston: Beacon Press. (Original work published 1922)
Weinstein, F., & Platt, G. M. (1973). *Psychoanalytic sociology: An essay on the interpretation of historical data and the phenomena of collective behavior.* Baltimore: Johns Hopkins Univ. Press.
Wilson, D. Sloan, & Sober, E. (1994). Reintroducing group selection to the human behavioral sciences. *Behavioral and Brain Sciences, 17,* 585–654.
Zakaria, F. (1997). The rise of illiberal democracy. *Foreign Affairs, 76,* 22–43.
Zilboorg, G. (1944). Present trends in psychoanalytic theory and practice. *Bulletin of the Menninger Clinic, 8,* 3–8.

Name Index

Albright, W. F., 204n
Anderson, B., xvii, 53n, 62
Andrews, G., 19
Armstrong, K., 217
Assmann, J., 84

Balter, L., 135
Bell, D., 66–67
Bell, J. E., 55
Bergen, B. J., 28
Berger, P. L., 6, 11, 12n, 13, 80, 85, 191, 203n, 204n, 238
Bernard, H. S., 54
Bertalanffy, L. Von, 55
Braudel, F., 237
Broderick, C., 55
Buhl, F., 114–115

Campbell, D. T., 7
Cohen, 19
Colley, L., xvii, 238
Comte, A., 34–35
Conrad, S. D., 19
Cooley, C. H., 13n, 38n, 57

Davis, K., 40
de Tracy, D., 66
Deutsch, M., 56
Donner, F. M., 157
Durkheim, E., xii, 5–6, 12n, 34, 35, 36, 37, 38, 52, 223

Eisenstein, E. L., 87n

Engels, F., 66
Erikson, E. H., xii, 5, 14–15, 16, 22, 30–33, 59–61, 64, 65–66, 67–68, 181, 189, 190, 191, 194, 195, 206, 209
Erikson, J. M., 194, 195
Ettin, M. F., 19
Evans, R. I., 31

Fiore, Q., 87
Freud, A., 195n
Freud, S., xii, xiii, 5, 9, 14, 15–16, 18, 19, 27–29, 38–39, 43–44, 45–54, 65–66, 66n, 67–68, 135, 181, 190, 208

Galanter, M., 59
Geertz, C., 66
Gellner, E., 62
Gibbon, viii, xi
Greenberg, J. R., 54
Greenfeld, L., xvii, 61–62, 207

Hare, A. Paul, 58
Hartmann, H., xii, 5, 28, 32
Herodotus, 135
Hitti, P. K., 221n
Hobsbaum, E. J., xvii
Hodgson, M. G. S., 82, 86, 228
Hofstadter, R., 19
Holt, P. M., 74, 75, 77, 79
Hughes, J. A., 35
Huntington, S. P., xvii, 34n, 59
Hutchinson, J., 50–51, 61, 62–63

Ibn al-Kalbi, 93
Ibn Ishaq, 92–96, 101, 102, 103–106, 107, 111, 112, 115–116, 117–119, 123, 125–126, 129, 139, 141, 144–145, 149–150, 151–153, 156–157, 162–164, 166, 170–173, 174–178, 183, 185
Ibn Sa'd, 144
Isaacs, H. R., xv–xvi, 63–64

Joffe, W. G., 9–10

Kaplan, R. D., 34n
Kedourie, 62
Kivnick, H. Q., 194, 195
Klein, R. H., 54

Lambton, A. K. S., 74, 75, 77, 79
LaPlanche, J., 47n, 148n, 218n
Lazell, E. W., 54
Le Bon, G., 44, 45, 48
Lewin, K., 56–57
Lewis, B., viii, ix, 74, 75, 77, 79, 101, 138, 148
Lifton, R. J., 55–56, 208, 222
Lings, M., 155–156, 190, 209, 210, 214–215, 218–219, 221
Luckmann, T., 6, 11, 12n, 13, 80, 85, 191, 203n, 204n

Mackay, C., 59
Mannheim, K., 6
Martin, P. J., 35
Marx, K., 34, 35, 36–37, 66
Maryanski, A. Z., 40
Maslow, A. H., 13
McDougall, W., 44–45, 48, 50, 51, 65, 68
McLuhan, M., 87
McNeill, W. H., 58–59, 220–221n, 221, 223
Mead, G. H., 13n, 38n
Meissner, W. W., 209–210
Merton, R., 6, 37, 40

Milburn, M. A., 19
Mills, C. Wright, xi, 10
Mitchell, S. A., 54
Munich, R. L., 53

Nairn, T., 63
Nicholson, R. A., 99
Nietzsche, F., 207

Olmstead, M. S., 58
Olson, M., 237

Pagels, E., 83n
Parens, H., 18
Parkin, F., 34
Parsons, T., xii, 5, 37–40
Perry, R., 14
Peters, F. E., 89–90, 97, 104, 105, 107, 112, 114, 116, 118, 120, 121, 129n, 133n, 142, 144, 161n
Pfaff, W., 63
Pickthall, M., 214
Pine, F., 5
Platt, G. M., xii, 4, 32–33, 41, 190–191, 194n, 203n
Pollock, C., 19
Pontalis, J.-B., 47n, 148n, 218n
Post, J., 19
Pratt, J. H., 54
Putnam, R. D., 237

Rapaport, D., 31–32
Redfield, R., 58
Reiss, I., 13–14n
Renan, E., 101
Rieff, P., 208
Ritzer, G., 20n, 37, 40
Rodinson, M., 114, 139, 193, 199, 203–204, 213
Rosenberg, S. D., 28
Rosenblatt, B., 5, 9
Ross, D., 37
Roth, B. E., 50
Rothstein, A., 3, 27, 28–29
Runyan, W. McK., xii, 4, 19

Name Index

Sagan, E., 19
Sandler, J., 5, 9–10
Saul, L. J., 18
Schafer, R., 17–18
Scheidlinger, S., 53–54
Scheler, M., 207
Schmidt, C., 20
Schwartz, R. M., 84
Shapiro, T., 14
Sharrock, W. W., 35
Singer, D. L., 54
Smith, A. D., 50–51, 61, 62–63
Smith, J., 55
Sober, E., 6
Stewart, G., 19

Al-Tabari, 91–92, 94, 95, 96, 101, 105, 107–111, 113, 117–119, 121–123, 124–129, 133–134, 136, 142–143, 149–150, 152, 159, 161, 169, 179–180, 183–184, 187

Tonnies, F., 58
Trotter, W., 45, 48–49, 51
Turner, B. S., 37n, 40

Vaillant, G. E., 19, 102n, 161n, 195n, 208, 228
Volkan, V. D., 19

Watt, W. M., 97–98, 99, 110n, 118, 120, 121, 124, 129, 139, 150–151, 155–156, 158n, 166–167, 179, 196, 202n, 209, 210, 212, 213, 215–216
Weber, M., xii, 5–6, 34, 35–36, 37, 81–82, 209
Weinstein, F., xii, 4, 32–33, 41, 190–191, 194n, 203n
Wilson, D. Sloan, 6

Zakaria, F., 240
Zilboorg, G., 7

Subject Index

al-Abbas, 176, 178
Banu Abd al-Dar, 107
Abdullah, 97, 102, 104, 189
Abdullah ibn Ubayy, 158
Abraham, 89, 203
   in history of Arabs, 90–91
   travels of, 89–90
Abyssinia, migration to, 123–124
Abyssinians, 75, 76
Acting out, 19
Action systems, 20n
Action theory, 38–40
Adaptive defense styles, 228
Adnan, 91
Adoption, changing views of, 212–213
Adulthood, definition of, 195
Affective group
   formation of, 15–16
   ties of, 59
Aggressive drive, *razzias* and, 217–220
Aggressive transformation, 207
AGIL scheme, 20n
Aisha, 195, 211
Akhenaten, 84
Alexander the Great, 86
Alexandria, 233
Ali, 116, 134
   as adopted son, 198–199
Allah, 100, 116
   daughters of, 119–120
Altruism, 19, 228
Altruistic sacrifice, 223
Altruistic suicide, 223n
American Indians, 61
Amina, 102

al-Anfal, 153
Anticipation, 228
Apostasy, Wars of, 231–232
Aqaba, Gulf of, 184
Arab empire, 233–234
Arab identity, development of, 79
Arab-Jewish conflict, first mention of, 127–128
Arab poets, pre-Islamic, 79
Arab settlements, 78
Arab states, pre-Islamic, 78–79
Arab tribes, ancestors of, 91
Arabia. *See also* South Arabia
   geography and climate of, 73–75
   pre-Islamic, xiii, 73–87
   pre-Islamic religions in, 99–100
Arabia haeresium ferax, 77
Arabiyya, 79
Arabs
   ancestors of, 89
   genealogy of, 89–91
Aramaic, 232
Arbitration, 235
   pre-Islamic, 137–138
Army
   distribution of booty in, 235–236
   as group, 46
   representational world of, 68–69
Artificial groups, 46
Asceticism, strictures against, 213–214
Ashura, 142–143
Atonement, Day of, 142–143
Attachment, 8
Aurelian, 78
Authenticity, 57

Subject Index

Authoritarian personality, 33
Autonomy, 15
Aw clan, 166–167

Badr, battle of, 151–158, 219, 220
    promise of martyrdom in, 221
Abu Bakr, 116, 134, 136, 139, 154, 185–186
    death of, 233
    as Muhammad's successor, 187–188, 231–232
Bakr tribe, 176
Banat Allah, 120
Barbarism, period of, 92–93
Barbary Corsairs, x
Basic group, 13–14
Basic needs, 13–14, 17, 68
    of group, 147, 236–237
    provided by Muhammad, 228–229
Bedouins, 23, 77–78
    clan life of, 191–192
    climate and, 73–74
    common culture of, 80
    pre-Islamic religions of, 99–100
Behavior, in groups, 56
Belief systems, synthesizing of, 83n
Berbers, 234
Bible
    identity and, 84
    impact of, on Quran, 201
Biblical prophets, 202
Biography
    based on psychoanalytic theory, xi–xii
    psychoanalytic theory in, 4
Biological development, 11
Blood feuds, 98–99
    banning of, 226–227
Body image, group identity and, 64
Book of Idols, 93
Boycott, 124–129
Bureaucratic corporations, 58, 59
Byzantine army, 233
Byzantine Empire, 183–184, 200–201, 232–233
Byzantines, 234

Caliph, 231–232
Capitalist society, factors affecting, 35–36
Caravan routes, 77–78
Celibacy, 213–214
Central Asia, 234
Chalcedon, council of, 77
Charismatic leader, 37, 67
    growth of, 189–229
    personality qualities of, 209–210
Childhood
    representational world of, 9–17
    sexual seduction, 27
Christendom
    forces of, ix
    Islam conflict with, ix–xi
Christendom-Islam confrontations, viii
Christian Abyssinia, emigration to, 123–124
Christian Arabs, 235
Christian Byzantine empire, 76, 78
Christianity
    demonization of outsiders by, 83n
    doctrines of, 204n
    impact of, 200
    pre-Islamic, 76
    printing and spread of, 87n
    prophets of, 202
    rise of, 86
Church, as group, 46
Cities
    universalist religion and, 80–87
    values of, 85–86
Clan family, 191–192
Clans
    early religious traditions of, 80
    life of, 191–192
    loyalties to, 59–60
    in Mecca, 97–99
    pre-Islamic, 224–226
    representational world of, 10–11
Climate, of Arabia, 73–75
Cold War, 59
Collective existence, forces of, 237
Communal feeling, 16

Communication, in groups, 57
Communism, transition to democracy of, 239–240
Community. *See Umma*
Complicity in common crime, 135
Constantinople, 232
　Greek defense of, ix
　imperial church of, 77
　Ottoman capture of, x
　as Roman capital, 76
Constitution, 52–53, 237
Constitutional democracies, 239
Contagion, 45
Coptic population, 232
Creativity, of adulthood, 195–196
Crisis, with loss of son, 198–200
Crowds, 44–45
　sociologic study of, 58
Cults, 59
Cultural contact, 80–81
Cultural values
　language in transmitting, 85–86
　religion in transmission of, 86–87
Cyprus, 234
Cypselas, birth of, 135–136
Cypselian paradigm, 136

Damascus, occupation of, 233
Abd al-Dar, 96
Deception, in warfare, 219–220
Decline and Fall of the Roman Empire, viii
Defense mechanisms, 208, 228, 237
　of denial, 19
　displacement, 19, 228
　of group, 19–20
　of leader, 21–22
Democracy, 239
　developmental origins of processes of, 22
　transition to, 240
Deputations, Year of, 185
Dereification, 12n, 192n
Developmental events
　in group formation, 49, 51
　in group origins, 68

Developmental experiences, representations of, 8
Developmental stages, 14–15, 30–33
　Freudian, 15–16
Dhimmis, 207
Dhu Awan, Mosque of Dissent in, 184
Dhu Yazan family, 76
Dialectical social psychology, 13n
Disadvantages, provision of needs of, 235–236
Displacement, 19, 228
Diwan, 235–236
Doubters, 205–206
Drill, 220–221
Dumat al-Jandal expeditions, 162–163, 170
Dyad, 7–8, 13–14

Eating practices, 204
Economic factors, 238
Economy, 14, 17
　shaping of, 35–36
Ego, 28–29
　definition of, 208
　executive role of, 29
　functioning of, 9–10
　group, 136
　parents in formation of, 17–18
Ego psychology, 31–32
Ego strengths, Muhammad, 208
Ego tasks, 208
Emigrants, 138–139, 141–142
　expedition to Nakhlah, 149–151
　razzias of, 147–149
Emotional ties, nationalist, 62–64
Encounter groups, 57
End of Ideology, 66–67
Enlightenment, 36
　values of, xvi
Environmental conditions, Arabian, 74
Envy, in family group, 50
Equality, expectation of, 16–17
Ethical code, 196–197
Ethnic conflict, 59
　revival of, 63

Ethnicity
　in global conflicts, xvi–xvii
　as group force, 63–64
　nationalism and, 63
Experienced person, 190
Extended clan family, 191–192
　dependency on, 224–226
Externalization, 12n

Fadak, 174–175
Fairness, expectation of, 16–17
False prophets, 186–187
Family
　affective group formation in, 15–16
　group development in, 50
　ideal shapes of, 17, 193
　representational world of, 10–24
　triad of, 14
Family group, 6–7
Family therapy, systems theory in, 55
Fantasy, sources of, 27
Fascism, 63
Fasting, 142–143
Fear, group denial of, 223–224
Feeling homeostasis, 9–10
Fertile Crescent, 74
　Arab conquest of, 232–234
　political conflict in, 78
　towns and cities of, 80
　trade routes through, 79
　universalist religion development in, 79–87
Fetishes, 52
Field theory, 56–57
Financial manias, 59
Folk society, 58
Followers
　link with charismatic leader of, 209–210
　role of, 8
French Revolution, 33–34
Friendship group, 57

Gabriel, 118
　visions of, 113

Gandhi, nonviolence of, 181
Gangs, 57
Genealogy, 91, 236
General Systems Theory, 55
Generativity, 181
Geography, of Arabia, 73–75
Gestalt, 56
Ghassanids, 78–79, 97, 201
Ghatafan, 164–165
Ghatafan tribe, 163
Global conflicts, xvi
Global tensions, xvii
God
　abstract representations of, 83–84
　as Creator, 201
　in history, xi
Good mother, 12
Good Pleasure, Pledge of, 172–173
Great Britain, as nation, xvii
Greek culture, dominance of, 86
Greek Macedonians, 75
Greek perspectives, xi
Greek religion, limited spread of, 83n
Gregariousness, 45, 48–49
Group behavior, 236–240
Group dynamics, 53–54, 56–57
Group ego, 136
Group feeling, 49
Group forces, 63–64
Group identification
　with Jewish customs, 203–204
　with leader, 204–205
Group identity, xiii, 47–48, 60–61, 67–68, 225
　ethnicity and, 64
　versus group mind, 65–66
　influences on, 64–65
　Muhammad and, xiv–xv
　in representational world, 147
Group immortality, 222–223
Group mind, 44, 65–66
Group Mind, 44–45
Group process, 56
Group psychology, 43–44
Group Psychology and the Analysis of the Ego, 43

Subject Index

Group psychotherapy, 53–54
Group relations, 19
Group solidarity, 135
   as mass military force, 220–221
Group techniques, 57
Group therapy movement, 54
Group unity, 205–206
Groups
   artificial, 50
   basic needs of, 147
   childhood developmental events in formation of, 51
   defense mechanisms of, 19–20
   differentiation of, 21–22
   formation of, xiii, 3–24
   genealogy of, xvi
   morphology of, 44, 46, 50
   needs of, 8, 68
   needs of, provided by Muhammad, 228–229
   origins of, 68
   reality testing for, 18
   religious identity and conflict of, 81–82
   representational world of, xiii, 18–24, 21–24
   retrogressed, 60
   rise and decline of, 237–240
   social purpose and, 55–56
   sociological studies of, 57–58
   specialized, 68–69
   structure of, 51
   synthetic or integrative function of, 20–21
   theories of formation of, 43–69
   ties binding, 46–48
   transient, 49–50, 65
   well-organized, 45

Habit, 91
Habitualized actions, reciprocal typification of, 11–12
Hadith, xv, 23–24, 101–102, 229
Hagar, 89
   in Mecca, 100
al-Hajj, 119

Hajj pilgrimage, 99–100, 121, 187
Halimah, 103
Hamzah, 124
Haram, 100
Hashim, 97
Banu Hashim, 124
Hashim clan, 192–193
Hawazin tribe, 178–179
Heavenly journey, 112–113
Hegelian-Marxism, xi
Hellenic civilization, 86
Helpers, 128, 139, 141–142, 180
Heraclitus, 183
Herd instinct, 48–49
Hierarchy, 51, 55
Hijra, xiv, 133–145
   ninth year of, 185
Himyar, house of, 76
Hinduism, limited spread of, 83n
Hippalus, 75
Hira, 78
Hisham, 125
History
   ideology in, xi
   psychoanalytic theory in, 4
   psychology and sociology in, xi–xii
Holocaust, 59
Holy Law. *See* Sharia
Holy Wars. *See Jihad*
Hope, 189–190
Host, unconscious transference onto, 206–207
al-Hudabiyya, treaty of, 170–172, 175–176
Human potential movement, 57
Humor, as defense, 228
Hunayn, victory at, 178–180
Hypnosis, 47–48
Hypocrites, 138–139, 206
   dissent of, 184

Icons, 52
Id, 28–29
Ideal shapes, in Muhammad's representational world, 192–193

Ideas, religion in transmission of, 86–87
Identification, 16, 19–20, 67, 190, 203–204
  binding groups, 46–47
  of childhood, 8
  in group formation, 50
  language in, 51–52
  with leader, 204–205
  with nation state, 50–51
  with prophet, 209–210
  vertical, 47–48
Identity
  at different developmental stages, 30–33
  formation of, 193–194
  group, 60–61
  with nation, 61–64
  violently exclusionary, 84
Ideology, 66–67
  in global conflicts, xvi–xvii
  in leadership role, 52–53
Idols, 93
  of Quraysh, 93–94
Ignorance, Era of, 92–93
Imagined communities, 62
  political, xvi–xvii
Imitation, 45
Immortality, promise of, 220–229
Imperialism, collapse of, 239
Incense route, 77–78
Individual identity
  group identity and, 64
  merged into group, 205–206
Individual rights, 16
Individualism, methodological, 7
Individuals
  basic needs of, in group, 17
  in group formation, 3
  representational world of, 5, 21
  social institutions and, 32
  sociological theory and, 33–37
  ties to society, xiii
Industrial Revolution, 33–34
Industrialization
  groups during, 58–59
  war and, 238–239
Infantile sexuality, 27–28
Inner world, 13, 29–30
Instinct theory, 27
Integrative capacities, 228
Integrative group functions, 20–21
Internalization, 204n, 205
  process of, 38–39
Interpolated Verses, 117–120
Intrapsychic experience, 29–30
Iraq, 233
Isaac, 89
Ishmael, 89, 91–92
  descendants of, 94
  in Mecca, 100
Islam. *See also* Muslims
  birth of, 101
  as center of civilization, ix
  conflict with Christendom, ix–xi
  converts to, 202
  decline of, x
  empire of, 231–240
  evolutionary development of, 203
  expansion of, xv
  factors in rise of, 237–238
  group identity of, xiii
  growing strength of, 185–186
  impact of Judaism on, 200–207
  military and political power of, vii–viii
Banu Israil, 119
Italy, Ottoman plan to capture, x

Jahada, 149
Abu Jahl, 123, 125, 134, 151
  death of, 152
Jerusalem
  Holy Rood in, 183
  as *qibla*, 203
Jewish customs, group identification with, 203–204
Jewish symbols, 203
Jewish tribes, 144–145
Jews
  Byzantine oppression of, 232
  execution of, at Qurayza, 165–167

expulsion of, from Medina, 160–162
growing distance between Muslims and, 156–158
at Khaybar, 173–181
in Medina, 137, 142–145, 206–207
Jihad, 24, 149, 189, 207
aggression in, xiv–xv
justification of, 218
phases of, viii–ix
from tribal raids, xiv
Judaism, 76
impact of, 200–207
relationship with, 142–145
Judeo-Christian scriptures, 201
Jurham, 91
Jurhum
early years of, 92
waywardness of, 92–93
Justice, 236–237
basic trust and, 17
expectation of, 16

Ka'b ibn al Ashraf, 155–156
Ka'ba, 90–91, 92, 95–96, 100
Muhammad at, 177–178
rebuilding of, 107–108
Khadija, 104
conversion of, 202
death of, 126
marriage to, 105–106, 194–200
support of, 109–111
Khaybar, 169, 235
conquest at, 173–181
siege of, 219
al-Khazraj, 169
Khuza'a tribe, 91, 92, 94–95,176
Banu Kinana, 94
Knowledge, sociology of, 6

Abu Lahab, 106
Lakhmids, 78–79, 201
Language, 12
of Arabia, 74
in identification, 51–52
transmitting beliefs and values, 85–86

al-Lat, 94, 117, 119
shrine of, 178
Latent function, 6
Leader-follower relationship, reciprocal, 209–210
Leader role, 8
Leaderless groups, 46
Leaders
charismatic, 189–229
defense mechanisms of, 21–22
emotional ties to, 204–205
functions of, 20–21, 69
group identity and, 64
individual and, 50
mother as, 51
parent as, 17–18
strength of, 52
Leadership
methods of, 56
of Muhammad, 207–212
sociology of, 58
Legal system, 17, 236–237
Libido theory, 27–28
Liwa, 98
Longue durée, 237

Madinat an-Nabi, 126–127
Maghrib, 234
Magic, 80
Mala, 98, 226
Abd al-Malik, 234
Maliks, 75
Abd Manaf, 96–97
Manat, 94, 117, 119
shrine of, 178
Manifest function, 6
Marib dam, 91
Marriage, 207
commitment to, 194–195
Quran reforms of, 215–217
Marriage alliances, 216
Martyrdom, promise of, 221–229
Marxism, 35–36, 238
collapse of, 59
failure of, 36–37
Mass behavior, 58, 236–240

Mass citizen army, 62
Materialism, 35–36
Matrilinearity, 215–217
Mecca, 79, 108
  attack of Medina by, 163–165
  conquest of, xiv, 169–181, 218
  early history of, xiv, 89–100
  founding of, 96
  pilgrimage to, 99–100
  polytheism of, 119–120, 121
  Quraysh return to, 94
  reconciliation with, 180–181
  social and ethical structures of, 97–99
  surrender of, 175, 177–178
  trade in, 97
  treaty with, 170–172
Meccan caravans, *razzias* against, 147–149
Medina, xiv, 126–127
  central organization of, 235
  consolidation of power in, 157–158, 162–163
  Constitution of, 139–140, 225–226
  hostility toward Jews of, 156–157
  Jews of, 142–145
  Meccan attack of, 163–165
  migration to, 23, 129, 133–145
  Muhammad support by, 127–129
  Muhammad's arrival in, 137–142
  warring factions of, 137–138
Merchant class, in universalist religion, 81–82
Messenger of God, 108
Military factors, 238–239
Military-industrial complex, 238
Military leader, 218–220
Mobs, 49–50, 59, 65
Monogamy, 214
Monophysite Christianity, 77
Monophysite churches, 232
Monotheism, 76, 82–84, 120, 189, 201, 204
Morality, 196–197
Morals, internalized, 38–39
Moses
  monotheism of, 84
  Muhammad's ties to, 143
Mother
  as leader, 51
  role of, 11–12
  as social object, 39
Mother-child dyad, 7–8, 13–14
  of Muhammad, 191
Motherhood, 12–13
Motivation, in groups, 56
al-Mughira, Abu Umayya ibn, 108
Muhajirun, 138–139
Muhammad
  acute senses of, 190
  adolescence and young adulthood of, 193–194
  adulthood and marriage of, 194–200
  amorous nature of, 213
  ancestors of, 89–100
  appearance of, 209
  arrival in Medina, 137–142
  attempt to kill, 134–136
  beginning of prophetic mission of, 108–115
  birth of, 102–108
  boycott of, 124–129
  challenges to, 186–187
  childhood identity of, 190–191
  childhood influences on, 23–24
  children and, 211
  clan of, 192–193
  conquest of Mecca by, 169–181
  controversial marriage of, 212–213
  death of, viii, 187–188, 231
  death of son, 198–200
  documented life of, 101
  early experiences of, 189–190
  early years and prophetic call of, 101–129
  gentleness of, 210
  humor of, 210
  Jewish community and, 206–207
  Jews of Medina and, 142–145
  last years of, xiv, 183–188
  matrilinearity and, 215–217

Subject Index

migration to Medina by, xiv, 129, 133–145
military leadership of, 147–167
misfortune in life of, 103–104
orphan status of, 191–192
personal charisma of, 209–210
personality and leadership role of, 207–212
poverty of, 107
public preaching of, 115–117
Quraysh opposition and persecution of, 121–124
representational world of, xiv–xv
sayings and actions of, 101–102
sexuality of, 213–215
as warrior prophet, 217–220
wives of, 211–212
Mukarribs, 75
Multicellularity, 51
Munafiqun, 138–139, 205–206
Muruwah, 99, 224
Musaylimah, 186–187
Muscular bonding, 221
Muslim calendar, starting point of, 138
Muslim scholars, ix
Muslims. *See also* Islam
armies of, in Europe, viii
conquests of, 232–235
formation of community of, 23–24
group identification and togetherness of, 205–206
growing distance between Jews and, 156–158
original community of, 139–140
Abd al-Muttalib, 97, 102, 103, 192
Mutual idealization, 209–210
Mutual trust, 22
Mutuality, 191
of function, 190
Myths, communication of, 21

Nabat, 92
Banu al-Nadir
expulsion of, 160–162
Jews of, 156

al-Nadir clan, 169
banishment of, 160–162
Najran massacre, 76, 78
Nakhlah, expedition to, 149–151
Naklah, ambush at, 218
Nasi, 98
Nation states
history of, 62
identification with, 50–51
stability of, 58–59
National culture, 6–7, 7
National Training Laboratory (NTL), 56–57
Nationalism, 51*n*, 61–64
Nations, xvi–xvii
constitution of, 52–53
relationships between, 59
rise and fall of, 237–240
Natural pleasures, 214–215
Nazism, 63
Near Eastern history, 75–76
Needs
basic, 13–14, 17, 68, 228–229, 236–237
of groups, 8, 51, 147
Negus, 124
Nestorian Christianity, 77
Neurosis, etiology of, 27

Oases, urbanization of, 77–78
Object-choice, 39
Object relations, 29, 39
in group, 19
Objectivity, 6
Odenathus, 78
Oedipal conflict, 14*n*, 28
Oedipus complex, 27–28
Old Testament, Quran and, 144–145
Oligarchies, 239
Oral culture, 193
Organizations, sociology of, 58
Orphan status, 191–192
Ottomans, x
Outer world, versus inner world, 29–30

Pagan polydaimonism, 204
Paganism, end of, 177–178
Palmyra, 78
Palmyrene Arabs, 78
Panic, 65
Parents
  as leaders, 17–18
  omnipotence of, 190–191
Parthians, 78
Patrilineal system, 215–217
Peacemaking religions, 82
Persian Empire, 85, 201, 232–233
Persian Sasanids, 78, 85
Persians, 76
Personal conflicts, 203
Petra, 78
Philosophes, xi
Phoenicians, 77
Pillars of Islam, 185
Poetry, as mass communication, 155–156
Poitiers, viii
Political community, xvi–xvii
Political revolutions, 33–34
Polygamy, 214
  sexuality and, 216–217
Polytheism, 83–84, 204
  end of, 189
  in Mecca, 100, 119–120, 121
  rejection of, 119–120
Prayer, 143–144
  customs of, 203–204
  rites of, 201
Primal horde theory, 49–50, 135
Primary groups, 57
  decline of, 58
Printing press, in spreading Christianity, 87n
Professional organizations, 58
Projection, 19
Projective screens, 28
Prophet
  function of, 140–141
  impact of, 37
Prophetic mission, beginning of, 108–115

Prophet's sayings, 23–24
Protestant Ethic and the Spirit of Capitalism, 35–36
Protestantism, impact of, 35–36
Provincial Arabia, 78
Pseudospeciation, 60, 64
Psychoanalysis, sociological implications of, 27–33
Psychoanalytic sociological position, 32
Psychoanalytic theory
  in biography, 4
  central elements of, 5
Psychobiological functioning, 10
Psychological historic analyses, xi–xii
Psychosocial development, 31–33
Psychosocial model, 30–31, 60
  of group formation, 3–24
Ptolemies, 75
Public preaching, 115–117, 196
Public worship, 143–144

Qadisiyya, battle at, 233
Qahtan, 91
al-Qasim, 106
Qaydar, 91
Qayls, 75
Qaynuqa clan, expulsion of, 157–158
Quran, xv, 23–24, 229
  on Abraham, 90
  authenticity of, 114–115
  on Badr battle, 154
  biblical material in, 201
  as divine revelation, 100
  on exile of al-Nadir, 162
  on function of Prophet, 140–141
  on idolatry, 93
  interpolated verses of, 117–120
  justifying raids, 148
  on life of the Prophet, 102
  marriage reforms of, 215–217
  Meccan chapters of, 196–197
  Old Testament scriptures and, 144–145
  real world in, 108
  on the rich, 121

Subject Index

on treacherous, 167
Quran reciters, 234–235
Quraysh, 97
  boycott of, 124–129
  clan of, 92
  idols of, 93–94
  Muhammad's warnings to, 116–117
  opposition and persecution by, 121–124, 133–134
  opposition to Muhammad, 117–120
  as peacemakers, 105
  rebuilding of Ka'ba by, 107–108
  reconciliation with, 180–181
  return of, to Mecca, 94–96
  trading relationships of, 98
  tribe, 192–193
Qurayza
  clan of, 163, 164
  execution of, 165–167
Qusayy, 92, 94–96

Race, loyalties to, 59–60
Racial conflict, 59
Racial imperialism, 63
al-Rahman, 116
Raids, against Meccan caravans, 147–149
Rajab, violation of, 149–151
Rationality, 36
Rationalization, 148n
Razzia, 189, 226
  aggressive drive in, 217–220
  first bloodshed in, 149–151
  against Meccan caravans, 147–149
Reaction formation, 8, 16, 19–20, 49n, 50, 67
Reality, adaptation to, 10
Reality testing, 18, 227, 228
Recognition stories, 103–104
Reconciliation, 180–181
Reference groups, 58
Reified role, 11–12
Relationism, 6
Religion
  in ancient Near East, 76–77
  communication of, 21

definition of, 81
group identity and, 64
nationalism and, 62
organized, 15
post-Enlightenment decline of, 50–51
pre-Islamic, 99–100
secular, 66–67
as social bond, 226–227
study of, 34
universalist, 79–87
Religious conflict, 59
Religious mission, 148–149
Religious tribe, 197–198, 226–227
Remarriage, waiting period before, 215
Representational world, xiii, 5
  of child, 8, 9–17
  of family and group, 18–24
  group identity in, 147
  of groups, 7, 18–24, 65–68
  ideal shapes in, 192–193
  in ideal shapes of *umma*, 204
  of Muhammad, xiv–xv
  of Muhammad's childhood, 191–192
  of nation, 52–53
  of *umma*, 228–229
  of universalist religion, 87
Ressentiment, 207
Revolutionary immortality, 222–223n
Ridda, Wars of, 231–232
Ridwan, 172–173
Rifada, 98
Righteous community, 82
Riots, 59
Rites, 201
Rituals
  communication of, 21
  Jewish, 203
Role deviant, 11–12
Roles, 11–12
  dereification of, 12n
  individuals as, 192
Roman Empire, 76
  Christianity in, 85
Russia, transition to democracy of, 240

Sabaic language, 74
Sacred books, 85
Sacred buildings, 90
Sa'd ibn Mu'adh, 166–167
Safety need, 14, 17
Said ibn Ahmad, ix
Salat, 143–144, 201
Sasanian Empire. *See* Persian Empire
"Satanic Verses," 117–120
Satyagraha, 181
Sawda, 139
Scriptures
   divine inspiration of, 144–145
   in leadership role, 53
Secondary groups, 58
   in industrialized state, 59
Security need, 14
Security structure, 17
Seduction hypothesis, 27
Seleucids, 78
Self, ideal shape of, 9–10, 190–191
Self representations, 9
Semitic consciousness, 110n
Semitic language, 74
Sexual drive, 207
Sexuality, attitudes toward, 213–215
Abd Shams, 97
Shared guilt, 136n
Sharia, 24
Sibling rivalry, 50
Significant others, representation of, 9–10
Sind province, 234
Sinful Wars, 104–105
Siqaya, 98
Sira, 101
Social bond, blood versus religion as, 226–227
Social change, 34
   modern society, xv–xvi
Social constructs, abstract, 11–12
Social institutions
   human life cycle and, 14–15
   impact of, on individual, 32
   impacting individuals, 6–7
   pathological, 36

Social object, 39
Social order, 11–12, 34
Social organization, 31
Social phenomena, 5–6
Social psychology, 55–56
Social purpose, groups and, 55–56
Social reality, subjective interpretation of, 36
Social roles, 31
Social symbols, 52
Socialization, 32
   starting point of, 39
Socially determined interference, 11–12
Societies of contract, 58
Societies of status, 58
Society, xiii
Sociological analyses, xi–xii
Sociological theory, 33–37
Sociology, 5–6
   criticisms of, 36–37
   development of, 34–35
   of groups, 57–58
   interpretative, 36
   psychoanalytic theory in, 4, 27–33
   structural-functional school of, 8, 37–41
South Arabia, 74–75
   anarchy of, 76
   decline of, 91
   dominance of, 77–78
Southern Italy, 237
Soviet Union, collapse of, 59
Spain, invasion of, 234
Specialization, 68–69
Specialized groups, 237
Specialized institutions, 21–22
Spoils of war, state ownership of, 152–153
Stones, worship of, 93
Striving, religious purpose of, 148–149
Structural functionalism, 37–41
   criticisms of, 40
Structural theory, 28–29
Subculture, 6–7

Subject Index 265

Subgroups, 8, 237
 specialized, 22
Subjectivity, 6
Sublimation, 228
Submission, 226
 hierarchy of, 186
Suffrage, universal adult, 239
Abu-Sufyan, 176–177, 180
Suggestibility, 45–46
Suggestion, in group formation, 48–49
Suicide, altruistic, 223n
Suleyman the Magnificent, Sultan, x
Super-tribe, 140
Superego, 28–29
 as bridge, 39
 formation of, 18
Surat an-Najm, 117
Sword of God, 233
Symbolic immortality, 222–229
Symbolic objects, 52
 sharing of, 204
Symbolic universe, 12–13
 of Bedouin clan life, 191–192
Syria
 campaign against, 183–184, 218
 expedition to, 232–233
 expeditions to, 175
 invasion of, 233
 journey to, 105–106
System, definition of, 55

Tabiya, 220
Tahannuth, 108–109
Ta'if, siege of, 179
Abu Talib, 104, 122, 124, 126, 192
Taxation, 236
Temple, destruction of, 76
Thaqif tribe, 126, 179
Theological immortality, 222–223
Theoretical concepts, xii–xiii
Theory, importance of, 3
Tolerance, religious, 83n
Totemic community of brothers, 135
Tours, viii
Trade, free, 238
Trade professions, 59

Traumatological psychology, 31
Trench, battle of, 163–165, 218, 220
Tribal identities, in cities, 80–81
Tribal raids, xiv
Tribes
 early religious traditions of, 80
 loyalties to, 59–60
 in Mecca, 97–99
 power and wealth of, 226
 pre-Islamic, 224–226
 of pre-Islamic Arabia, 75
 values of, 226
Trust, 227
 basic, 15, 17, 236–237
 mutual, 22
Trust-mistrust, 193–194

Abu Ubaida, 231
Uhud, battle of, 158–165, 219, 221
Umar, 124, 231, 233
Umma, xiv, 237
 building of, 189
 creation and shaping of, 207
 formation of, vii
 framework of, 140–142
 growing strength of, 162–163, 185
 hierarchy of membership in, 185–186
 ideal shapes of, 204
 in Medina, 140–142
 religious mission of, 148–149
 representational world of, 228–229
 Shiekh of, 226–227
 values of, 226
Umra, 170, 175–176
Unconscious transference, onto host, 206–207
Universal authority, 232
Universalist religions, xiii
 development of, in Fertile Crescent, 79–87
 rise of, 73–87
Urban society, 58
 tribal identities and, 80–81
Urwah, 121, 128–129

al-Uzza, 117, 119
    shrine of, 178

Values, transmission of, 85–86
Visions, 108–111, 112–113
    criticisms of, 114–115

al-Walid, Khalid ibn, 232, 233, 234
Waraqa, 110, 111
Warfare
    justification of, 217–220
    Muhammad in, 147–167
    in social expansion, 238–239
Warnings, 116
Warrior prophet, 217–220
Well-being, 9–10
    in group, 18–19
    with meeting of basic needs, 17
    need for, 14

World wars, 59
    nationalism in, 62–63

Yathrib, 78, 127
Yemen, invasion of, 102
Yemenites, 91
Yom Kippur, 142–143

Zakat, 185, 232
Zamakhshari, 90
Zamzam, 97
Zayd, 116, 212
Zaynab, 106
    marriage to, 212–213
Zenobia, 78
Zoroastrian-Mazdeism, 85
Zoroastrianism, 77
Zoroastrians, 76, 82
Zuhayr, 125